D0360708

2008

McCain
THE MYTH OF A MAVERICK

Matt Welch

palgrave
macmillan

McCain
Copyright © Matt Welch, 2007, 2008.

All rights reserved.

First published in hardcover in 2007 by PALGRAVE MACMILLAN®
in the US—a division of St. Martin's Press LLC, 175 Fifth Avenue,
New York, NY 10010.

Where this book is distributed in the UK, Europe and the rest of the
world, this is by Palgrave Macmillan, a division of Macmillan Publishers
Limited, registered in England, company number 785998, of Hound-
mills, Basingstoke, Hampshire RG21 6XS.

Palgrave Macmillan is the global academic imprint of the above companies and has companies and representatives throughout the world.

Palgrave® and Macmillan® are registered trademarks in the United
States, the United Kingdom, Europe and other countries.

ISBN-13: 978-0-230-60805-4
ISBN-10: 0-230-60805-1

Library of Congress Cataloging-in-Publication Data is available from
the Library of Congress.

A catalogue record of the book is available from the British Library.

Design by Scribe Inc.

First PALGRAVE MACMILLAN paperback edition: September 2008

10 9 8 7 6 5 4 3 2 1

Printed in the United States of America.

For Emmanuelle

CONTENTS

Acknowledgments		vii
Preface	*The Unexamined Candidate*	xi
1.	Cowboys and Indians	1
2.	The Defiant One	21
3.	The Elitist	39
4.	Maverick vs. "Maverick"	57
5.	The 12-Step Guide to Becoming President	71
6.	Forgive Them, Father, For I Have Sinned	85
7.	Anger Management	105
8.	Healing Vietnam	119
9.	Theodore Redux	135
10.	Bomb Bomb Bomb, Bomb Bomb Iran	153
11.	The Crooked Talk Express	173
Epilogue	The Thirteenth Step	189
Afterword		205
Notes		221
Index		237

ACKNOWLEDGMENTS

Thanks first and foremost to Nick Gillespie, editor of *Reason*, which for my money is the best and most consistently interesting political magazine in the United States. When I came back from a summer vacation babbling about how John McCain's writing was drenched in the language and themes of 12-Step Recovery, Nick actually found it more interesting than crazy. When I failed to finish my article on the subject before jumping ship to the *L.A. Times*, he took both developments better than most. When I hired away his best writer . . . OK, he threatened to shoot me in the back but only at first. When I finally wrote the McCain piece for the *L.A. Times* instead, he calmly asked me to expand it for the magazine, and then made it much better through the editing process. And when I got the book deal, he offered up his apartment, plenty of contacts, and invaluable encouragements. Thanks, Nick.

The whole *Reason* extended family was kind and helpful. Jesse Walker, Dave Weigel, and Brian Doherty provided good suggestions; Shikha Dalmia related a killer anecdote I couldn't use, Chris Mitchell is giving pro bono promotions help, and David Nott was his generous and inscrutable self.

Emmanuelle Richard is a terrific researcher, conscientious journalism adviser, and one hell of a wife; that last skill received a particularly strenuous workout. Agent Kate Lee of ICM found the opportunity and made quick work of complex negotiations. Editor Jake Klisivitch of Palgrave handled an impossible deadline and tumultuous summer with humor and class. At the *L.A. Times*, Jim Newton was gracious and accommodating with my sudden leave, and Janet Duckworth, Paul

Thornton, Swati Pandey, Linda Hall, and Tim Cavanaugh picked up after me without complaining too much. Well, except for Cavanaugh.

There are numerous people within John McCain's orbits (both tight and extended) who provided the kind of help that cannot be thanked by name; you know who you are. In Arizona, a special *gracias* goes out to Linda Whitaker of the Arizona Historical Foundation's Goldwater Archive, both for guidance and intellectual interest. McCain's official handlers were of no help at all, but mostly polite.

Back in Los Angeles, Roman Genn gave me leads; Ken Layne, as always, was an intellectual foil and source of much-needed laughter. Steve Coulter brought music, Ben Sullivan and Ken Basart provided their particular form of moral support, as did Jeff Solomon, Amy Alkon, David Rensin, Tony Pierce, Charlie Hornberger, and Bonnie Bills. My father, Peter Welch, tempted me with Angels games and ragged me about my due date, and the cast of characters at HalosHeaven.com were the unwitting recipients of much blown-off writing steam in the wee small hours. Long ago and far away, Joel Brand introduced me to "The Big Blue Book," though I doubt he imagined it manifesting like this.

Everybody interviewed for the book or simply harrassed in conversation has my grateful thanks as well.

There have been two sets of father-son admirals in U.S. Navy history, as far as I have been able to determine: John Sidney McCain I and II and Hugo Wilson Osterhaus I and II. The latter are my great-great grandfather and great-grandfather's brother, both of whom went on to command sailors named John McCain. My grandmother, Elizabeth Osterhaus Bobbitt, gave me useful insight into the family's former business, particularly how it affected poor Hugo Osterhaus III, our analogue to John McCain III; and my mother, Mary Bobbitt

Townsend, the world's foremost Osterhaus scholar, helped by lending me Hugo II's unpublished mini-memoir.

Back when the smart money was against me, four people in particular took the short bet and helped me believe. They are: my aforementioned mother, Patrick Byron Whalen, Catherine Anne O'Mara, and Bashkim Ademi.

A final thanks goes out to the subject of this book. Rare indeed is the politician who sustains his or her interesting-ness after lengthy study. This book would not have been written had his two-part memoir not been such a fascinating, question-begging read. By subjecting his political philosophy and practice to critical scrutiny, I am attempting, in my way, to treat him and the office he seeks with the seriousness both have long since deserved.

Matt Welch
Los Angeles, California
August 21, 2007

THE UNEXAMINED CANDIDATE

The shock of finding a Republican outside the Democratic con-
vention is followed by a disturbingly pleasant sensation. I'm
beginning to understand the war that must occur inside a 14-
year-old boy who discovers he is more sexually attracted to boys
than to girls. The longer I hang around McCain the harder it is
to fight the feeling that just maybe I'm . . . Republican.

—Michael Lewis, *The New Republic*, Sept. 30, 1996

Best Snookering of a National Journalist by an Arizona Pol:
Michael Lewis by U.S. Senator John McCain.

—*Phoenix New Times*, Sept. 18, 1997

As he had all spring, John McCain looked uncomfortable in
his own skin. It was the first debate of the 2008 Republican
presidential primary campaign at the Ronald Reagan Library
in Simi Valley, California. MSNBC's Chris Matthews had
just asked the 10 candidates to stare into the twinkling eyes
of popular Gov. Arnold Schwarzenegger, who was sitting
next to Nancy Reagan in the front row 20 feet away, and say

yea or nay to a constitutional amendment allowing natural-
ized citizens to become what McCain had dreamed of since
his days as a prisoner in Vietnam: president of the United
States.[1]

Most of the contenders gave a quick no or made a joke.
McCain paused a beat and then deadpanned, "Depends on
whether he endorses me or not." The crowd laughed. The
Arizona senator smiled and finished his thought, "He and I
have many similar attributes, so I have to seriously consider it."

John McCain is one of the great preemptive joke-tellers
in American politics. To audiences awestruck by his heroic
war record, he breaks the ice by saying, "It doesn't take a hero
to intercept a surface-to-air missile." To supporters worried
about how he might cope with electoral defeat, he says:
"When we lost the 2000 primary in South Carolina to
George Bush, I slept like a baby—sleep two hours, wake up
and cry; sleep two hours wake up and cry." And at every stop
in Iowa this time around he makes sure to tell listeners that
he's had his "glass of ethanol before breakfast."

Who can deny the charm of a powerful man willing to
poke fun at himself? Certainly not the national press corps,
who were swooning to McCain's flattering attentions and
good-time flyboy humor even before he was taken prisoner
in Hanoi. (Legendary *New York Times* correspondent R. W.
"Johnny" Apple Jr. shared a close friendship with McCain for
four decades, starting when the two first enjoyed the bright
lights of Saigon together on a little R&R.[2]) "McCain is so
much fun to be around it almost shouldn't be legal," his first
biographer, Robert Timberg, has said.[3]

Besides seducing reporters, McCain's jokes also contain—
in both senses of the word—uncomfortable truths. His
record as a pilot *was* unimpressive: he partied through flight

school, crashed at least three planes during his career, and was present at the center of the deadliest Naval disaster since World War II.[4] His South Carolina defeat in 2000 *was* a devastating, perspective-rattling blow, one that reoriented his basic campaign approach to 2008. And the candidate *has* cravenly flip-flopped on his contempt for the corn-based fuels that have become synonymous with primary-season pandering.[5]

But by joshing about his foibles—or, alternatively, by soberly confessing them, as he does early and often in all five of his books[6]—McCain pulls off the neat trick of removing them from the conversation. Journalists are far less likely to explore the truth behind the wisecracks than his *bonhomie* in delivering them. Thus the ethanol sellout becomes a story about how the candidate "couldn't resist lampooning the need to support subsidies," showing off one of "the sharper senses of humor in Washington."[7] When McCain jokes that the Constitution is subject to something so base as his endorsement considerations, we're expected to laugh it off, even though in 2006 he indicated a potential willingness to reverse his long-standing opposition to a constitutional amendment restricting marriage to opposite-sex couples, announcing this shift to the same Jerry Falwell he famously called one of the country's "agents of intolerance" six years earlier.[8] Faced with such displays of unprincipled opportunism, the many pundits still sympathetic to McCain will say, as *The New Republic*'s Jonathan Chait put it in April 2006, "Go ahead, senator, flip-flop away. I know you're with us at heart."[9]

But the John McCain who became a national icon was supposed to be better than all that. "You will always hear the truth from me . . . no matter what," he promised on the night of his stunning New Hampshire victory in January 2000. It was a vow that stirred people long deadened to politics by Bill

Clinton's heavily lawyered tongue and the shrill rhetorical excesses of divided, incremental government. "This election season has produced the McCain Independents," *Weekly Standard* Editor William Kristol and star writer David Brooks co-trumpeted a few days after New Hampshire. "The Republican establishment . . . cannot save a faltering [Bush] campaign no matter how well funded it might be."[10] Like many *Weekly Standard* predictions about a candidacy the magazine helped concoct, this would not exactly come to pass.[11]

But even in defeat, McCain, like Obi-Wan Kenobi from his beloved *Star Wars*, only seemed to get stronger, attaining the status of some kind of National Uncle. There he was, after the September 11 massacre, calming American nerves on Jay Leno's *Tonight Show* in a way President Bush wouldn't dare try. Or on *Saturday Night Live*, mocking John Ashcroft and Barbra Streisand alike. Or on the Senate floor, cashing in his political chits by forcing through a Democratic-backed campaign finance reform package that his perturbed vanquisher did everything but veto. So seriously did McCain take his career-making pledge of truthfulness that he apologized extravagantly after dropping out of the 2000 race for having "lied" during the campaign when he said that the Confederate flag flying over South Carolina's capitol was a "states' rights" issue instead of the untenable "symbol of racism" his heart knew it to be. "The politician who promises to put patriotism before selfishness, who promises not to lie, and then reneges," he reflected in his 2002 political memoir *Worth the Fighting For*, "does more harm to the public trust than does the politician who makes no issues of his or her virtue."

So how could this man who "walks on water"[12] have fallen from the heavens with such a resounding thud? How could a

shoot-from-the-hip senator who thrilled reporters by reck-
lessly speaking their favorite kind of truth to power—criticism of Republicans, by a Republican—stoop to having his
lieutenants issue robotic dodges about South Carolina's policy
of flying the Confederate flag? ("A bipartisan solution to this
issue was developed by the General Assembly, and the senator
applauds their efforts," one said.) How could the politician
perennially voted most likely to mount a third-party challenge
now lunge so desperately for the coattails of California's
"post-partisan" governor?

A grieving chattering class, not yet prepared to renounce
faith, has pinned the blame on the ugly necessities of winning
Republican primaries. "Yes, he has pandered to the Bush
crowd and religious conservatives," MSNBC's Howard Fineman wrote.[13] "Though he seems uncomfortable doing it, or
overcompensates by being too enthusiastic, and all in all
looks like he is following a dance-step chart."

But neither the straight-talking maverick of 1999–2000
nor the fallen saint of 2007 was a very revealing caricature to
begin with. Both are functions of an intriguing and little-
understood paradox of modern politics: that John McCain,
both in spite of and because of his overexposure in the media,
is one of the most journalistically under-examined major candidates running for president.

We all know the dazzling highlights from his larger-than-
life biography—the torture in Vietnam, the Straight-Talk
insurgency, the campaign finance reform, maybe even some
traces from the Keating Five scandal and the 1990s tobacco
wars. But how might these experiences translate into future
performance as president (or as a key player in another candidate's administration)? Based on how McCain is usually
presented, we can only make crude, wish-fulfilling guesses,

positive or negative. More than perhaps any presidential contender since John F. Kennedy—a man McCain resembles much more than he does his idol Teddy Roosevelt—the Arizona senator is a willing construct of the media industrial complex. To understand what he believes, why he's talking so crooked, and what kind of president he would make, it's important to untangle the truth of his life from the selective mythology of its depiction.

At the time of McCain's creation myth, he was introduced as a virtuous, high-minded Tourette's case of Truth. While that image does overlap some with reality, McCain had already compiled a readily discoverable record of unsavory behavior, petty recriminations and media puppeteering long before he ran for president. When *60 Minutes* went to Phoenix in 1997 to vet his background, they discovered what most investigators (this author included) found after asking around about Arizona's senior senator: evidence of a punitive temper, a local press corps burned (and often frozen out) after years of detailing his questionable activities, and political skeletons buried (figuratively) in the desert. But instead of airing any of that, executives went with a worshipful profile entitled "The Maverick from Arizona."[14] Explained Mike Wallace at the time: "I'm thinking I may quit my job if he gets the nomination. . . . I'm impressed by his independence, by his willingness to take on the tough ones. By his honesty about himself. As I look at the current crop, there's something authentic about this man."[15]

In that first formative flush of attention, liberal writers approached McCain as they would their first schoolboy crush. Literally. "A feeling is building up inside me, and, rather than continue trying to keep it to myself, rather than deny it any further, I think it's time finally to open up and discuss it publicly," wrote *The New Republic*'s Charles Lane in October 1999, in one of many such confessionals that year. "I didn't want this to happen. I know it shouldn't be happening. But it is: I'm falling for John McCain."[16]

There were many understandable reasons for these initial public displays of affection, not the least of which was the man's undeniable charisma. But the timing was perfect, too, in a way that only time and distance make clear. McCain was an authentic hero in an age of inauthentic, draft-dodging Clintonism. His stunning war record was only then becoming widely known, through Robert Timberg's acclaimed 1995 book *The Nightingale's Song* (expanded in 1999 to a McCain-only bio),[17] and the senator's own brilliant, best-selling, just-in-time-for-the-presidential-campaign POW memoir *Faith of My Fathers* (1999). For a generation of reporters who came of age opposing the Vietnam War, largely alienated from military life, McCain offered not just proximity to martial virtue, but reconciliation and even forgiveness across the great Cold War divide, a ceremonial function he has performed with mostly commendable relish. It also helped that he spoke the Fourth Estate's language when it came to getting money out of politics, fighting Big Tobacco, and cleaning up the environment, while also expressing boredom and even hostility toward conservative perennials like abortion, tax cuts and—this may be hard to remember—isolationism.

With such an epic bio to convey, and the happy, anecdote-generating distraction of constant access, there wasn't much time or space to analyze McCain's actual political philosophy and track record. So journalists either pretended he didn't have any (an easy dodge, given his military disdain for partisanship and evident disinterest in ideological theory), or suggested his beliefs were unformed but promising, ready to be molded either by sage counselors or a new citizen army. Understandably, the candidate did nothing to discourage these notions.

As a direct result, much of what we think we know about John McCain is wrong. He does not, for instance, talk particularly straight. McCain lied to his young second wife about his age until their wedding day, shaving four years off (she lied, too, adding three), and probably wasn't especially truthful with his first wife while famously tomcatting around Washington, D.C., and various ports of call in the 1970s.[18] On issues of more national import, he disobeyed President Jimmy Carter and worked behind his back to save an aircraft carrier project the commander in chief wanted scuttled.[19] To this day, he campaigns one way while voting another (sometimes in the same week), and serially mischaracterizes his own stated positions on everything from immigration to Iraq.[20] When angry, he has knowingly slimed critics and political opponents (detailed in chapter 6). He is prone to ridiculous hyperbole; in March 2000, he declared that if two pro-Bush Texas millionaires were allowed to keep running their anti-McCain attack ads, "it will change the nature of American politics forever. It will destroy it."[21] (Not only did this sadly fail to destroy American politics, McCain later accepted money from the same two millionaires on behalf of his Straight Talk America political action committee).[22] And he frequently makes absolutist declarations about his own personality ("I would never, ever hold a grudge," for example[23]) that practically scream out that the opposite, in fact, is true.

In few of these regards is McCain much different from the average politician. But the average politician doesn't base his or her appeal on being courageous enough to tell the truth.

McCain is also not a "Man of the People" (as suggested by the title of a 2002 biography by Paul Alexander[24]); nor is he "One of Us" (as headlined in an *Esquire* piece from August 2006). He's third-generation Navy royalty, prepped in an elite boarding school, married (as his namesake father was before him) to an ambitious, moneyed millionairess of refined taste and regal bearing. He's lived or worked within 30 miles of Capitol Hill for more than 40 years and is infamous through-out his home state as someone who studiously avoids mixing with the little people. "The more I got to know John McCain, the more I didn't like him," says Don Hesselbrock, who was active in local GOP politics before attending John McCain's first-ever political rally in Arizona. "Couple things bothered me. Number one was . . . John McCain was always much more of an elitist."[25]

Nor is McCain much of a reformer, hard as that might be to accept. His two most significant reform laws—the line-item veto and McCain-Feingold—were both judged to be largely unconstitutional by the Supreme Court. (Indeed, most of McCain's ideas for reform involve increasing federal power at the expense of individual liberties.) A third law, the Military Commissions Act of 2006, will be adjudicated by the high court in the fall of 2007, and is a classic example of a legislative cure being arguably worse than the disease. The bill was intended to strengthen the Geneva Conventions, but ended up denying habeas corpus—for the first time in U.S. history—to a class of detainees.

Then there is McCain's signature initiative, the Biparti-san Campaign Reform Act of 2002, which predictably fell short of his promises to "get dirty money out of politics" and unleash a Teddy Roosevelt-style wave of D.C. housecleaning. It also amounted to the most grievous assault on the First

Amendment since World War II. Even the PAC that McCain created to fight the corrupting influence of money has itself become a fund to pay for McCain's travel for speeches and to reward Republican candidates who just happen to be clustered in the early primary states of South Carolina, New Hampshire and Iowa.[26] And Straight Talk America—as well as McCain's Reform Institute, a legally non-political tax exempt organization—is financed through the generous support of mega-corporations, like AT&T, that have frequent business before the Senate Commerce Committee, which McCain chaired for six years.[27]

None of these details are hard to find, and they do show up in the reporting from time to time. But they barely chip away at the one-dimensional maverick frame that was cemented a decade ago, despite a relatively new treasure trove of primary source material furnished by John Sidney McCain III himself.

Consider for a moment McCain's South Carolina *mea culpa*. Not only does he perform ritual self-criticism in *Worth the Fighting For* for having chosen personal ambition and power-lust over keeping his word, he lays out in damning detail how he compounded the sin in its commission. Whenever asked about the Confederate flag he would theatrically pull out a crumpled piece of paper and woodenly read the politically correct states' rights message, as if he were being held hostage. "I wanted to telegraph reporters that I really didn't mean to suggest I supported flying the flag, but political imperatives required a little evasiveness on my part," he wrote. "I wanted them to think me still an honest man, who simply had to cut a corner a little here and there so that I could go on to be an honest president."

McCain's 34 years of voluminous on-the-record verbiage—the best-selling books, the hundreds of appearances on Sunday chat shows, the inspirational speeches—are positively cluttered with cautionary tales about what happens when he elevates his own self-interest over what's good for the country. "All lives are a struggle against selfishness," he wrote, tellingly in *Worth the Fighting For*, a phrase he recycles on the graduation circuit. "I've made plenty of mistakes since [Vietnam]. And I have many regrets. But only when I have *separated* my interests from the country I've been privileged to serve these many years are those regrets profound." His has been a long and not always winning public battle between ambition and virtue, narcissism and selflessness, exhibitionism and modesty. We really have been warned.

McCain learned the secret to overcoming selfishness at the lowest point in his life. It came when his broken, dysentery-wracked body and soul could no longer withstand the rope-torture, isolation captivity and savage beatings at the hands of his jailers, driving him to sign and tape-record a confession about his "black crimes" against the Vietnamese people. Shamed by his inability to live up to the letter of the American Serviceman's Code of Conduct[28] and devastated at the thought of his father—then a four-star admiral in charge of prosecuting the Vietnam War—ever hearing his traitorous words, McCain contemplated suicide. It was only after regaining his will to resist, through the ministrations of his fellow prisoners and the memory of his family's patriotic honor, did he begin to understand what he later described as "perhaps, the most important lesson" of his life. "I discovered in prison that faith in myself alone, separate from other, more important allegiances, was ultimately no match for the cruelty that human beings could devise," he wrote in *Faith of My Fathers*. "Nothing in life is more liberating than to fight for a cause larger than yourself, something that encompasses you but is not defined by your existence alone."

This idea that a "cause greater" can trump "selfishness" is the taproot of all of McCain's politics. It propels his efforts at reform, provides rhetorical flourish to his oratory and serves as a conscience-booster when self-interest leads him astray. And it's also nearly word-for-word the same description of the concept that underpins 12-Step Recovery programs like Alcoholics Anonymous.

In A.A.—whose meetings McCain's father attended late in life[29]—addicts are encouraged in Steps 1 and 2 to first admit their problem, then invest faith in "a Power greater than ourselves." Those familiar with *The Big Book* of A.A. will be startled at how often its themes (confession, then testimony) and even vocabulary (narcissism, egotist, etc.) crop up in McCain's own books. The senator is intimately familiar with 12-Step programs; his wife Cindy has said she's attended Narcotics Anonymous meetings weekly ever since she publicly confessed her addiction to pain medication in 1994.[30] She told *Dateline*, "the best thing I've ever done is go into recovery and stay drug-free."[31] It's notable that although McCain says he learned his great life's lesson in Vietnam, the "cause greater" articulation of it didn't really become part of his stump speech until 1998, as he was finishing *Faith of My Fathers*. Since then, he hasn't stopped talking about it.

In McCain's repurposing of 12-Step Recovery principles, the deliberately vague and individually defined "Higher Power" is replaced with a specific entity—not God, but the United States of America. The front page of his campaign Web site, for instance, features a Cause Greater link, at which he declares, "I am running for President of the United States because I believe in the greatness of this nation as a beacon of goodwill throughout the world. My friends, each and every one of us has a duty to serve a cause greater than our own self-interest." Belief in the ideals of America, and in the brotherhood of those who share that belief, saved McCain's life and has inspired people worldwide to emulate or immigrate to that "shining city on a hill" of Ronald Reagan's formulation. So maintaining and improving upon U.S. "greatness" becomes not just a way for more Americans to experience the transformative healing that McCain enjoyed, but also a quasi-militaristic imperative of citizenship. "Those who claim their liberty but not their duty to the civilization that ensures it, live a half-life, having indulged their self-interest at the cost of their self-respect," he said at a Boston College commencement ceremony in 2006. "But sacrifice for a cause greater than your self-interest, and you invest your lives with the eminence of that cause, your self-respect assured."

This is not just idle jargon. It's the reason McCain does what he does. When pushing through campaign-finance reform, McCain said, "How are we going to motivate young people to serve if you have to spend a million dollars to win an election?"[32] Faith in government for McCain is synonymous with faith in country, and any perceived threat to that belief—whether it be campaign mudslinging, corporate scandals or even unregulated steroid use in baseball—becomes the target of his considerable wrath. "Our greatness," he writes in *Worth the Fighting For*, "depends upon our patriotism, and our patriotism is hardly encouraged when we cannot take pride in the highest public institutions, institutions that should transcend all sectarian, regional, and commercial conflicts to fortify the public's allegiance to the national community." And what about good old-fashioned, don't-tread-on-me cynicism? "Cynicism threatens to become a ceiling on our greatness."[33]

At this point, it is hard not to start to detect in McCain a belief system antithetical to, or at least heavily skeptical toward, the rights of individuals; and many have. Libertarians, personified within the Republican Party in the figure of Arizona's own Barry Goldwater, have long been among the harshest critics of Goldwater's successor in the Senate. The libertarian Cato Institute, after years of battle, is prone to producing such exhausted headlines as "John McCain Is Wrong." *Reason* magazine has published more than 100 articles and columns critical of McCain over the years, including an April 2007 cover story on the "frightening mind of an authoritarian maverick."[34] Grover Norquist's Club for Growth in March 2007 summed up the Arizonan thusly: "Senator McCain's outspoken pursuit of anti-growth and anti-free-market policies in the realms of taxes, regulation, and campaign finance reveals a philosophical ambivalence, if not hostility, about limited government and personal freedom."[35]

It is not surprising, then—though almost completely unreported—that despite McCain's occasional half-hearted claims of being a "Goldwater conservative," the relationship between the two iconic men was strained. Goldwater viewed government through the lens of maximizing individual liberty and local autonomy. McCain, while allegedly holding views that "defy categorization" (*Baltimore Sun*, 1996; *Los Angeles Times*, 1999), actually has a consistent record of using the federal government as a means to the end of reigniting patriotism and expanding "national greatness."

Nowhere is this approach more coherent, and less timely, than in the realm of foreign policy. Put simply, McCain's national greatness program for fighting foreign wars and maintaining the United States' unipolar supremacy would be the most openly militaristic and interventionist platform in the White

House since Teddy Roosevelt first started waving his Big Stick around the Americas and the Pacific Rim. McCain wants more boots on the ground in Iraq, and he envisions U.S. forces there for at least the next half-century. He advocates intervention in Darfur, makes jokes about bombing Iran, and has championed a policy of "rogue-state rollback" since 1998. He initially maintained some Vietnam Syndrome-style reticence about sending U.S. troops abroad, opposing deployments to Lebanon, Haiti and Somalia (and even insisting as late as August 1990 that "we cannot even contemplate . . . trading American blood for Iraqi blood").[36] But all that evaporated by the late 1990s after the success of the first Gulf War and the U.S. interventions that brought a halt to ethnic bloodshed in the former Yugoslavia.

This interventionist approach, which is considerably more hawkish than anything George W. Bush has ever practiced, is one of the better-documented aspects of McCain's belief system, even if it is routinely portrayed not as the radicalism it is, but as evidence of his "strong credibility on national security."[37] But much less understood is the extent to which interventionist hegemony has been literally seared into McCain's skull and then reignited late in life after the long intellectual detour of Vietnam.

Voters know McCain comes from a strong navy background and may have even heard that his two paternal forebears were the first father-son four-star admirals in U.S. history. But even that only begins to scratch the militaristic surface. His direct ancestors served in every major U.S. war from the Revolution to World War II, and his two sons from his second marriage will likely both see action in Iraq.[38] Dad led the invasion of the Dominican Republic in 1965, Grandpa commanded all naval air power during World War II, and Grandpa's uncle created the modern military draft.

But as important as the exalted responsibility was the robust ideology that fueled it. McCain's grandfather came of age right as Theodore Roosevelt, under the sway of historian Alfred Thayer Mahan's *The Influence of Sea Power Upon History* (1890), was pushing America to become an imperial power. "For the McCains of the United States Navy, as well as for many of our brother officers, presidents just didn't get much better than Teddy Roosevelt," McCain wrote in *Worth the Fighting For*. "He transformed the American navy from a small coastal defense force to an instrument for the global projection of power." McCain's father, a great admirer of colonial Britain, became known as "Mr. Seapower," giving popular alarmist lectures about America's potential naval gap with the Soviet Union. This was the McCain clan's basic template—brawling Scots-Irish temperament brought to high-level military service, then ennobled by the intellectualism of empire. The only chink in the armor of ever-expanding U.S. might was the single thing McCain is most famous for: Vietnam.

Here we begin to understand the *why* of one of McCain's most intriguing and lauded *whats*. From literally the moment he touched down on U.S. soil, Lt. Cmdr. McCain has been actively working to heal the divisions of Vietnam. "Now that I'm back, I find a lot of hand-wringing about this country. I don't buy that," he wrote in *U.S. News & World Report* just two months back in the country.[39] "I've received scores of letters from young people, and many of them sent me POW bracelets with my name on it, which they had been wearing. Some were not too sure about the war, but they are strongly patriotic, their values are good, and I think we will find that they are going to grow up to be better Americans than many of us."

Such magnanimity was not just for show—McCain has forgiven draft-dodgers, peace activists who declared his Hanoi prison as humane[40] and even Vietnam's foreign minister (who was deputy foreign minister for the government that held McCain prisoner). He and John Kerry worked tirelessly (if impatiently) to put the POW/MIA issue behind them and then normalize relations with Vietnam. *Faith of My Fathers*, in addition to crystallizing McCain's "cause greater" concept, reads like an attempt to put this tragedy, at long last, in the national rearview mirror. The war, he writes at the end of the book, "left some Americans bereft of confidence in American exceptionalism—the belief that our history is unique and exalted and a blessing to all humanity. . . . That was a pity, and I am relieved today that America's period of self-doubt has ended." Putting Vietnam behind us was the essential precondition for creating a new American century. Until that project hit the rocks in Iraq.

So what happened to this, the more complicated version of John McCain in the first half of 2007? Longtime friends say it's that age-old political story: a candidate determines that the country's fortune depends on his becoming president. It is clear that McCain believes passionately in the greater cause of American exceptionalism. It is also clear—because he's told us over and over again—that he's had trouble in life sorting out where his ambition ends and the good of the country begins. What's more, he has repeatedly maintained (as documented in chapter 4) that acting like a real sonofabitch is forgivable, even commendable, as long as it's in the service of a truly great cause. Once McCain believes that his presidential ambition is a cause greater unto itself, then the same man who can be so haunted by an eight-year-old lie in South Carolina becomes capable of the same low politics as any other presidential contender.

Though as an incisive man once wrote, "It is hard to succeed if the public is convinced that you lack conviction or honesty."[41] Especially when the toll it takes is plainly visible on your face.

This book examines the under-examined philosophy and track record of presidential candidate John McCain, teasing out his views on the proper role of government. It's not a biography or a campaign memoir so much as it is a user's guide or decoder ring for deciphering a supposedly inscrutable candidate. There will be biographical details along the way, in rough chronological order, but only insofar as they shed light on what a McCain presidency would look like. My hope is that it will remove the surprise of what this allegedly unpredictable maverick does between now and November 2008, and maybe afterward.

As I write (in mid-August 2007) McCain is submerged in the polls, far behind schedule in fundraising and working with a drastically reduced staff. The Internet is teeming with "McCain Death Watches."

But I would not count him out just yet. Nothing puts more spring in this scamp's step than being an outnumbered underdog, one against the world, especially if he believes in his heart of hearts that his unpopular stance is morally just. Rudolph Giuliani, the only competitor with anything approaching McCain's national profile and cross-partisan appeal, is always one campaign gaffe away from imploding. Mitt Romney is a slick, flip-flopping lightweight (in my view, anyway), and Fred Thompson has shown little in the way of motivation or energy. What's more, even in defeat McCain may well end up as vice president or secretary of defense in either a Giuliani or a Thompson White House (McCain and the actor are close friends). And all three of his main competitors promise to dish up helpings of the "national greatness" foreign policy approach discussed at length in chapters 9 and 10.

This being a book about politics, you deserve to know mine, such as they exist. In some respects, I'm the ideal McCain voter—politically independent, proudly western and a member of the press. I would have voted for the guy in 2000 if he had appeared on any of my ballots (though that's back when I believed in campaign finance reform. I have been called an "*Economist*-style conservative liberal,"[42] and while I appreciate the surrealism, there's not much "conservative" about me (no matter what my *Los Angeles Times* colleagues might think), unless you count hating communism and having a default preference for free markets. I'm basically a Central European-style liberal: I don't care so much for government or political parties. (If you really want to know my incoherent voting record, please consult www.mattwelch.com/votingrecord.)

More to the point, my approach to politics and ideology is more journalistic than polemic; I'd rather discover and explain than proselytize. It is not at all necessary—and definitely not recommended—that you share my beliefs in order to find use for this book. Why did I write it? Because I took some McCain books on a vacation (being interested in his character) and was flabbergasted by the amount of 12-Step language in them. Also, I'm especially drawn to subjects who grapple consciously with the concept of capital-T Truth, from Ralph Nader (whose 2000 campaign I covered), to

Vaclav Havel. I've also spent much of my career writing about (and criticizing) the media, which plays such a central role in the McCain story.

So I hope you enjoy, and please tune into *mccainbio.com* for follow-up news and information.

COWBOYS AND INDIANS

Robert Jordan, with his fearlessness, with his service to a flawed cause, with his courage and his self-confidence but yet his fatalism, was everything I ever wanted to be in life. And he was as real to me as any real person that I've ever known . . . [He was] willing to fight and die for what he believed in, die for his comrades and, by the way, also have a wonderful love affair with a beautiful Spanish girl.

—John McCain, *Air Talk*, KPCC-FM 89.3
Los Angeles, Nov. 8, 2002[1]

The whole thing has the too-perfect felicity of a youthful erotic dream.

—Edmund Wilson, *The New Republic*, October 1940[2]

The question from the audience would have been a slam-dunk for John McCain eight years ago: What would you do to include moderate Republicans and to bring back to the party those independents who were formerly registered Republicans? It was at the end of the third GOP presidential debate in 2007, in the independent-minded state of New Hampshire that had given McCain his storybook upset victory in January 2000, and the candidates were trying to cram in their best closing sound bites. San Diego Congressman and presidential long shot Duncan Hunter, a Vietnam vet and border-fence hawk who earlier in the year won a straw poll of Republican activists in McCain's home county of Maricopa, Arizona (the local boy finishing a dismal fourth[3]), used the opportunity to call front-runners Rudolph Giuliani, McCain and Mitt Romney a bunch of damned Teddy Kennedys. Given chances to respond, the triumvirate of "Rudy McRomney" all ignored Hunter's immoderate baiting and addressed the underlying query. Well, sort of.

"Protect the family, that's one of the questions earlier," McCain said distractedly when it came his turn. "Protect our American family; it's under assault in many respects, as we all know." Not even a gift-wrapped opportunity to reinforce his considerable independent bonafides was going to deter McCain from the urgent business of throwing more red meat to a GOP base long suspicious of his conservatism. Even more interesting, though, was the way he chose to wrap up his pitch. After talking about the "transcendent struggle" against "radical Islamic extremism," he said: "I am prepared to lead. My life and my experience and my background *and my heroes inspire me and qualify me to lead* in this titanic struggle." (Emphasis added.)

Everybody has heroes. Some of us (including Giuliani[4] and former *New Yorker* editor Tina Brown)[5] list McCain among them. But does the quality of our chosen inspiration "qualify" us for the highest office in the land? McCain apparently takes that curious notion seriously enough that he made the same comment on Bill O'Reilly's TV show just days before ("I believe my whole life, my inspiration, my heroes, and my experience have qualified me to serve"),[6] then quickly sent out press releases highlighting that line, and repeated the idea yet again in interviews just following the New Hampshire debate. Such is the senator's fixation on role models that his three most recent (and least readable) books— *Why Courage Matters* (2004), *Character Is Destiny* (2005), and *Hard Call* (2007)—are all collections of heartfelt mini-hagiographies glorifying the people who have inspired him most. More than just about any other contemporary politician, McCain's heroes are fundamental to his political persona and sense of self. So just who are these people?

Drunks, bastards, rule-breakers, cold warriors, coaches, Vietnam vets and martyrs, mostly.[7] (Many, especially members of his family, belong to multiple categories.) But the oddest wing in the McCain pantheon is one that might best be labeled "fictional characters from macho melodramas about pre-World War II warfare." Prominent among them is Marlon Brando's brown-face characterization of Mexican revolutionary Emiliano Zapata in McCain's favorite film, Elia Kazan's *Viva Zapata!* Even more central to his life is a figure that sprang from the fertile and romantic imagination of Teddy Roosevelt's most literarily accomplished fan, Ernest Hemingway.

"The first hero of mine outside of my father and grandfather," McCain told radio interviewer Larry Mantle in 2002, "[was] Robert Jordan, the protagonist of *For Whom the Bell Tolls*."[8] Jordan, a stoic American who volunteered to blow up Fascists in the Spanish Civil War, was no mere boyhood fling. Hemingway's blockbuster remains McCain's favorite novel, his go-to recommendation for the accurate depiction of war,[9] and an ongoing source of comportmental inspiration. "There is nobody I'd rather be than Robert Jordan," he told the *Arizona Daily Star* in 2002.[10] His political memoir, *Worth the*

Fighting For, devotes its entire second chapter to the Montana writer-turned resourceful guerilla fighter clearly recognizable as Hemingway's idealized alter-ego. "For a long time, Robert Jordan was the man I admired above almost all others in life and fiction," McCain writes. "He was and remains to my mind a hero for the twentieth century." In fact, the purple title of McCain's memoir comes from the final chapter of *For Whom the Bell Tolls*, when Jordan tries to stave off death long enough to machine-gun down the soldiers pursuing his comrades: "The world is a fine place and worth the fighting for and I hate very much to leave it."

McCain encountered Robert Jordan at an opportune time. He was 12 years old and had finally settled down in Arlington, Virginia, after spending most of his early childhood as an itinerant navy brat. The future presidential wannabe was actually born in the Panama Canal Zone in 1936 (he's eligible for the White House since his parents were U.S. citizens) and lived stints in naval pit stops like Long Beach, Coronado and New London. His taciturn father, a submarine commander, had been absent during the war and distant upon return. And young John McCain's first great hero, his grandfather Admiral John Sidney "Slew" McCain, had died just days before John III's ninth birthday.

Slew sounds like basically the best grandpa ever, minus the early death. "In today's slang, he lived large," McCain wrote in *Faith of My Fathers*. "He smoked, swore, drank and gambled at every opportunity he had." He was a wiry, hooknosed runt with a booming voice, scrappy energy, and natural ease with enlisted men (his underlings called him "Popeye the Sailor Man"). He was notoriously disheveled, with false wooden teeth he'd take out to horrify the grandkids, and a beat-up old cap that his great friend Admiral Bull Halsey called "The most disreputable one I ever saw on an officer."[11] He hunted and fished, rolled his cigarettes with one hand, and spent his spare time at the racetrack, sometimes dragging along McCain's equally vivacious mother Roberta, "who was enchanted by him."[12] When advised once about a new treatment for his presumably persistent ulcers, legend has it that Slew yelled, "Not one dime of my money for doctors. I'm spending it all on riotous living!" He rode in Teddy Roosevelt's globe-spanning Great White Fleet,[13] escorted supply ships to Europe during World War I, learned to fly at age 52 to qualify for aircraft carrier command, and sunk hundreds of Japanese ships during World War II.[14] Between the wars he served—just as his son and grandson eventually would—at key bureaucratic posts in Washington, D.C., navigating the minefield of Beltway politics to effect lasting change on how the Navy is organized. Though little Johnny didn't know it at the time, Slew was also a prolific and mostly amateur writer, penning technical essays about force structure, unpublished novels about the Ku Klux Klan fighting communism in New York City, and polemics against the prohibition of alcohol and gambling.[15]

"My memories of him are few but vivid," McCain wrote in the introduction to the Slew McCain biography *A Leader Born*. "My mother would rouse us from our beds and hurry us downstairs for a few stolen moments and a quick snapshot with our busy grandfather. He would greet us as effusively as ever, tease our grogginess away with his high spirits, joke and kid with us for a few minutes, tell us not to be any trouble to our mother, and then, as he gave us a few quick pats on the head, he would make for the door and the waiting car outside that would carry him back to a world at war. After I returned to bed, unable to sleep, I would imagine our next meeting when I might be able to coax a few war stories out of the old man."

That's a hard act to follow, and John McCain Jr. (known more commonly as "Jack") seemed haunted, if determined, by the challenge. (He would manage to eventually surpass his father in flag rank, rising to the second most prestigious position in the Navy.[16]) To this day John III understandably identifies much more with his swashbuckling grandfather than his dutiful dad. "As a boy and a young man," he wrote in *Faith of My Fathers*, "I found the attitude his image conveyed irresistible. Perhaps not consciously, I spent much of my youth— and beyond—exaggerating that attitude, too much for my own good, and my family's peace of mind." The tension between McCain's Slew-inspired rambunctiousness, his more maternal sense of ambition, and his father's iron commitment to honor has been gnawing at his soul ever since.

After grandpa left the picture, there was a glaring lack of available male role models. "The relationship of a sailor and his children is, in large part, a metaphysical one," McCain wrote wistfully in *Faith of My Fathers*. "As any other child would, I resented my father's absences, interpreting them as a sign that he loved his work more than his children." Striving to please his dad eventually became his greatest motivation as a naval aviator. And in a twist only a Greek tragedian could love, the biggest single point of pride McCain takes in his dad's long military record is the fact that he ordered Hanoi to be bombed by low-accuracy B-52s even though he knew his imprisoned son was in the line of fire. "That is a very hard decision for a father to make," he wrote, with staggering understatement, in *Character Is Destiny*. "The memory of him and the example he set for me helped to form my own conscience, and shame me when I disobey it. I don't think there is anything greater a parent can do for you."

Years later, McCain made the great symbolic step of retiring from the Navy on the same day of his father's funeral (he died a young but decrepit 70). As John Karaagac observed in the useful and rarely referenced *John McCain: An Essay in Military and Political History*, "McCain's own political career was characterized by a strong identification with established, almost quasi-father figures—John Tower certainly, perhaps Ronald Reagan, and, to a lesser extent, Barry Goldwater."[17] A metaphysical paterfamilias was enough to keep McCain in the family's line of work, but not enough to fire his restless imagination.

Into this void strode the muscular charms of Ernest Hemingway. In his too-perfect telling, the always-superstitious McCain one day found not one but *two* four-leaf clovers in his Arlington front yard, and then, he explains, "[I] raced into the house and headed straight for my father's study, where I grabbed the first book I could reach off his library shelves to press my prize in."[18] That book was *For Whom the Bell Tolls*, Hemingway's sober, mid-career meditation on the confusions of the Spanish Civil War, focusing on the last three days in the life of an explosives expert who becomes increasingly convinced that his latest assignment will end in death. McCain says he opened the book to a particularly gruesome flashback scene in which Spanish revolutionaries formed a gantlet outside a town hall to bludgeon local leaders—including a priest—and toss them over a cliff. "The chapter . . . should disabuse the most immature reader of any romantic notions about the nature of organized bloodletting," McCain wrote. "But it cast an immediate spell on me."

Robert Jordan, if he had been real, would have been one of the estimated 1,000 American volunteers who died in Spain fighting on the side of the Republican (and largely communist) revolutionaries, in a losing battle against General Francisco Franco's Hitler-backed Nationalists. The Spanish Civil War was an initially bracing, eventually bewildering 1930s *cause célèbre* among European and American intellectuals, Hemingway included, in which World War II's seemingly inevitable battle lines of fascism vs. communism drew first blood and tested out weapons. Many writers and former pacifists signed up for the cause, most enduringly a grim young British socialist and unsuccessful novelist named Eric Blair (pen name George Orwell), whose *Homage to Catalonia*, a nonfiction account of his comrades and the treacherous political intrigues he observed within the anti-Fascist factions, has long since lapped Hemingway's runaway bestseller in critical estimation.[19]

But McCain wasn't, and isn't, very interested in all of that. For the 12-year-old boy and 70-year-old man alike, the political machinations in Madrid were noteworthy mostly in that they *didn't* discourage Jordan from carrying out a mission he knew to be futile. "They were dedicated to the cause," he wrote in *Worth the Fighting For*, "willing to sacrifice their lives for it, but vulnerable to disappointment at the hands of cynical politicians who controlled their fate and the weary realism of the people they had come to save. Their heroism was a beautiful fatalism."

It's hard to read that paragraph without thinking about Vietnam. Or even Iraq. There is something especially noble and professional about a soldier not wavering in his duty when the cause isn't necessarily just or well-thought out, the civilian leadership is corrupt and the natives aren't particularly grateful. As McCain put it in a May 2007 *Wall Street Journal* piece, the novel "helped bring home to me one of the fundamentals of military experience: what it is that moves soldiers in battle." When all else fails, there is not the tragedy of soldiers being used as political pawns, but the bond of brothers, and of the ideals they share, just as there was when McCain hit rock bottom in Hanoi after taping his confession. "In the end, Jordan voluntarily sacrifices his life for the sake of the people he fought alongside, the people he had come to love."[20]

But even though it *looks* like the perfect Vietnam allegory—McCain even once told an interviewer, "I knew that Robert Jordan, if he were in the next cell to mine, he would be heroic. . . . He would be stoic, he wouldn't give up; and Robert would expect me to do the same thing"[21]—it doesn't mean his *For Whom the Bell Tolls* obsession is a product of the Hanoi Hilton. When seeing or listening to interviews with the senator about Hemingway's story, it's apparent that what really gets his pulse up is not the tragedy of the soldiers being used as political pawns, but the utter romantic hopelessness of it all. "They were doomed to failure," he told Tim Russert on *Meet the Press* in 2002.[22] "But he still went to blow the bridge . . . in an attack that he knew could not succeed. It's a—it's a wonderful story."

McCain is the patron saint of lost causes. Aside from his controversial Bipartisan Campaign Reform Act, which finally squeaked through in 2002 after a quixotic, seven-year struggle, the bills he is most famous for all failed: the line-item veto that the Supreme Court struck down in 1998, the never-passed $1.10-a-pack tobacco tax he proposed the same year, and 2007's comprehensive immigration reform debacle. Every year McCain stands up on the Senate floor to denounce line items of congressional pork; every year the budgets pass and the earmarks continue to increase. Rather than discourage him, setbacks and long odds put a noticeable spring in his step, while victory leaves him uncertain.

David Grann, one of the few reporters to write perceptively about McCain's psyche during the Straight Talk Express days, noted in *The New Republic* back then that the candidate looked deathly the night he won New Hampshire, and positively buoyant when he got drubbed in South Carolina (to the point that he was trying to cheer up a despondent press corps).[23] "Is McCain trying to lose?" Grann asked in his analysis. The question has come up again this year. When the buzzards were circling Bob Dole's run in 1996, it was Senator McCain who jumped on the campaign trail and kept his friend in good spirits to the bitter end. "Beautiful fatalism" for the Arizona senator is not just a throwaway phrase; it's a credo to live by. *For Whom the Bell Tolls* is almost leaden in its portent of constantly foreshadowed death. Twelve-year-old John must have giggled while reading it.

The McCain household was fertile soil for the romance of battlefield fatalism, preferably exercised in faraway lands full of beautiful women. Presuming the worst is almost an act of self-preservation when your family business is war and fighting is a question of when, not if. McCain's forebears, "bred to fight as Highland Scots,"[24] include John's great-great-grandfather William Alexander McCain (who died in the Civil War), and William's three sons—Henry Pinckney McCain, father of the Selective Service; Confederate solider Joseph Watt McCain; and great-grandfather John Sidney McCain, who was too young to fight in the Civil War but served as a sheriff and raised his two sons to be military officers. That first John Sidney McCain married a woman who the senator says had an even *more* militaristic family background, and together they produced his four-star admiral of a grandfather and the notorious Wild Bill McCain, an Army cavalryman who chased Pancho Villa around through Mexico.

McCain's grandfather was the first in the clan to switch from Army to Navy, a fortuitous bit of timing that literally and figuratively expanded the family's horizons. Teddy Roosevelt, first as assistant secretary of the Navy and later as president, was in the process of transforming the U.S. Navy from a glorified Coast Guard into the strutting instrument of a hungry young empire. Slew McCain cut his teeth on a Spanish gunboat leisurely putting down the Philippine Insurrection, a low-intensity guerilla resistance to U.S. occupation that top military brass to this day cite as the single best analogy for the ongoing operation in Iraq. Though U.S. brutality in the Philippines was notorious, triggering a backlash at home from the likes of Mark Twain, none of this registers in McCain's Huck Finn–style portrayal of his grandfather's early career. "Their mission allowed them to sail virtually wherever they pleased, call on whatever ports they chose, showing the flag, in essence, to the Filipinos at a time when the United States feared a Japanese challenge for control of the Philippines," he wrote in *Faith of My Fathers*. "They cruised an immense expanse of the archipelago, putting in for fresh water and supplies at various ports, arbitrating minor disputes among the locals, and generally enjoying the exotic adventure that had come their way."

Slew, like his son Jack who would later follow in his path, was a great fan of Lord Admiral Nelson, Rudyard Kipling, and the colonialist literature of the British Empire. Both were disciples of Alfred Thayer Mahan's *The Influence of Sea Power Upon History*, a book arguing that global supremacy could only be achieved through a dominant Navy. At a time when the western frontier was closing and cities were filling up with factories and immigrants, it was Roosevelt's Mahan-inspired Navy that became the vehicle for youthful dreams of adventure and conquest. Hemingway, an ardent admirer of Roosevelt (down to aping his mustache and flannel shirts, and taking up boxing), heeded Roosevelt's call to live the "strenuous life," which eventually took him across the Atlantic to observe wars, exaggerate his contributions to them, and write classic pieces of modernist fiction in a new American idiom. The riddle is not that a 12-year-old McCain embraced *For Whom the Bell Tolls*; it's that it took him so long.

And that embrace hasn't slackened with age. Robert Jordan's tale remains for McCain "*the* great American novel,"[25] and the character is still vivid enough that the senator has name-checked him on *Larry King Live* at least four times.[26] So what does this relationship tell us about McCain the grandfather and presidential candidate?

For one thing, that his requirements for great fiction don't include anything resembling a human love story. As the great critic Edmund Wilson put it, in an otherwise favorable review, "The hero falls in with an appealing little girl who has been captured and raped by the Fascists, who has never loved before and who wants him to teach her love. She adores him, lives only to serve him, longs for nothing but to learn his desires so that she can do for him what he wants, talks of her identity as completely merged in his. She is as docile as the Indian wives in the early stories of Kipling." The affair, central to both the story and McCain's affection for it, is just embarrassing to the contemporary reader. Maria, as a character, has all the depth of a liquor store advertisement.

The anachronisms don't stop there. Though Hemingway was derided by his artistic predecessors as a nihilist of questionable patriotism, he was actually applying a modern twist on themes popular in gung-ho, turn-of-the-century literature: martial glory, cross-cultural love, western vigor, and the White Man's Burden. He may have shown more sensitivity to local concerns and the horrors of war, but he still fit comfortably in a Teddy Roosevelt ethic that portrayed American globe-trotting as rebellious adventurism and didn't shed too many tears over the trampled locals. Many of McCain's real-world heroes—the obsessively driven Antarctic explorer Ernest Shackleton, Colorado River explorer John Wesley Powell, Navajo chieftain Manuelito, Teddy Roosevelt—were the kind of hyperactive, larger-than-life, late-nineteenth-century frontier characters who Hollywood so successfully mythologized (and sanitized) in the movies of McCain's youth. There are entire museums (the Gene Autry in Los Angeles, most notably) dedicated to unpacking the long-seared lies of western mythmaking and uncovering the more complicated realities behind *The Winning of the West* (which is the name of Roosevelt's racially exuberant, multi-volume history[27]). Historiography, and the culture, have long since moved beyond the facile pleasures of cowboys-and-Indians. McCain, though he's become a well-respected advocate for Native American affairs in the Senate (following in the footsteps of his predecessor Barry Goldwater), is still a sucker for the ersatz frontier spirit that coursed through Ernest Hemingway's veins.

While it could be expected for McCain the soldier to appreciate noble fighters like Robert Jordan, who carry out flawed orders issued by venal military leaders of ruthless governments, one searches in vain for McCain the powerful legislator divining a single useful political conclusion from Jordan's largely pointless death. Though the senator loves quoting the "worth the fighting for" line, Hemingway's real twist of the knife comes right before: "I have fought for what I believed in for a year now. If we win here we will win everywhere." What Jordan believed in had already begun to rot and would only get considerably worse in Spain and the rest of the world. His side wasn't going to win, and even if they had, they surely would not have won "everywhere," given the cataclysms and duplicitous diplomacy to come. It's reasonable to conclude that he's dying for no good reason at all.

McCain sincerely believed when he was in Vietnam that he was fighting to prevent Southeast Asian countries from falling like dominoes to the communist menace. That faith proved groundless, but the senator has seen little reason in the last three decades to reassess where his naïveté ended and Washington propaganda began.[28] Modern readers of *For Whom the Bell Tolls* are like high-school students learning about Vietnam: impatient to jump through the deliberative recitation of facts to get straight to the question of *why*. Unless, as the late Hemingway biographer Michael Reynolds argued, modern audiences just take official lying as a given. "Any reader born around 1936, the first year of the Spanish Civil War, has gone through more political promises made and broken than he or she can remember," Reynolds wrote in the *Virginia Quarterly Review* in 2000. "This disillusionment, which has become an American rite of passage, is also part of Robert Jordan's political education." McCain, who was born in 1936 and experienced that disillusionment firsthand, is nonetheless much more interested in lauding the sacrifices of soldiers than ripping the mask off deceitful government planners. It's the literary interpretation of a loyal grunt, not a skeptical decision-maker.

But it wasn't a mere Company Man that first captivated the preteen McCain; it was an improvisational, courageous lone wolf and martyr who got the girl while leading a ragtag band of mountain rebels against a heavily armed dictatorship. Which is also the same basic premise behind his still-favorite film, *Viva Zapata!*, whose Brando-portrayed title character merits a chapter of his own in *Worth the Fighting For*.

McCain caught *Viva Zapata!* in a Washington, D.C., movie theater a couple of years after discovering Hemingway. This was his introduction to the revolutionary hero Emiliano Zapata, a brooding horseman and explosive charismatic who battled autocrats in early twentieth-century Mexico just so that his local villagers could once again plant corn on their land. McCain's instant attraction to the film will sound familiar. "For the most part, the movie is filled with a foreboding of recurring misfortune. And while it celebrates the heroism of one man with courage, independence, and an ardor for doing justice, its central theme is the futility—a glorious futility, to be sure, but a futility nonetheless—of expecting one person to save us all from iniquity."[29] Another generous helping of beautiful fatalism.

Like Robert Jordan, Brando's Zapata (complete with sombrero, dark makeup, and the most comical droopy mustache this side of Snoopy's cousin Spike) dynamites trains, rolls around with a raven-haired girl (without letting it distract him from the cause), navigates corrupt politics in the capital, grapples with drunken treachery, shoots his friend, and dies in combat. He's a devil-may-care underdog, a ragged rebel who chooses to fight hopeless odds with no superpower army to back him. (It is worth noting, though McCain never remarks on it, that his Annapolis-trained grandfather and father spent their lifetimes battling the communism that Robert Jordan supported, and that his grandfather's brother hunted down Zapata's greatest military ally.)

Quite unlike Robert Jordan, Zapata was an emotional and physical brawler, rough with the ladies, and illiterate. "His manner—humorless, unyielding, and violent—needed a good cause to make it tolerable," McCain wrote. "The experience [of seeing the film] enlivened my dreams of fighting for justice as fearlessly as Zapata had. But even more important to me was my hope that by doing so I would provoke the right sort of enemy. I wanted to be a good man, of course, and fight in a good cause. But what was the point of being good if it didn't gain the attention of the bad? To do that, I reasoned, the good man has to know how to be a little bad sometimes, as long as his misbehavior is for the right cause."

Here we see the contemporary purposes for McCain's ongoing discussion of his fictional boyhood heroes. There are essentially three possible morals, all of them overlapping, to any serious McCain story, whether fiction or nonfiction: (1) that the rugged individualist on his own is no match for life's hardest challenges; (2) that enlisting in a cause greater than yourself (preferably that of American exceptionalism) elevates your life without submerging your individualism; and (3) that the excesses of selfishness are forgivable—even desirable—when channeled in the service of that greater cause. So not only does Zapata's unseemly behavior (throwing his wife in the dirt, slamming his prospective father-in-law's chin on the kitchen table, using saleswomen as suicide bombers) become "tolerable," we are expected to forgive a young McCain for actively trying to emulate Zapata's badness, as long as it was for the "right cause." (And given that he was bred from birth to join the U.S. Navy, his causes' righteousness can be safely presumed.)

This formulation provides an ingenious way out of an otherwise awkward contradiction. For just as his exaggerated impersonation of his grandfather's charisma became a conflicting source of high tribute and personal regret, so too are McCain's enduring heroes of youth symbols of the two competing sides of his personality. He originally loved Jordan and Zapata because they were vigorous and violent martyrs who fought for doomed causes and died with their boots on in far-flung lands. In fact, he *still* loves them for that reason, occasional protestations to the contrary notwithstanding. But the adult McCain feels like he has to reject some of those childish things even while forgiving his younger impulses. "I had not the wit," he writes in *Worth the Fighting For*, "to articulate the truth [*For Whom the Bell Tolls*] taught or the wisdom to really understand it. . . . [I was] heedless of the book's warning not to carry individualism so far that it becomes egotism."

Now older and wiser in the way of greater causes, McCain thinks he has finally cracked the mystery of the "worth the fighting for" phrase that he can't get out of his mind. "To me it means everything," he told radio interviewer Dick Gordon in 2005. "Maximize your time, be associated with a cause greater than your self-interest. Care about the world—not just your own self, care about the entire world—which is the opportunity that the United States has as a nation today, because we're the most powerful nation in history, going back to the Roman Empire."

It takes real message discipline to convert the fuel of an essentially anti-imperialist novel into the fire of virtuous empire, but the flatness of McCain's voice betrays a perfunctory enthusiasm about slapping his one-size-fits-all moral

onto a book that initially thrilled him for an altogether different reason. "He's a man," McCain said earlier in the same
interview, with considerably more brio, "who's willing to sacrifice his life for what he believes in, even if what he believes in
he realizes is flawed in many respects. Remarkable, remarkable
story." Save that "cause greater" stuff for later—bring on the
climactic shoot-out!

The penultimate scene of *Viva Zapata!* is the kind that
sticks with you for years. After 90 minutes of frenetic and
exuberant action, with a constant flow of *campesinos*, horses,
children, pigs, soldiers, and schemers, the film slows down to
a spooky, impressionistic crawl. Brando's Zapata, who has for
so long evaded capture and staged guerilla raids, is lured out
of the mountains by an offer of ammunition and materiel
from a turncoat soldier. His wife, her nerves worn to nubs
after 10 years of struggle, is sure it's a trap, but he goes anyway. In a dusty plaza of a forgotten pueblo, Brando, all alone
and utterly serene, is then ambushed from all sides. As he
crouches like a pill bug in the center of the courtyard and is
plugged with hundreds of bullets, you half expect him to rise
up again, stronger than ever. The peasants, in fact, don't
believe it's Zapata's dead body—no mere 100-to-1 disadvan-
tage is enough to cut down *this* warrior.

On July 10, 2007, McCain encountered a political am-
bush of his own. After desultory second-quarter fundraising
results, his longtime political guru John Weaver, who is to
McCain what Karl Rove is to George W. Bush, resigned
from the senator's campaign, along with campaign manager
Terry Nelson and two other senior executives. Even Mark
Salter, the candidate's alter-ego, confidant, and co-author of
his five books, announced he was going off payroll and cutting down his activities. "If that's true," one shocked McCain

loyalist told the *National Review*, "no one is left in McCain world." *Newsweek*'s Richard Wolffe cracked that "the last person left is the candidate himself." The comedic political blogger known as Baseball Crank took it one step further: "John McCain's campaign today announced that Senator McCain has been let go from his role in the campaign."

That last bit was satire, but the beleaguered senator himself might have been the one laughing the most. Nothing is more beautiful to this 70-year-old boy than a truly hopeless cause. Now that half the political world is ready to give his candidacy up for dead, he may have finally hit his sweet spot. His heroes, certainly, have seen much worse.

2

THE DEFIANT ONE

A rebel without a cause is just a punk. Whatever you're called—rebel, unorthodox, nonconformist, radical—it's all self-indulgence without a good cause to give your life meaning.

—John McCain, *Worth the Fighting For*[1]

"Fuck you," he yelled at the guards as they hurried him along, aware that other prisoners could see him and were loving every minute of it. "Fuck you, you goddamned slant-eyed cocksuckers."

—Robert Timberg, *John McCain: An American Odyssey*[2]

On January 10, 2007, after months of speculation that the White House was finally considering a plan to withdraw from Iraq, President George Bush gave a prime-time address announcing instead the deployment of 20,000 additional U.S. troops, who would be given more aggressive rules of engagement. The new surge strategy went over like a lead balloon in public opinion, but within minutes John McCain popped up on *Larry King Live* to praise the speech as "excellent." This was hardly surprising given that McCain had been calling for more boots on the ground in Iraq for more than three years; but still the enthusiasm stuck out like a buoy in a sea of skepticism. King then asked the senator whether his support for an unpopular war threatened to hurt his political ambitions. "Well," McCain said, "I don't know what's going to happen a year from now, Larry, but I can tell you"—and here he let slip a weirdly inappropriate grin—"I would much rather lose a campaign than lose a war."

Why was this man smiling? Well, for one, he knew that his stance would be greeted as a refreshing return to straight-talking form by journalists who'd spent the previous year bemoaning his less-convincing suck-up to the social-conservative Right. (Three days later, sure enough, the *Chicago Tribune* ran the headline: "Defiant McCain Back as Maverick.") He might have also been registering pleasure at testing out a winning campaign catchphrase, one that he and his supporters would go on to repeat scores of times in the ensuing months. McCain, after all, has a long history of reaping political benefit from declaring himself above politics, especially during times of war. He delayed announcing his candidacy for president in 1999 in deference to the seriousness of the Kosovo crisis, and then was on television more in the following few months than any other contender, backing President Clinton's decision to intervene, decrying Republican isolationism, and calling for more boots on the ground. In mid-July 2007, longtime backers such as the *Weekly Standard's* William Kristol[3] were recommending that McCain suspend his foundering campaign to focus on holding the Senate line on Iraq, and then see if the field was ripe for re-entering come the fall.[4]

But the most likely reason McCain was smiling on Surge Night was that once again he found himself in his favorite position—outnumbered on all sides, defending an unpopular and perhaps hopeless cause, sticking defiantly to his guns. Emiliano Zapata would have been proud. About the only other time during the 2008 campaign that McCain looked more ebullient featured conditions that were strikingly similar. It was at the end of the third GOP debate, after the candidate had glumly taken an hour-long thumping from all nine of his competitors over the comprehensive immigration reform bill that he had spent years trying to shepherd through Congress, over the furious objections of the GOP base, especially in Arizona. At one point, immigration restrictionist and Colorado Congressman Tom Tancredo warned that English needed to be made the official language of the country "to hold us together." Then McCain's rival Mitt Romney, former governor of Massachusetts, slickly evaded a question about how he could support English-only laws while also running Spanish-language commercials. McCain, suddenly looking relaxed for the first time in months, said "Governor, *muchas gracias*," then uncorked a moving extemporaneous speech about the Hispanic names "engraved in black granite" at the Vietnam memorial, and the "green-card holders who are not even citizens of this country, who love this country so much that they're willing to risk their lives in its service in order to accelerate their path to citizenship and enjoy the bountiful, blessed nation." Love or hate the immigration bill, it was an inspiring patriotic soliloquy, and McCain's ear-to-ear smile after the debate betrayed a man pleased with once again delivering a knockout punch with his back up against the wall.

John McCain's most attractive quality is also his Achilles' Heel. He's a spirited, defiant rebel, not only unafraid to speak his mind, but instinctively drawn to minority causes he can portray as a fight between good and evil. He takes impish delight in gratuitously telling his own allies what they don't want to hear, whether it's making sure a pro-life audience understands that he supports stem cell research, or hectoring environmentalists about the benefits of nuclear power. He will insist that his motivation is to merely do whatever's right for the country, and that's certainly an important part of the story, but he's also been hardwired since childhood to find the underdog's corner and come out swinging.

The three famous John Sidney McCains of the U.S. Navy (there's a fourth now, he's just not famous yet) shared many things in common. Each was short and runty for his age and occupation; Slew was 5 foot 7, Jack 5 foot 6, and John is 5 foot 7. Each had an outsized temper, would fight in a second, and took more umbrage than most at hazing rituals. While each was well-read and curious and would achieve some distinction in the world of letters, none was much of a student: Grandfather graduated 80th in an Annapolis class of 116, father 423rd out of 441, and the senator an almost heroically dreadful 894th out of 899. They were all first-class hell-raisers, drinkers, and cussers, even by Navy standards, earning nicknames like "Good Goddamn McCain" and "McNasty." And each married above his social station: Slew to his own language instructor at Ole Miss, Jack to the vivacious daughter of a millionaire oil wildcatter, and John (in his second and current marriage) to the educated daughter of one of Arizona's richest men.

When John McCain writes about his dad (with whom he had a much frostier relationship than Jack had with Slew[5]), it's hard to know where father leaves off and son begins. "His irregular childhood, the constant disruptions occasioned by his father's transfers, were a challenge to him, as, I suspect, was his small stature," he wrote in *Faith of My Fathers*.[6] "It intensified an adolescent compulsion to prove his courage and daring to his peers in whatever new social circumstances he found himself in. The quickest way to do so was to exhibit a studied indifference to the established order, devise imaginative circumventions of the rules, take your punishment, show no remorse, and fight at the drop of a hat." Part of this surliness came from what McCain termed a "secret resentment" that his life "seemed preordained" with the Navy. "For most of us I think our strong sense of predestination made us prematurely fatalistic. And while that condition gave us a kind of confidence, it was often a reckless confidence. We started with small rebellions against the conventions of our heritage. And as we grew older and coarser, our transgressions became more serious."

It is startling to contemplate how violent John McCain was well into his 20s. "When I was disciplined by my teachers, which happened regularly, it was often for fighting," he wrote in *Faith of My Fathers*. At every new school he would "fight the first kid who provoked" him, not really caring whether he won or lost. At Episcopal High, his elite boarding school in Arlington, Virginia, even McCain's friends (for example, Malcolm Matheson, as told to Robert Timberg in *John McCain: An American Odyssey*) remember him as "a hard rock kind of guy, a tough, mean little fucker." Another Episcopal alumnus told Timberg: "He prided himself on being a tough guy. He was seemingly ready to fight at the drop of a hat. He was easily provoked, ready to be provoked." He even yelled "Shove it up your ass!" to some unimpressed housing development girls he and two buddies were trying to pick up one summer night, an outburst that led to his friend being wrongly fingered in juvenile court for verbal assault. (McCain told Timberg he did not recall the events.) He wrestled in high school and boxed at the Naval Academy, making up for lack of technique with bulldog aggression and the ability to take a beating. Even while maturing at the Academy, he and his friends were constantly sneaking off grounds, where they "drank a lot of beer, [and] occasionally got in fights." One of his treasured memories as a midshipman was being drunk on shore leave in Cuba and charging into the middle of a huge brawl between Marines and sailors. "We loved it," he recalled.[7]

But there were more debonair sides to his rebellions, too. He'd ape James Dean, buy Elvis Presley records, and hang out in jazz clubs. Episcopal had a strict dress code, so McCain would flaunt it by sporting filthy Levi's, motorcycle boots, a beat-up trench coat, and an ever-present cigarette when the coast was clear. As former headmaster Dick Thomsen recalled to Paul Alexander, "He walked around with his jacket and tie all messed up. The tie would be at half-mast and jacket collar turned up. He'd have this sort of surly look on his face, that 'Don't tread on me' type of expression. He traveled with a gang that was, I guess you could say, dissidents. He may have broken every rule in the book but he got away with most of them."[8] Most legendary among his gang's feats of derring-do were their nocturnal raids on the bars and burlesque houses of Washington, D.C.'s 9th Street. "Their sins were more fancy than ours, whatever they were," classmate Bentley Orrick told Timberg. "If we went over the wall to see a movie, they'd walk over the wall to get laid, or at least that was the projection." McCain, in *Faith of My Fathers*, demurs.

"Our exploits there were tame compared to my more reckless conduct at the Naval Academy. But because we exaggerated them for the benefit of our rule-abiding classmates we were granted some prestige for our daring, and for the welcome fallacy that our excursions were somehow leading us to romantic opportunities that were only imagined in our all-male society." McCain was creating the persona that would stick to him until he was shot down in Vietnam and continue influencing his life long afterward.

Episcopal was modeled on a military academy, took its honor code seriously, and aimed to mold well-bred sons of the South into disciplined future leaders (McCain, as a cosmopolitan navy junior whose parents entertained frequently on Capitol Hill, was not typical for the school). As he would in the Naval Academy, McCain learned through crude trial and error how to make the system (and his tenuous place within it) bend but not break. While cloaked in rebellion, this cycle itself was something of a tradition, argued the historian John Karaagac in *John McCain: An Essay in Military and Political History*. "McCain's description of himself," he wrote, "suggests an ethos of laconic disinterest, not of the antihero, but the anti-striver, the rebel against externally imposed constrictions and (within limits) authority. In his memoir, everything becomes a kind of game of adolescent brinkmanship, how much one can press the limits of the acceptable and elude the powers that be. This itself conforms to an unwritten code of geniality and group camaraderie. . . . Defiance of the rules was even a test of martial fiber and, implausibly, leadership."

Ask modern servicemen to name their favorite military movies, and there will be a surprising the number of votes for counterculture classics like Stanley Kubrick's *Full Metal Jacket* and especially Bill Murray's *Stripes*, as opposed to more traditional character-building exercises like *An Officer and a Gentleman*. Navy fliers like John McCain will also frequently pull the lever for *Top Gun*. What all these films have in common is an antihero protagonist, a slacker and/or hothead rebel who chafes against the system's small-minded discipline, clashes with the C.O. to the point of almost getting kicked out, and yet ends up developing into an unlikely hero and leader of men in battle. This is not just a fable, it's the storyline of all three John McCains—and an intentional design component of officer training. At the Naval Academy, Karaagac wrote, "the cadet or midshipman feels compelled to break lesser rules, not in spite, but because of the code of personal honor and conduct. . . . Hard as it is to appreciate, the Academy's concept of personal honor actually encompasses minor truancies that are turned into a type of lesser code within the context of an adherence to the institution and its professional mores. . . . It becomes a type of gamble or dare at the fringes of the oppressive systems of rules and regulations. If caught, the violator pays the penalty without complaint or griping, which allegedly shows a certain manly virtue."

Still, as Karaagac wrote, "one is altogether astonished by McCain's breaking the rules," and his "streak of recklessness and lack of prudence." Astonished, yes, but also hugely entertained. A full five chapters of *Faith of My Fathers* is dedicated to what a cussed and outrageous sonofabitch McCain was between high school and Vietnam, a formative stretch of 15 years. It would be an opposition researcher's dream come true if it weren't for the fact that McCain cheerfully and preemptively offers up the damning evidence himself. Among the many highlights:

- At the Naval Academy, ensign McCain "embarked on a four-year course of insubordination and rebellion," leading a group of miscreants called the Bad Bunch, who escaped "over the Academy walls on many an evening," breaking untold numbers of regulations and laws. "Women were just drawn to him," Annapolis roommate Jack Dittrick told Timberg.

- Scheduled to meet a girlfriend in Philadelphia one summer, he instead got plastered at the train station, arrived at her parents' house several hours late, crashed through her screen door and was sent home after a few minutes. "I never saw the girl or her family again."[9]

- During his sophomore year, when midshipmen of his class were still supposed to be seen and not heard, McCain broke all protocol by ripping into an upperclassman for verbally abusing a Filipino waiter.

- On leave in Rio de Janeiro he and his pals indulged "in the vices sailors are infamous for," and over the course of "excessive drinking, nightclubbing, and little or no sleep" hooked up with a Brazilian fashion model from a "wealthy and socially prominent family." The two had a torrid five-day affair and kept up a long-distance relationship for a number of months. McCain still never tires of talking about her on the campaign trail.

- After graduation, he took up with a tobacco heiress in Europe. (McCain's women seemed mostly to be heiresses, models, or strippers.) During other stints in Europe, he became a regular at Monte Carlo casinos.

- At flight school in Pensacola, Florida, McCain tells how "I enjoyed the off-duty life of a Navy flyer more than I enjoyed actual flying. I drove a Corvette, dated a lot, spent all my free hours at bars and beach parties, and generally misused my good health and youth." Among his girlfriends was a stripper known as Marie, the Flame of Florida.[10]

- In Spain, doing an unauthorized flyby, he knocked down some power lines and caused a blackout, creating "a small international incident."

- At Mississippi's McCain field (named after his grandfather), John "organized a number of legendary bacchanals" under the auspices of the "Key Fess Yacht Club," an ad hoc party shack where he brought in girls, bands, and togas.

As Karaagac shrewdly laid out, this seemingly inappropriate behavior actually had a useful and well-worn function when it came to the business of flying warplanes on and off aircraft carriers: "In fact, McCain's personality traits seemed rather well-suited to the life of the naval aviator. The very characteristics that made McCain 'worst rat' at prep school and problem plebe at the Academy turned out to be assets in a military branch that prized a certain extroverted aggressiveness, personal valor, and even daring bravado. Ultimately, the flyer needed good nerves and an inner-directed confidence. He needed an element of professional strut and bravado. All formed the psychic barrier against the creeping fear and trembling that shakes even the most sturdy of warriors when least expected."

The beautiful fatalism helped too. McCain ditched one plane in Corpus Christi Bay and another somewhere between Maryland and Virginia, without losing his nerve. In July 1967, just before takeoff from the *USS Forrestal* on what was supposed to be his sixth bombing run over Vietnam, an electrical power surge set off a Zuni missile from a nearby F-4 Phantom, ripping straight into McCain's A-4 Skyhawk while he was in the cockpit. With planes exploding all around, McCain climbed onto the nose of his jet, jumped and rolled through the flames, then ran like hell. The fire killed an appalling 134 men and took days to put out. Though it was the deadliest military accident since World War II, and became the subject of a full-length book and annual study at the Naval Academy, McCain exhibits a striking lack of introspection about the carnage: just five pages in *Faith of My Fathers*, two of them dedicated almost callously to what he fretted at the time was its negative impact on his combat career. "It appeared that my time at war was to be a very brief experience, and this distressed me considerably," he wrote. "As the crippled *Forrestal* limped toward port, my moment was disappearing when it had barely begun, and I feared my ambitions were among the casualties in the calamity." A new assignment to the *USS Oriskany* proved his fears unfounded and provided practical use for his compartmentalization of horror. Two months later, at the age of the 31, he was shot down over Hanoi harbor.

It's useful here to step back and consider how McCain the presidential candidate portrays his extended adolescence. On the one hand, there is evident pride and good, self-deprecating humor in detailing his youthful excesses (which he explores in considerably greater detail than, say, the mechanics of flight instruction, or whatever it was he may have thought about Cold War politics or popular culture between "The Sun Sessions" and "Sgt. Pepper"). On the other hand, the willful egotism of the whole period is set up as a literary device, a lengthy bit of foreshadowing about how an interesting but ultimately unserious rugged individualist is about to learn the most valuable lesson of all, changing him forever. "Most of my reminiscences feature the frivolous escapades with which I once established my reputation as a rash and prideful nonconformist," he writes of his Annapolis days. In his 20s, when he began to itch for combat and promotion, "I worried that my deserved reputation for foolishness would make command of a squadron or a carrier, the pinnacle of a young pilot's aspiration, too grand an ambition for an obstreperous admiral's son, and my failure to reach command would dishonor me and my family." His despair was such that he even talked of quitting the Navy at some point and joining the

French Foreign Legion instead, losing interest only after he found out how severe the requirements were.

After learning his life's lesson in captivity, McCain was "no longer the boy to whom liberty meant simply that I could do as I pleased, and who, in my vanity, used my freedom to polish my image as an I-don't-give-a-damn nonconformist." It looks like a clean character arc. It was anything but.

McCain's combative and rebellious personality, molded and channeled by Navy traditions and lacquered in third-generation fatalism, had served him surprisingly well (if sloppily) as a Navy flier and combat pilot with 22 bombing runs under his belt. Though it was this character trait that he said was changed by Vietnam, there is plenty of evidence to suggest that it propelled him through much of his defiant tenure in enemy hands. "There are only a few short causal leaps from McCain the Academy truant, quick to uphold honor but also defy the upper class lackeys, to the aggressive noncollaborator and problem prisoner in Hanoi," Karaagac wrote. "Clearly, McCain's role in the 'bad bunch' of Annapolis set the precedent for his status in the 'Hell's Angels,' those prisoners of war incarcerated in a separate compound and solitary confinement for their disruptive behavior."

McCain's remarkable prison story, though very well known by now, is always worth retelling. On September 29, 1967, he was shot down by an antiaircraft missile during a bombing run over Hanoi. He ejected into a piece of his own plane, breaking both arms and his right knee, and splashed down in Truc Bach Lake. He blacked out, almost drowned, and then was pulled ashore by more than a dozen angry Vietnamese, who commenced kicking and screaming and stabbing. Somebody broke his shoulder with a rifle butt, another bayoneted his ankle. Finally, an army truck came and took him to the Hanoi Hilton, where he was interrogated and beaten for another four days. He likely would have been left for dead, but the Vietnamese learned that his father was an admiral, so they took him to a hospital for stabilization and yet more interrogation and beating. Eventually, he coughed up the name of his ship, squadron, and bombing target. For that, he received a cast for one of his broken arms and was told to give an upbeat interview to a visiting French journalist in order to receive treatment for his wrecked knee. In December, they operated, hacking through all of his ligaments. He was malnourished, wracked with dysentery, and 50 pounds underweight when they dumped him in a cell with two Americans, George "Bud" Day and Norris Overly. They thought he wouldn't survive the night.

Instead he yakked all day and the next, grateful for interaction with Americans, and began to very slowly get better with the help of his new cellmates (especially Overly; Day was pretty busted up, too). "I can remember thinking that night, My God, this guy's got a lot of heart," Day later told Timberg. "You've been involved in sports and games and things where people kind of rise to an occasion, and that was him. He was rising. And if he hadn't been, he'd have been dead."

In April 1968, with his condition much improved (although still miserable), McCain was moved into solitary confinement, a brutal blow to a man so dependent on communication and chatter. "It's an awful thing, solitary," he wrote in *Faith of My Fathers*. "It crushes your spirit and weakens your resistance more effectively than any other form of mistreatment." In June, he was given a surprise offer of early release (a few months before, Overly had accepted a similar deal, in noncompliance with the Code of Conduct for American Prisoners of War, which states that

POWs shall demand they be released in the order of their capture, unless they have life-threatening medical conditions). McCain, who was very much injured and somewhat sick, considered the offer, but eventually turned it down. Two months later, he was brought in to sign and tape-record a confession of his crimes against the Vietnamese people, and when he refused, was tortured severely through beatings and rope holds. After four days, he finally cracked. He confessed, then was thrown back into solitary for two weeks. It was McCain's rock bottom.[12]

"They were the worst two weeks of my life. I couldn't rationalize away my confession. I was ashamed. I felt faithless, and couldn't control my despair. I shook, as if my disgrace were a fever. I kept imagining that they would release my confession to embarrass my father. All my pride was lost, and I doubted I would ever stand up to any man again. Nothing could save me. No one would ever look upon me again with anything but pity or contempt."[13]

If this story were a conventional, orderly narrative, a fellow prisoner would then bring McCain back from the brink; he would see all at once that his youthful rebellions were just pointless acts of selfish defiance, and then be emboldened thereafter by a newfound strength derived from the greater cause of comrades and country. But McCain has never told the story in anything like linear narrative. In *Faith of My Fathers*, which zigzags all over the place during the Hanoi chapters, he jumps from rock bottom to "the end of 1969" in the very next paragraph. In his 12,000 word essay for *U.S. News & World Report* two months after his return, he goes from confession to his generalized tools for coping: prayer, hatred, and communication. And it wasn't until more than 30 years later that McCain started using the "cause greater" formulation. "In prison, where my cherished independence was mocked and assaulted, I found my self-respect in a shared fidelity to my country," he wrote in *Faith of My Fathers*. "I thought glory was the object of war, and all glory was self-glory. No more. For I have learned the truth: there are greater pursuits than self-seeking. . . . Glory belongs to the act of being constant to something greater than yourself, to a cause, to your principles, to the people on whom you rely, and who rely on you in return. No misfortune, no injury, no humiliation can destroy it."

No one should begrudge a soldier his interpretation of his own prisoner-of-war experience. But since this lesson is the through-line of McCain's politics, of his purposes for using the government and conducting U.S. foreign policy, it's worth asking at least one question: Is he giving his own considerable rugged individualism short shrift?

There was no motivational speech to pick McCain up off the floor after his confession. Prison neighbor Bob Craner did his level best to cheer him up, "but I couldn't shake it off," McCain reports. Yet after two weeks of this misery, when the Vietnamese brought him back in to sign another confession, he refused and would go on resisting their demands for the next 15 months of beatings, torture, and solitary confinement. "I had recovered enough to resist," McCain explains simply.

Meanwhile, there were numerous occasions when the adolescent brawler-turned Navy flyboy gave his comrades great cheer not by solemnly renouncing his individualism, but by brazenly spitting in the eye of his tormentors. These include:

- On Christmas Eve of 1968, a couple of months after breaking McCain, the Vietnamese arranged a Potemkin Christmas service for the prisoners with the propaganda cameras rolling. The inmates, many of whom had never seen one another, were under strict orders not to talk. In Timberg's marvelous telling:

"Fuck that," said McCain. Turning to the nearest American, he said, "Hey, pal, my name's John McCain. What's yours?"

"McCain, stop talking," cooed a smiling guard called Soft Soap fairy, aware that he was on camera.

"Fuck you," said McCain, louder than before. "This is fucking bullshit. This is terrible. This isn't Christmas. This is a propaganda show."

McCain hastily briefed his new friend. "I refused to go home. I was tortured for it. They broke my rib and rebroke my arm. . . . "

"No talking!"

"Fuck you!" said McCain, momentarily interrupting his briefing. Resuming, he said, "Our senior ranking officer is—"

"No talking!" said the Prick, who had rushed to a spot just outside camera range to try to control his favorite prisoner.

"Fu-u-u-u-ck you, you son of a bitch!" shouted McCain, hoisting a one-finger salute whenever a camera pointed in his direction.[14]

- After being interrogated and tortured in the awful October 1968–December 1969 period, McCain recalls, I "always shouted greetings to the prisoners whose cells I passed, smiled, and flashed a thumbs-up."

- When dignitaries would visit, and/or whenever there were cameras on the premises, McCain would let loose with "some of the most colorful profanity that you would ever hope to hear," prisoner Jack Van Loan told Timberg. "Here's a guy that's all crippled up, all busted up, and he doesn't know if he's going to live to the next day, and he literally blew them out of there with a verbal assault. You can't imagine the example John set for the rest of the camp by doing that."[15]

- Punished repeatedly for communicating with fellow prisoners by using tap code, McCain would just keep on using tap code and take his punishments. "Acts of defiance felt so good," he explained, "that I felt they more than compensated for their repercussions, and they helped me keep at bay the unsettling feelings of guilt and self-doubt that my confession had aroused."

Looking at the events McCain portrays, rather than his interpretation of them, what emerges is the same old sonofabitch, with the familiar reservoir of back-against-the-wall defiance, manufactured courage and potent charisma, who (like almost all POWs) fell short of perfection under extreme duress and then found extra strength and a new sense of humility from the brave and patriotic men around him. Like many, in his deprivation he fell in love with his country all over again and developed a more sober sense of purpose to serve it upon return. But instead of merely deepening his appreciation for his band of brothers, McCain has—slowly, and over time—interpreted this mix of messages as a rebuke to the rebellious, just-for-the-hell-of-it nonconformity that he brought with him to prison. "I learned in Vietnam how short a distance separates the individualist from the egotist and how neither can match the strength of a community united to serve a cause greater than self interest," he wrote in the prologue to *Worth the Fighting For*. "I have not forgotten the lesson."

You can still be a rebel. But it don't mean jack without a cause. And that goes for non-soldiers, too.

THE ELITIST

*McCain has evolved over his 20-year political career into the one
current politician who best articulates the hopes and dreams of
the common man, the citizen out there in Kansas or Oklahoma
or Alabama who wants to see a return to populism in America.*

—Paul Alexander, *Man of the People*[1]

*He is so arrogant, and so above it all, and it just permeates his
staff. He's so enamored with himself about running for president,
about being the senior senator from Arizona, and the power that
he has, which is a good godawful lot, that I think he's just turned
his back on the people that have elected him.*

—Lyle Tuttle, chairman, Maricopa County
Republican Committee[2]

The event couldn't have been more tailor-made for that populist man of the people, John McCain. More than 50 proud
veterans, most of them from the Vietnam War, were gathered
in a historic Sonoma, California, park to commemorate Flag
Day 2007. As they do each year, the grizzled-looking vets and
other local volunteers solemnly recreated the 1846 raising
of the Bear Flag, symbol of the effort to extract California's

independence from Mexico. Century-old fraternal organizations cheerfully sold barbecue, poured local microbrews, and auctioned off posters of such McCain heroes as Pat Tillman to help raise money for one of the McCains' favorite causes—cleft-palate surgery for children. (The procedure saved the life of the McCains' teenage daughter Bridget, who they adopted from Bangladesh, and Cindy McCain is very active in a global nonprofit called Operation Smile.) Tattooed teens and misfit bikers sat at long picnic tables with New Age art-sellers and patriotic grandmothers, mixing amiably and listening to a blues band called The Hellhounds. "This is 100% genuine, grade-A, locally produced community volunteerism at its finest!" beamed one of the main organizers, George Webber. At the anointed hour a ramshackle, all-amateur cast, decked out in period costume and elaborate mustaches, performed a hilarious yet educational re-staging of the Bear Flag Revolt on its 161st anniversary. Sonomans, Webber bellowed in conclusion, have been "ornery and independent ever since!"

Only one ingredient was missing from this made-for-McCain moment: the candidate himself. He was in Sonoma all right, but not with the little people in the plaza. Less than four miles away, up on a hilltop with 360-degree views, the senator was holding a $2,300-a-head luncheon at a $35 million manse called Villa Shanel, one of eight McCain fundraising events during a four-day California swing. The 11,600-square foot faux-Tuscan residence, perched on 360 acres in the heart of wine country, is famous throughout the Bay Area for its high society bacchanals, and large enough to have its own fire department.[3] Estate owner Gary Shansby, a consumer products venture capitalist and fine-arts philanthropist who makes frequent appearances in the *San Francisco Chronicle*'s Swells column, reported to the *New York Times* that McCain was seen bucolically grazing on the property's ample berry bushes, even as the crusty vets in VFW caps held dignified salutes down in the lowlands.[4]

Not only was it an odd choice of venue that day for a celebrated populist, it was hardly the most Republican of locations, either, being in the heart of where San Francisco's rich go to summer. Shansby, one of McCain's national fundraising co-chairs (despite having been mostly removed from national politics for the past two decades), expressed frustration that his candidate keeps insisting on red-state themes while trying to pass the hat. "I tell him all the time, 'Everyone knows where you are on Iraq,'" Shansby told the *Times*. "'Let's talk about the environment, pork-barrel spending, health care, dependence on foreign oil.'"

The myth that John McCain is a "man of the people," a natural-born genius at retail politics, is so all-pervasive that one feels like an atheist at Jesus Camp suggesting otherwise. In mid-July 2007, for example, with his campaign in heavily publicized tatters, poll numbers in the tank, and less money in the bank than the Republican Party's only real populist sensation this season (long shot Libertarian Congressman Ron Paul), a stripped-down McCain went back to New Hampshire's town hall circuit and was greeted with a national press chorus of "returning to his roots" stories. McClatchy News Service declared he was back "in his element" taking "question after question at a free-wheeling town hall meeting."[5] Reporters took at face value McCain's assertions: "We will continue to campaign the way I do best, which is not with money, but with town-hall meetings and face-to-face encounters with the voters."[6] As for the buzz-killing impact of his various campaign implosions, that was just "an inside-the-Beltway kind of thing," the candidate clucked.[7]

The facts, alas, say otherwise. From the beginning of his political career, McCain has never won an election without outspending his opponent, usually by massive amounts. He has engaged in intensive door-to-door politicking just twice (Phoenix in 1982, New Hampshire in 1999–2000). And he has lived the bulk of his life inside the very Beltway he's so fond of campaigning against. With the notable exception of the soldiers he's served with and the staffers he's employed, McCain has favored the company of corporate bigwigs, powerful politicians, and nationally known journalists since before he ever ran for office.

Ask Arizonans whether their senior senator is a "man of the people" and those who have an opinion will laugh. "He's just above it all; he doesn't have time to mess with peons," said Lyle Tuttle, chairman of the Maricopa County Republican Committee. Don Hesselbrock, who has been active in the Arizona GOP since the 1970s, says McCain avoids contact with the unwashed, in direct contrast to junior Republican Senator John Kyl. "[Kyl] would rather have a packed room of a thousand people paying ten dollars each, where John McCain always seemed much more comfortable having a room of a dozen people paying a thousand dollars each," Hesselbrock said. "Almost every fundraiser I've ever known McCain ran just tend to be a very high-dollar affair, and a fairly exclusive group."

The genesis of McCain's populist myth comes from his first campaign for Congress, in 1982, when the uprooted Beltway resident ran for the Phoenix-area seat being vacated by retiring Republican John Rhodes. During the primary, in Robert Timberg's telling, McCain "campaigned door-to-door six hours a day, six days a week, personally knocking on twenty thousand Republican doors. By the end of the campaign he had gone through three pairs of shoes—Cindy had the third pair bronzed—and developed skin cancer."[8] An impressive display of McCain's famously boundless energy and determination, to be sure. But a Cinderella story of personal politics trumping money and connections? Not quite. "Many have told the tale of John McCain winning the 1st Congressional District by wearing out three pairs of shoes," the *Arizona Republic* wrote in its 19,000-word biographical pull-out section on the senator in October 1999. "McCain's footwear definitely took a beating during the race, but it was more greenbacks than soles that swept McCain into the U.S. House of Representatives."

The carpetbagger spent $313,000 that year ($670,000 in 2006 dollars) on the primary campaign alone, more than any of his more locally renowned rivals.[9] Just over half of that came from loans to himself, using his rich young wife's considerable collateral (Cindy McCain's father Jim Hensley was one of the wealthiest men in the state, his wealth derived from owning the Maricopa County franchise for distribution of Anheuser-Busch beer). When asked by the *New York Times Magazine* in July 2007[10] whether he'd consider borrowing $5 million from his wife, McCain snorted that he'd "never do such a thing" because it's more "appropriate" to focus on small donors, but in fact he would never do such a thing because the practice is now *illegal*. But McCain back then had other important assets on his side as well. Savings & Loan tycoon Charles Keating, McCain's first major political sponsor and close personal friend, helped raise more than $100,000 for the campaign.[11] Another powerful new friend, *Arizona Republic* Publisher Duke Tully, took McCain under his wing, introduced him to Phoenix-area bigwigs, and delivered his newspaper's endorsement.[12] McCain also had the backing of such Washington-cultivated friends as Sen. John Tower, R-Texas, and even the president of the United States.

"Thanks to my prisoner of war experience, I had, as they say in politics, a good first story to sell," McCain recalled in *Worth the Fighting For*. "And with my connections to national political figures, including the Reagans, the money I believed I could raise . . . and an increasing number of new friends in my adopted hometown willing to get involved, I knew I had a pretty good shot at it." It would be the last seriously contested campaign McCain would run until losing the Republican presidential nomination to George W. Bush in 2000.

John McCain knew before puberty that he came from a special family, and he was groomed from age 10 for elite leadership. His grandfather was in those famous surrender pictures from the deck of the *USS Missouri* at the end of World War II, and when he died days later it made the front page of the *New York Times*. His father, a well-regarded submarine commander during the war, became the Navy's first chief of information and then the branch's liaison officer to Congress. "My parents kept a house on Capitol Hill," McCain wrote in *Faith of My Fathers*, "where they entertained leading political and military figures. My mother's charm proved as effective with politicians as it was with naval officers. The political relationships my parents forged during this period contributed significantly to my father's future success."[13]

Roberta Wright McCain, still alive at age 95 and traveling the world with her identical twin sister Rowena, was and is a regal, high-spirited woman determined to iron out the considerable rough edges on the McCain men, grooming them for political aspirations higher than their unpolished manners and indifferent education would suggest. (In this she shared a common trait with her mother-in-law, Katherine Davey

Vaulx McCain, who met her husband while teaching him at Ole Miss, and was forever supplementing his literary education and challenging him intellectually.) Roberta is the daughter of an Oklahoma oil wildcatter who moved to Southern California after making his fortune to send his daughters through school. McCain's father Jack, unlike his grandfather Slew, was socially awkward, had a problem holding his liquor, and showed little enthusiasm for all things non-Navy. Through Roberta's classy entertaining and gentle encouragements, she helped coax Jack into a more assertive, politically astute persona, one that became well known on Capitol Hill and the lecture circuit, where he championed the cause of an ever-stronger Navy.

"Her complete devotion to my father and his career contributed more to his success than anything else save his own determination," McCain wrote. Jack's posts in D.C. "helped to broaden his circle of acquaintances outside the Navy," and made him a regular figure in congressional hearings. During McCain's childhood, the family breakfast table included people like the chairman of the House Armed Forces Committee, and nighttime meant cocktails with generals, senators, and journalists. "Given my parents' many friendships with politicians," McCain wrote of his own experience as Navy liaison to Congress, "I was not over-awed to find myself in the company of the hundred powerful souls to whom I would now report."[14]

Like Al Gore and George W. Bush, McCain was the kind of Beltway offspring destined for elite, all-boys prep schools. First up was St. Stephen's middle school, then the more demanding boarding-school environment of Episcopal High, both in Arlington, Virginia. Though he stuck out at both institutions as a feisty military brat in a sea of well-bred southern preppies, McCain was being groomed for entrance into the Naval Academy; it was his introduction to a culture that would continue the evolutionary march of the McCain men. "EHS gave me a sense of what life could be like were I somehow to elude a Navy career," he wrote in *Faith of My Fathers*. "On a school holiday, some friends and I visited Princeton University. Long afterward, I would daydream about enrolling at Princeton, joining one of its stately eating clubs, and sharing in the romance of a place that seemed to me to offer equal parts of scholastic excellence and gracious leisure. But I was never so enthralled by the attraction of such a life that I deluded myself into sincerely believing it would be mine."

Being the namesake of a four-star admiral and an upwardly mobile Navy captain left McCain vulnerable to charges of nepotism, especially during his first decade of barely skating by in the armed services. Establishing a pattern that continues to this day, what set off McCain's considerable temper most quickly were accusations containing at least an element of truth—in this case, that he benefited from family connections. At the Naval Academy, on the verge of being kicked out for too many demerits, he was summoned to the commandant's office and informed that he was "spoiled." It was a charge McCain "greatly resented," and he risked his career by making that clear. "The commandant was neither the first nor the last person to accuse me of being spoiled, implying that my parents had greased my way in the world," McCain wrote in *Faith of My Fathers*. "Later in my career, as I rose through the ranks, some would attribute my advance to my admiral father's benefaction. I suppose it is an accusation that many children of successful parents learn to ignore. I never did, however. I grew red-faced and angry every time some know-it-all told me how easy a life my father had made for me."

What makes this passage especially interesting is that on several occasions McCain goes on to undermine his own protestations. He *did* receive special treatment because of his father, especially (ironically enough) in Hanoi, where he likely would have been left for dead had his captors not learned of his identity. Of the 591 POWs who came back to the United States in the first months of 1973 as part of Operation Homecoming, only one was offered an extraordinary 13-page spread in *U.S. News & World Report* in which to write about his experience, thereby launching a national profile. This certainly wasn't because of McCain's own rank, flight record, or length of imprisonment. His parents certainly *did* help grease his way in the world on occasion. For example, upon returning from Vietnam, McCain was denied entrance into the National War College because he was still a lieutenant commander, and only commanders and captains were eligible to enroll. So McCain explains: I "appealed [the] decision all the way to the secretary of the navy, my father's friend and now my Senate colleague, John Warner, who ordered the navy to grant my request and, by so doing, probably saved my career."[15] McCain become a trusted adviser to Warner on POW issues, a status most of the other 590 men likely did not enjoy.[16]

Although McCain had help getting his foot in the door, he made the most of his opportunities. The *U.S. News* piece may have fallen into his lap, but it was a remarkable, gracious, and nearly bitterness-free bit of writing, foreshadowing the literary success he would have with *Faith of My Fathers*. (Near the end of the piece readers are presented with a man already inflating political trial balloons—"My own plans for the future are to remain in the Navy, if I am able to return to flying status. That depends upon whether the corrective surgery on my arms and my leg is successful. If I have to leave the Navy, I hope to serve the Government in some capacity, preferably in Foreign Service for the State Department. I had a lot of time to think over there, and came to the conclusion that one of the most important things in life—along with a man's family—is to make some contribution to his country.") McCain may have had the benefit of a lowered bar when recertifying his fitness to fly an airplane, but he pushed himself through nine months of excruciating physical therapy to get within range. He may have been technically unqualified to become commanding officer of the Replacement Air Group in Jacksonville, Florida, but by all accounts he worked like hell, inspired his men, and won one meritorious citation after another. And all along he maintained that winning combination of his grandfather's charismatic derring-do and his mother's ambition-fueled social grace. When Ronald and Nancy Reagan held a series of homecoming events for the returning POWs in 1973, it was McCain who dazzled them with his presence and inspiring patriotic stories, building a friendship that would later lead to his wife Carol getting a job in the Reagan White House. "I had," he wrote later, "used my professional advantages well since I had come home from war."

By the time he was appointed to his father's old post as Navy liaison to Congress in 1977, McCain was champing at the bit to get into politics. He had already considered running for the House from Florida in 1976, but deemed the competition too tough. Long accustomed to Washington socializing and the Navy's organizational concerns, and still possessing plenty of his rakish charm (which led to a series of extramarital affairs during this period), he was ideally suited for a job that largely involved accompanying senators on long-distance trips and making sure the Navy's interests were being represented on Capitol Hill. Unsurprisingly, he proved to be one of the most popular Navy liaisons in history. "Under McCain," Timberg wrote, "the Navy's small liaison office on the first floor of the Russell Senate Office Building became a late-afternoon gathering spot where senators and staffers, usually from the Armed Services and Foreign Relations committees, would drop in for a drink and the chance to unwind. The magnet was McCain, a fun-loving, irreverent, mildly impetuous figure."[17] The party would often spill over to John and Carol's Alexandria house, where they entertained several times a week.[18] "John McCain, as a Navy captain, knew on a personal basis more senators and was more warmly received than virtually any lobbyist I have ever known in this town; they loved to see him," McCain's liaison-office colleague and future Air Force Undersecretary James McGovern told Timberg.

McCain made fast friends with two senators his own age: antiwar liberal Gary Hart, D-Colo., and moderate northeasterner William Cohen, R-Maine, both of whom served as groomsmen at his 1980 wedding to Cindy Hensley. "He was a fascinating character," Hart recalled to Nicholas Kristof in February 2000.[19] "He was current on the issues and could engage on every level. And he was very funny." Sen. John Tower, R-Texas, became McCain's senatorial father figure, talking foreign relations and encouraging him to run for elected office. "Late in the afternoon, on almost every day that the Senate was in session," McCain wrote, "his secretary would call me to say, 'The senator would like to see you.' I would drop whatever I was doing and join him in his office for a drink. It was unusual for a liaison officer to be on such close personal terms with a member of the Senate, especially such an influential member."

A Google search of "John McCain" and "Mr. Smith Goes to Washington" yields more than 13,000 hits. Yet far from being a morally pure outsider, an ethically sound nonpolitician who comes to D.C. from the hinterlands to restore common-sense virtue, McCain was raised, trained, and repurposed as politician smack dab in the muck of Capitol Hill, leveraging his name and personal connections to cut corners, jump lines, and even disobey orders. Such was the case in 1978, when President Jimmy Carter, a former submarine officer, decided that land defense capabilities were more important than expanding the Navy's carrier fleet, and so decided not to replace the USS Midway after it had been decommissioned. "For the next two years," Timberg wrote, "McCain, assisted by Jim McGovern, quietly but effectively lobbied for the new carrier in secret defiance of Secretary W. Graham Claytor, for whom he worked, and President Carter." Congress approved a $2 billion carrier in 1978, prompting Carter's veto, but with McCain's quiet lobbying passed it again the next year, and the weakened president signed it into law. How did McCain justify his duplicity? "We knew all the uniformed Navy agreed with us," he told Timberg. "We had enlisted petty officers with families on food stamps. We had ships that couldn't leave port. The problems were just incredible." The ends, in other words, justified the means.

But historian John Karaagac pointed out that McCain's arguments were bogus, and eventually hypocritical. "The huge carrier, so dear to the heart of the Navy's air wing and in many ways so questionable to the U.S. defense posture as a whole, had absolutely nothing to do with military families," he wrote in *John McCain: An Essay in Military and Political*

History.[20] "It is particularly ironic that the debate from the 1970s has a strange political foreshadowing in the context of the late 1990s. The only difference is that the political tables have been turned. Today it is Senator Lott . . . who has been an advocate of the carrier, which happens to be built in his home state and, more to the point, in his home town of Pascagoula, Miss. Today McCain rightly criticizes this as a boondoggle which does, in fact *detract* from the service-man's pay."

Prodded by driving ambition, and intoxicated by the influence of Capitol Hill, McCain "quickly became intrigued by the enormous power over the nation's security exercised by senior members of the Armed Services Committee." The most well-connected Navy liaison in modern history wanted to enter Congress through the front door. He moved to Phoenix with his new wife Cindy in the spring of 1981, days after burying his father and quitting the Navy; he was far too impatient to slog through the drudgery of slowly building a political profile. "Finding a political base in a community usually takes years of work, building recognition and respect for your civic-mindedness, associating with a local political party and volunteering your time to its causes, and running for local and state offices," he wrote. "I had neither the time nor the patience to follow a ten-year plan for election to Congress. I was in my forties and in a hurry, ambitious for the kind of influence I had seen wielded by the country's most accomplished politicians."

So at the dawn of his political career, the notion of John McCain being a plain-folks public official wasn't just laugh-able, it was an affront to the truth. McCain didn't have *time* for the people; he was too busy chasing after power. Before even moving to Arizona, he told Thad Cochran, Republican senator from Mississippi, that he'd win a House seat in 1982, and then pounce on the Senate seat when Barry Goldwater retired.[21] McCain thought he could just run for whatever new House jurisdiction was created by the 1980 census, but mapmakers drew up the new seat in faraway Tucson. Luckily for him, Rep. John Rhodes decided to retire. Cindy bought a house in Rhodes' district the very day of the announcement,[22] and McCain set about running to represent his brand new neighborhood.

The senator from Maine hooked him up with local political fixer Jay Smith; the senator from Texas flew out to raise money, and local grandees Charles Keating and Duke Tully made sure McCain had access to the Valley's powerbrokers. Aside from knocking on doors, it was about as much of a grassroots campaign as Hillary Clinton's first run for Senate.

McCain's blatant ambition, and lack of firsthand knowledge about his district's concerns, was his most obvious vulnerability. True to his nature, he responded to the justifiable criticism by lashing out in anger. "I was becoming pissed off by the carpetbagger label, and my temper was getting the better of my judgment (as it often has)," he wrote in *Worth the Fighting For*. What happened next has become the stuff of legend. At a candidates' forum, after months of stewing over the charge without formulating an effective response, McCain was asked about his carpetbagging again and became irate. "Listen, pal," he snapped, as the audience grew quiet. "I spent twenty-two years in the Navy. My father was in the Navy. My grandfather was in the Navy. We in the military service tend to move a lot. We have to live in all parts of the country, all parts of the world. I wish I could have had the luxury, like you, of growing up and living and spending my entire life in a nice place like the First District of Arizona, but I was doing other things. As a matter of fact, when I think about it now, the place I lived longest in my life was Hanoi."[23]

It was a beautiful line, neutralizing the criticism once and for all, maybe even delivering that first election to McCain. It was also, transparently, a lie: McCain lived in Arlington, Virginia, for at least five years as a kid, and several years later as Navy liaison. His grandfather had worked on Capitol Hill, his father worked on Capitol Hill, and he had worked on Capitol Hill. Called out as a carpetbagger—which he was by any definition of the word, and in fact by his own admission—he lied, wrapped himself in his imprisonment, and made his interlocutors feel like ungrateful chumps for even asking about it.

Once in office, unsurprisingly, McCain didn't magically morph into a grassroots populist. Don Hesselbrock, who has attended or organized hundreds of Arizona GOP meetings over the decades, said: "I can remember Kyl being in the room numerous times, I remember [ex-Governor] Fife Symington in the room; I remember both of those guys would show up, they'd sit through the whole meetings, they'd participate, they'd be one of the crowd. I never ever ever EVER remember McCain ever doing that." And it's not just a passive disinterest in small-scale party activities, Hesselbrock said: McCain can show active hostility to what people have to say. At one fundraiser more than a decade ago, Hesselbrock recalled how an elderly man had walked up to McCain to express disagreement over a policy position. "Instead of listening to this man, or hearing him out, John McCain began to yell and scream at him . . . just yell and berate this poor little old man; I mean he was a frail little guy. . . . I remember all of us standing around amazed, and at least in my case very put off that somebody would treat any old guy like that, especially a constituent. This was not a Democrat, this was a Republican who was paying money to the party at a Republican fundraiser, and instead of listening to him and hearing him out, or at least appreciating his point of view, McCain just became irate."

So how did "Citizen McCain" (title of a 2002 book by Elizabeth Drew) get his reputation as a retail-politicking man of the people? Largely by giving maximum access to just about every national journalist who has a question. Reporters, long beaten down by handlers and spin, become so grateful to hear a real-sounding politician that they confuse his on-the-record availability with constituent press-fleshing and populist politics. "I have liked John McCain ever since I met him almost a decade ago," John Judis wrote in *The New Republic*, at the beginning of an otherwise critical and perceptive essay about McCain's foreign policy evolution.[24] "I had been playing phone tag with the press secretaries of senators friendly with [Fred] Thompson and was getting nowhere. I decided that, instead of calling McCain's office, I would drop by. I spoke to one of his aides, who asked me whether I had time to see the senator then. To my amazement, I was ushered into McCain's office, where, without staffers present, he answered my questions about Thompson.

"Talking to a senator in this manner, and on such short notice, is unheard of in Washington. . . . But McCain is different. It is a difference that he refined after being caught up in the Keating Five scandal in the early '90s, but it fits his personality and jibes with his public-minded advocacy of campaign finance reform."

Just as the national media seemed to genuinely like McCain at first blush, the feeling was clearly mutual. The candidate feels comfortable talking to journalists and authors, discussing books and foreign policy and movies. As the *Arizona Republic* reported during the 2000 Republican Convention, "The first private dinner McCain hosted upon arriving in Philadelphia wasn't for his dedicated delegates or donors—or even for anybody remotely connected to Bush—but rather for the often-fawning national press, including such Big Feet as Dan Rather, Tim Russert and R. W. Apple Jr."[25]

The terrific feature writer Michael Lewis (*Liar's Poker*, *Moneyball*) was one of the first to come under McCain's spell, beginning when he bumped into the Arizonan at an airport while writing political diaries about the Bob Dole campaign: "I am still floored by the idea that a senator will take the time to talk to me, even when he has no one else to talk to," Lewis wrote. "I am amazed that any reporter in this situation can bring himself to ask a difficult question. Certainly I cannot."[25] Lewis would go on to pen several more diary entries about McCain, followed by a 7,300-word profile in the *New York Times Magazine* ("The Subversive"),[27] and eventually another 3,000-word *NYT Magazine* piece, "I Liked a Pol," in which he revealed that McCain had invited him to stay in his apartment to cover the 2000 presidential campaign, and confessed almost ruefully that instead he was deciding to no longer write about a man who had become too close a friend.[28]

Arizona journalists, used to a senator who keeps the press at arm's length and occasionally refuses to talk to critical reporters, have treated such national hero-worship with a mixture of bemusement and frustration. "The Arizona media have been cataloguing his meanderings for years, building a case that John McCain—despite his status as a war hero—is a mean-spirited, hot-tempered, opportunistic, philandering, hypocritical political climber who married a comely beer heiress and used her daddy's money to get elected to Congress in a state he can hardly call home," wrote Amy Silverman of the *Phoenix New Times* way back in 1997.[29] "Still, the eastern media elite doesn't seem to care."

Or maybe they just recognize him as one of their own. As Michael Lewis once told the *Hartford Courant*, "But why should the Arizona papers know McCain any better than the national media? He lives in Washington. He's never really lived in Arizona. We know who he really is."[30]

4

MAVERICK VS. "MAVERICK"

I'd love to be remembered as a Goldwater Republican.

—John McCain, *Mr. Conservative*,
HBO documentary

I can't see those two being in the same universe. I'm sorry.

—Don Hesselbrock, Arizona
Republican Party activist

John McCain was panicked. The Keating Five scandal, a slow-burning ethics investigation into improper meetings McCain and four other senators held with banking regulators on behalf of his first political sponsor, thrift tycoon Charles Keating, had become synonymous with the Savings & Loan debacle that was then ripping through the headlines. "My popularity in Arizona was in free fall, dropping in one poll nearly twenty-five points by September from my standing two years earlier," he would later recall.[1] "Numbers like that usually indicate a nearly mortal wound, and I expected a rough, and quite possibly unsuccessful reelection campaign in 1992." This would be a brand new experience for a man whose political career to this point had been as charmed as Moses' crossing of the Red Sea—almost no opposition since that first contested primary, even when storming the hallowed U.S. Senate. But as 1990 turned into 1991, with televised hearings making McCain's face a national symbol of Beltway corruption, it was time to call in the big guns.

"Dear Barry," he wrote to his predecessor in the Senate, the conservative icon Barry Goldwater, "I have a very special favor to ask you."

Goldwater and McCain had never been particularly close. The two had started off on the wrong foot. During McCain's first primary campaign, the Arizona newcomer tried to "steal a little of the public joy" over the Army's selection of a Mesa-based contractor to build Apache helicopters, even though (1) McCain had nothing to do with the decision; (2) he had been a Navy man, not Army; and (3) he was working as a PR flack at the time for his father-in-law's beer distributorship. It was, he reflected later, "a bit of a stretch." Especially since local legend Barry Goldwater happened to be as intimately involved with defense procurement as any American alive. Two days before the primary, Goldwater's office tweaked McCain for trying to take undeserved credit. McCain says they sent out a telegram to his three opponents in the primary, who gleefully piled on right before the vote. In McCain's telling, it was long-time Goldwater aide Judy Eisenhower who had it in for him, a theory later bolstered by a story in the *Washington Post* in 2000. According to Lois Romano, during the 1982 primary, Eisenhower called McCain's first wife Carol to arrange a conversation with GOP candidate Jim Mack to see if there was juicy extramarital dirt he could use against her ex-husband.[2]

The day after winning the primary, McCain banged out a tense letter to Arizona's most famous Republican. "Notwithstanding what information you may have received from others, I did *not* claim credit for Congressional approval of the Apache helicopter," it said. "And I most certainly would not have been so presumptuous as to suggest that my influence in this matter was comparable to your own. You are in my opinion 'Mr. Defense' in the U.S. Senate. To even imply that my role as a mere candidate in the matter was comparable to your own would have been ludicrous and I did not do so." McCain blamed the misunderstanding on flattering comments made about him on the stump by Sen. John Tower and the mayor of Mesa, and then added "I want you to know that I bear no bad feelings toward anyone in this campaign. I have always had the highest respect for you personally, as I know my father did."[3]

Hardly an auspicious beginning. And the remark about Jack McCain was particularly suggestive. John's driving motivation in the Navy, by his own admission, was to please and live up to the example of his distant four-star admiral father. Returning from Vietnam, as he watched his retired dad wither and die after "long years of binge drinking" and the sadness of losing command, McCain sought out father-figures in the Senate such as John Tower and Cold War hawk Henry "Scoop" Jackson (D-Wa.).[4] In Phoenix he immediately gravitated to energetic older ex-military men like Charles Keating and *Arizona Republic* Publisher Duke Tully, but the figure who bestrode state politics like Paul Bunyan was Barry Goldwater. He was a man's man, a Republican's Republican, a blunt-spoken former Air Force pilot and don't-tread-on-me westerner who made ladies swoon and grown men bow and scrape. He had nerdy glasses, the strongest handshake this side of John Wayne, and a salty vocabulary. Goldwater "was irascible and principled, fiercely independent and patriotic," McCain wrote. "He was his own man always and his country's loyal servant. He appealed to every principle and instinct in my nature. And I really don't think he liked me much. I don't know why that was."

In his writings McCain has spent much more time puzzling over Goldwater's lack of embrace than he has describing, say, courting his wives, or living through the USS *Forrestal* fire. If anything, he sounds even more disappointed and genuinely befuddled than when reporting on his arm's-length relationship with his father. "As a politician, I was gaining a reputation for candor and outspokenness, qualities Barry was famous for," McCain nearly whined in *Worth the Fighting For*. "I always showed him great deference. . . . I admired him to the point of reverence, and I wanted him to like me. . . . Whatever he thought of me, he was never outwardly hostile, just a little reserved and occasionally a little short in our conversations. . . . He was usually cordial, just never as affectionate as I would have liked."

What made the sting worse was that the new congressman in town knew Goldwater expressed precisely that kind of affection to John McCain Sr. The correspondence between Goldwater and Jack McCain, also available at Arizona State University's Goldwater Archive, is a mere fraction of that between the two senators, yet it positively radiates in warmth by comparison. "Once Again," Senator Goldwater wrote Commander-in-Chief for the Pacific Jack McCain in January 1972, "I am indebted to you for not only a brilliant discussion of our troops in the Pacific, but also for a beautiful evening with your charming family."

Goldwater shared with the senior McCain an all-encompassing hatred of global communism. Jack, known as "Mr. Seapower" for his lectures on how to combat the Soviet threat through an aggressive naval buildup, was happy to brief the senator on everything from the minutiae of gunnery systems to the big-picture progress (and lack thereof) in Vietnam. They were fellow World War II vets, reserved one moment and gregarious the next, and took their hawkishness as a point of Republican pride. (At an Annapolis graduation ceremony in 1970, Jack McCain famously criticized the "make love, not war" slogan by pointing out that naval officers "were men enough to do both.")

John McCain, by contrast, did not have a reserved bone in his body. He loved being at the center of attention, demanded constant stimulation (a result, he says, of those long years of solitary confinement), and filled any silences with voracious reading. He inherited militarism from his family, as well as a terrific resentment against the Democratic Congress for defunding obligations in Southeast Asia, but his taste for interventionism during his first 15 years of office was tempered greatly by Vietnam. When he and Goldwater made joint appearances, they would frequently joke away their foreign policy differences with a little one-two bit:

GOLDWATER: If I had been elected president in 1964 you wouldn't have been a prisoner of war in Hanoi.

MCCAIN: True. I would have been a prisoner of war . . . *in China!*

But the biggest differences between McCain and Goldwater were so obvious, so destined to keep the two men out of each other's arms, that McCain's inability to identify them borders on self-denial and political tone-deafness. Goldwater was as authentically western as the red Sonoran dirt, a third-generation Arizonan with the tastes of a gunslinger (he was no stranger to whorehouses, mobsters, or Old Crow). He once said "Sometimes I think this country would be better off if we could just saw off the Eastern Seaboard and let it float out to sea." He grew up speaking Spanish, fighting labor unions, fraternizing with Navajos, working in his grandfather's department store, and learning to live and let live. Unlike McCain, he had a decades-long, hands-on interest in Arizona Republican politics, working precinct by precinct to transform a Democratic state into a reliable Republican stronghold. He despised Richard Nixon ("the most dishonest individual I have ever met in my life") and encouraged him to resign in the wake of Watergate (McCain, on the other hand, thought that "in the context of history, Watergate will be a very minor item as compared with the other achievements of this Administration, particularly in the area of foreign affairs").[5]

Most importantly of all, Goldwater took his mix of values and articulated an ideology of freedom in which the individual citizen was liberated by the removal of the federal government from his or her affairs. His 1960 book *The Conscience of a Conservative*, which sold an astounding 3.5 million copies, became the political bible and ideological manifesto of a new libertarian wing that it helped create within the Republican Party. Though he was no intellectual—a college dropout, in fact—Goldwater's ideas nevertheless propelled him to the Republican nomination for president in 1964. There he was trounced by President Lyndon Johnson, who portrayed him as a dangerous extremist; Johnson won more than 61 percent of the vote.

McCain's first sin in the eyes of the four-term senator was probably his presumptuousness in flying out from Washington, D.C., and declaring himself qualified to represent Arizonans based on his money, connections, and war record.

"Goldwater, according to people who knew him, was initially suspicious of McCain and viewed him as an opportunist with little knowledge of or loyalty to the state," the *Washington Post* reported in its March 2000 article. "'When he does finally come to see me, he hasn't lived here long enough to know what I'm talking about,' Goldwater would tell his aides." Even McCain is self-aware enough to acknowledge this possibility. "Maybe he too thought I was too junior, too little accomplished, and too new to Arizona," he wrote.

But when it came to Goldwater's bedrock libertarian principles, McCain just never showed much interest. The longer he has remained in office, the more that disinterest has turned into outright hostility. Even at first, he displayed very little ideological curiosity. His was conservatism by default, not passion—his dad was a Republican, and so was he. His district and state were safely GOP, so he never really had to defend his party's faith from a minority point of view. Stump speeches would include appeals to patriotism, homilies from Vietnam, and arguments for a stronger national defense. He could be safely relied upon to make cheap cracks about Democrats' defense credentials, such as his comment at the 1988 Republican Convention that "Michael Dukakis seems to believe that the Trident is a chewing gum, that the B-1 is a vitamin, and that the Midgetman is anyone shorter than he is." To this day, his books go on for hundreds of pages about politics without ever giving a sense of his own philosophical beliefs about the ideal role of government; instead plenty of ink is spent on friendships, skirmishes, and the nuts-and-bolts of his ambitions to achieve ever-higher political rank.

Finally, after his biography meanders through his first years in Congress, a clue: "No one had a more pronounced influence on my political convictions than Ronald Reagan," he wrote. "Most important [was] his eloquently stated belief in America's national greatness, his trust in our historical exceptionalism, the shining city on the hill he invoked so often, in which I heard the echoes of my great political hero Teddy Roosevelt." Reagan spoke the language of restoration, of healing the wounds of Vietnam so that America could get back to the business of leading the world by example and force. His "revolution," which was widely seen as the popular flowering of Goldwater's unpopular seeds of 1964, included healthy doses of libertarianism that McCain also endorsed at the time—"faith in the individual; skepticism of government; free trade and vigorous capitalism." But what lit his eyes up from the beginning was not what the government *shouldn't* do, but what Americans together *could* do.

Untethered to Goldwater's convictions about limited government, McCain was lured by federalizing shortcuts to greatness. One of his only core beliefs before entering public office was that Americans can be better led through the consolidation of power in the executive branch. Like Goldwater, McCain was a staunch opponent of the War Powers Act, but unlike Goldwater, that was just the beginning. McCain lionized Roosevelt partly because he "invented the modern presidency by liberally interpreting the constitutional authority of the office to redress the imbalance of power between the executive and legislative branches that had tilted decisively toward Congress."[6] Post-Watergate restraints on the executive, McCain thought, went too far. Contrast that to Goldwater's 1964 campaign tract, "My Case for the Republican Party," which argued: "Some of the current worship of powerful executives may come from those who admire strength and accomplishment of any sort. Others hail the display of Presidential strength . . . simply because they approve of the *result* reached by the use of power. This is nothing less than the totalitarian philosophy that the end justifies the means. . . . If ever there was a philosophy of government totally at war with that of the Founding Fathers, it is this one."

Slowly, McCain started asserting himself in the Senate, usually backing blunt uses of government. He supported giving the president a line-item veto to cut pork and shackling Congress with a balanced-budget amendment. Still, John Karaagac wrote in *John McCain: An Essay in Military and Political History*, "At this stage of his political career, and frankly through much of his Senate career, McCain was a beneficiary of the intellectual and political strides of other conservatives, not an initiator of advantages. It was only after the Bush defeat in 1992, and the rise of Clinton, that McCain seemed to fully find a distinct voice on domestic issues."

By the early 1990s two events that occurred more or less simultaneously began shaping McCain's yearning for "greatness" into a coherent approach: the stunning Gulf War victory in driving Saddam Hussein out of Kuwait, and the Keating Five corruption and campaign-finance scandal that for the first time threatened to derail his fast-track ambitions. The first event would begin to cure his Vietnam Syndrome, whetting his appetite for further faraway uses of power; the second converted him into a champion of reform. But before anything else, he had to win what he thought would be his first-ever seriously contested election. It was at that point that McCain reached out to Goldwater, who had over the years finally begun to warm to him.

"As you know," McCain wrote in his January 31, 1991 letter, "1992 is my year to stand for re-election. I'm anticipating and ready for a tough campaign. . . . I'd like to ask you to consider my request to appear as guest of honor at a fundraising dinner for my 1992 campaign, featuring President Bush and possibly President Reagan. The event will be a tribute to you and the 50 years of proud service to America that are your life and career." A week later, coincidentally or not, McCain read a glowing tribute to Goldwater on the Senate floor, crediting his leadership on the Armed Services Committee for developing the weapons used so well in the Gulf War. "I doubt that Barry Goldwater is much impressed by testimonials," McCain said. "I suspect that were he here, I would be treated to another display of his well-earned reputation for candor."

Goldwater, who was 82 years old and growing frail, agreed to attend the event, but President Bush's planners kept rescheduling. "The White House is screwing us around," McCain complained in a letter of August 1. "To say I'm frustrated over the complete lack of response from the White House," he wrote the following March, "would be the understatement of the year." McCain finally nailed down the president, and then excitedly sent out form letters to the state's entire Republican establishment, asking for donations of $1,000, $500, $250, and so on. One of the recipients sent a letter to Goldwater, signed "An Embarrassed Friend," slamming the one-term senator.

"I just received a splendid invitation to a 'salute to Barry Goldwater,' which I had planned to attend until I discovered what the evening is to be all about," it read. "It is nothing but a fund-raiser for John McCain, and not a salute to you at all. You are being used by McCain, who has brought such discredit on himself and the party that he must use your name to get people to come to his party. McCain doesn't care about this state, or the party—only McCain."

Goldwater was livid and insisted 10 days before the event that "the so called salute to Barry Goldwater" split the proceeds 50-50 with the Republican Party. "On top of that, when I got home this afternoon, I found copies of letters that you had mailed asking special friends of mine, to join in this effort. John, this is not the way I've operated in my political life, and I don't want to start it in my retired life. So, you agree to give half the money to the Republican Party, and this thing can go along. If you don't agree to it, then I'm going to have to give it a lot of good hard thinking."

McCain had lusted after Goldwater's seat from D.C., come to his state, bought a house in the district the day the incumbent congressman announced his retirement, run for office within months, claimed some dubious credit for a local weapons contract, turned his nose up at the nitty-gritty of party building, splashed around the kind of campaign money the state had never seen, and now insulted his friends with crass form letters for a "tribute" night whose proceeds would all go in his campaign's pocket. And yet to John McCain, why Barry Goldwater didn't hug him with both arms was a mystery.

McCain pulled the dinner off—1,200 people came out to salute Barry, hear old war stories, and listen to President Bush say "the nation needs an infusion of fresh, new Republican congressmen and senators who will be statesmen, like Barry Goldwater, like John McCain, leaders willing to try out new ideas."[7] All seemed smoothed over, until another Goldwater letter of September 25: "You will recall, during my speech at the dinner for the President in Phoenix, I announced that you were going to give half of the funds you raised to the State Republican Party. I am told by the Party, that you still owe them $35,000, and unless you pay all of it, or most of it, they cannot meet their payroll next Wednesday. . . . Don't ignore this."

As for trying out "new ideas," once McCain sailed to re-election with a 55–31–10 percent vote in a three-way race and got acclimated to the Clinton 1990s, his ideas largely consisted of "reform" efforts—the line-item veto, campaign-finance reform, cracking down on video-game violence—that involved giving more power to the government at the expense of citizens. In other words: the opposite of Goldwaterism. Meanwhile, his retired predecessor was following his principles to their logical conclusion in supporting an end to the ban on gays in the military, saying "You don't have to *be* straight to be in the military; you just have to be able to *shoot* straight." (McCain opposed, and continues to oppose, letting gays serve openly.) Goldwater also supported medical marijuana, denounced the "extremists" in his own party who dared rally around his name and railed against the rise of the Christian Right. When Jerry Falwell reacted to Reagan's Supreme Court appointment of Arizonan judge Sandra Day O'Connor by saying, "Every good Christian should be concerned," Goldwater replied: "I think every good Christian ought to kick Falwell right in the ass." All of Goldwater's positions were considerably more "maverick" than those of McCain more than a decade later.

By the mid-'90s, McCain was beginning to openly flout Goldwater's concept "that government should stay out of people's private lives," supporting intrusive regulatory schemes from his perch on the Senate Commerce Committee, placing regular if not constant pressure on Hollywood to clean up its marketing to children under 17, and warning about the slippery slope of the GOP being too fixated on individual rights. "The same 'leave us the hell alone' attitude that characterized the Republican approach to the federal government's intrusions on individual liberty began to assert itself in the world-view of some Republicans," he wrote in *Worth the Fighting*

For. When he ran for president in 1999, *Weekly Standard* writers David Brooks and William Kristol—who were providing a sort of running shadow intellectual rationale for his campaign—kept suggesting that McCain, in fact, was coming to bury Goldwater libertarianism as we know it. "John McCain and George Bush too are trying to move the party away from New Gingrich and Dick Armey and Barry Goldwater—that whole movement of conservatism which was an anti-government movement," Brooks said on the *Jim Lehrer News Hour* in October 1999. "The rebels believe the conservative movement has cracked up, the Republican establishment has ossified, and the Goldwater-Reagan ideological message needs to be overhauled," Brooks wrote for the *New York Times* in February 2000. "In New Hampshire, Mr. McCain showed signs of running as head of the rebel alliance."

As for Goldwater himself, McCain treated his libertarian cries from the wilderness with a somewhat condescending tolerance. "I am often asked by people inside Arizona, and outside of Arizona, about Barry," he told the *Washington Post*, in what the paper described as "a tone that suggests he's apologizing for a crazy uncle in the attic."[8] "I always say that Barry Goldwater has the right to say whatever he wants to." The end of the article suggests that Goldwater's replacement never did fully grasp the original maverick's lifelong commitment to individual liberty. "Some, like John McCain, attribute much of Goldwater's outspoken contrariness, which occasionally makes him sound like a raving liberal, to [his wife] Susan Goldwater's influence."

When Barry finally died, in May 1998, John McCain wrote a fond and typically self-revealing appreciation for the *Washington Post*. "I am both blessed and burdened to have succeeded Barry Goldwater to the United States Senate. I am blessed by the honor of it, but burdened by the certain knowledge that long after I have left public office, Americans will still celebrate the contributions Barry Goldwater made to their well-being, while I and my successors will enjoy much less notable reputations. Barry Goldwater will always be the Senator from Arizona, the one history recalls with appreciation and delight. In all the histories of American politics, Barry Goldwater will remain a chapter unto himself. The rest of us will have to make do as footnotes."

But it was at the funeral where McCain seemed to be staking out new rhetorical territory. Having boldly launched his second life on the day of his own father's funeral, symbolically kicked off a new phase of his politics at the burial of arguably his second-most important father figure. For his last quarter-century of public life, the Navy lieutenant commander-turned politician had managed to discuss his experiences and ideas about service without almost ever using the phrase "cause greater." But now it came tumbling out of the top of his eulogy for Barry Goldwater:

"The best thing that can ever be said of anyone is that they served a cause greater than their self-interest. All the well-earned testimonials and accolades to Barry Goldwater that have filled the nation's newspapers and airwaves since his death can be summed up in that one tribute: he served a cause greater than his self-interest." Thus was being submerged within the greater good one of the true champions of the individual in modern U.S. history. Soon the rest of us would have that opportunity, too. Or else.

THE 12-STEP GUIDE TO BECOMING PRESIDENT

All lives are a struggle against selfishness. All my life I've stood a little apart from institutions I willingly joined. It just felt natural to me. But if my life had shared no common purpose, it wouldn't have amounted to much more than eccentric. There is no honor or happiness in just being strong enough to be left alone.

—John McCain, speaking at Boston College,
Sept. 18, 2006

The alcoholic is an extreme example of self-will run riot, though he usually doesn't think so. Above everything, we alcoholics must be rid of this selfishness. We must, or it will kill us!

—Alcoholics Anonymous

On March 9, 2000, less than six weeks after having his face plastered on the cover of all three national newsweeklies, John McCain withdrew from the presidential race. The punishing loss in George W. Bush's firewall state of South Carolina had knocked the wheels off the Straight Talk Express, after which the demoralized and cash-poor campaign crashed into Super Tuesday, losing such independent-friendly, delegate-rich states as California, New York, and Ohio. In his concession speech, McCain yielded to that eternal temptation of politics—conflating his own earth-bound candidacy with a more exalted movement to revive the Land of the Free. "Millions of Americans have rallied to our banner, and their support not just honors me, but has ignited the cause of reform, a cause far greater and more important than the ambitions of any single candidate," he said. "I ask from you one last promise. Promise me that you will never give up, that you will continue your service in the worthy cause of revitalizing our democracy."

It was standard hyperbole for a losing insurgent—similar to the exit statements of Ross Perot in 1992, Ralph Nader in 2000 and Howard Dean in 2004—but with one notable twist: By invoking a "cause greater" as redemption for the vice of ambition (a sin he cops to repeatedly in his books and speeches), McCain was dressing this last rebel yell in the language and structure of 12-Step Recovery. Like a participant in Alcoholics Anonymous, McCain seemed almost compelled all campaign long to volunteer his flaws and declare fidelity to what A.A.'s Step 2 calls "a Power greater than ourselves." Like a successfully recovered participant in Narcotics Anonymous (as his wife Cindy has been since the early 1990s), he was forever channeling his character flaws into the service of that greater cause and trying to convince others to follow him down the path.

Two weeks later, *Good Morning America* asked McCain the question that would be on every interlocutor's lips for the next six years: Will he run for president again? "Being a recovering presidential candidate, it's very hard for me to assess that," he quipped, adding that he was "still only at Step 2."[1]

This would be his running gag until the GOP convention in August. "I think I am in Step 3 of this 12-Step Recovery program," he told Fox News on April 16.[2] (The official Step 3 includes "a decision to turn our will and our lives over to the care of God as we understood God.") He remained at "about at Step 3" in mid-May,[3] but by the end of the month he was telling the *Washington Post* that he had graduated to "about Step 8" ("Made a list of all persons we had harmed, and became willing to make amends to them all"). This wasn't long after McCain had gone to South Carolina to make amends for dissembling on his Confederate flag position during the 2000 primary campaign. "The best cure for a recovering presidential candidate is other challenges, so I've tried to hurl myself into them," he told the *Post*.[4] His self-assessment remained at Step 8 while entertaining reporters on the Straight Talk Express in his last hurrah en route to the Republican Convention, after which he buried his nose in the greater cause of reform for the next calendar year.

Twelve-Step programs are ingeniously contrived. Steps 1–3 (admitting to being "powerless" over the addiction, then turning your life over to a "Power greater" than yourself, which can be God or some other spiritual concept) are designed to get the addict's foot in the door by effectively (if temporarily) absolving him of responsibility for his troubles. Even Steps 4 and 5 are comparatively pain-free: taking a "searching and fearless moral inventory," then admitting "the exact nature" of your wrongs to another person. All of these stages are reinforced by a community, typically a support group of recovering addicts, who give each other strength by ritually admitting their addictions ("my name is Jack, and I'm an alcoholic"), discussing the challenges of their sobriety and ending each meeting with the recitation of the Serenity

Prayer: "God, grant me the serenity to accept the things I cannot change; courage to change the things I can; and wisdom to know the difference."

There are plenty of nonaddicts who have taken sustenance and insight from pieces of the 12-Step process, especially those who have loved ones in recovery. We don't know for sure if John McCain is one of them. But we do know that he is one of the most preemptively confessional politicians in America, both in public and private. In an insightful February 2000 *New York Times* profile of McCain's pre-congressional days, Nicholas Kristof described how this tendency played out during the messy dissolution of his first marriage. "Some family friends were appalled that a man who seemed so decent, so full of compassion for anyone who needed help, could treat his own wife in a manner they regarded as brutal," Kristof wrote. "But Mr. McCain gradually won everyone around again, with the same traits he now displays after making a mistake: a combination of charm and penitence. . . . It helped that Mr. McCain always accepted blame—embraced it— rather than making excuses. 'He has always felt very guilty about it,' [James] McGovern said. 'I have never talked with him for more than 40 minutes when he didn't bring it up, saying he felt badly about it.'"[5]

For real alcoholics, a little knowledge of the 12-Step program can sometimes be a dangerous thing. They learn the disarming power of admitting their faults, garnering both sympathy and a reputation for honesty, even if they haven't yet truly changed their ways. McCain first discovered the value of the media *mea culpa* in the wake of the Keating Five scandal, when, with his back against the wall and his hometown paper battering him on a daily basis, he said he "decided right then that not talking to reporters or sharply denying even the appearance of a problem wasn't going to do me any good. I would henceforth accept every single request for an interview from any source, prominent or obscure, and answer every question as completely and straightforwardly as I could. . . . I talked to the press constantly, ad infinitum, until their appetite for information from me was completely satisfied. It is a public relations strategy that I have followed to this day."[6]

Though there would be plenty of exceptions to this rule—various members of the Arizona press,[7] *Time* reporter Karen Tumulty[8] and myself,[9] for example—the general strategy took root and was central to McCain's christening by the national press as "Washington's last honest man." Journalist Michael Lewis, who fell first and hardest, had this reaction after first encountering McCain's self-effacing frankness: "A politician who lived dangerously! A politician who spoke his mind! It was all I could do to stop myself from shouting: Lie! Lie for your life! Lie or some journalist will take a quote from you and twist it around your neck! The man clearly needed to be protected." Lewis, whose power of insightful observation is even stronger than his attraction to overachieving men in public life, went on to report: "One of the traits McCain's staff finds most maddening in their boss is his tendency to recall for journalists only his most damning moments. Ask him about Vietnam and he'll tell you about the time he stole a washrag from the guy in the adjoining cell. Ask him about his first marriage and he'll leap right to his adultery."[10]

McCain's ritual self-criticism produced spectacular results, but that doesn't mean his confessions were necessarily calculated. Like many reared in the military tradition, he has always taken honor codes with grave seriousness, whether as a defiant high school student, rule-breaking Navy plebe, brash young flier or tortured POW. "An officer must not lie, steal, or cheat—ever," McCain declared in *Faith of My Fathers*.[11] He remains viscerally haunted and guided by the high example set by his father, "the most honest man I've ever known," he wrote in *Why Courage Matters*.[12] "He wouldn't tell a lie, ever. He wouldn't shift the blame for his own mistake to a subordinate. He wouldn't seek to escape an uncomfortable situation by offering a contrived excuse or telling a comforting untruth. He would stand the consequences for his honesty, whatever they were. And he never remarked on it. I have not lived as honestly as he did. It's a struggle. But whenever I've been less than honest, I've felt ashamed and much worse than had I told the truth and taken the consequences."

Perhaps it was this finely tuned shame that spurred McCain to kick-start campaign-finance reform in the wake of the Keating Five campaign-finance scandal, a response that the *New York Times'* Bill Keller later described as the only act of "restitution" he recalled seeing by a U.S. politician.[13]

Still, McCain's one-two-three punch of admitting flaws, noisily sublimating them under a greater cause, and then taking that cause to the people, didn't really coalesce until about the same time he started seriously thinking of running for president. And even then, the two weren't tied together at first. "I didn't decide to run for president to start a national crusade for the political reforms I believed in or to run a campaign as if it were some grand act of patriotism," he wrote in *Worth the Fighting For*, copping to a base motive once more. "In truth, I wanted to be president because it had become my ambition to be president." McCain's relentless flagging of his constant, driving ambition goes almost unnoticed in the coverage of his political endeavors, which is particularly odd, considering it's routinely presented as a semi-warning: "I have craved distinction in my life. I have wanted renown and influence for their own sake. That is, of course the great temptation of public life. Few are immune to its appeal. The desire to be somebody has driven many a political career much further than the intention to do something. I have never been able to conquer it permanently, but I have tried."

A Lexis search on "John McCain" and "cause greater" prior to 1998 turns up exactly one relevant quotation—his speech at the 1996 Republican Convention, in which he said Americans "want a president willing to fight for a cause greater than personal glory." He began using the phrase in earnest at two spring 1998 events rich in personal symbolism: the opening of a prisoners-of-war museum in Andersonville, Ga., and the funeral of Barry Goldwater.

At that same time, he was working with chief aide Mark Salter on his first book, *Faith of My Fathers*, covering his life story and family history up until the day he came home from Vietnam. At age 62, contemplating a long-gestated run at the highest office in the land, it was time to finally sear an indelible meaning onto the singular experience of his life. The first drafts were filled with so many unflattering admissions that editor Jonathan Karp asked his author to tone it down.[14] The book, McCain said upon its September 1999 release, was intended to "inspire Americans of the redemptive powers of imperfect people."[15]

This was a far cry from the purpose of the 12,000-word piece McCain wrote a quarter-century earlier for *U.S. News & World Report*. There, covering the same events as the Vietnam chapters in *Faith of My Fathers*, McCain's personal introspections were limited to insights like: "I had learned what we all learned over there: Every man has his breaking point. I had reached mine." His other lessons at the time were all pointed outward toward the country he was coming home to. There was irritation at peace groups, high praise for Richard Nixon, endorsement of the domino theory and a remarkable sense of wanting to unite a divided nation. "Now that I'm back, I find a lot of hand-wringing about this country. I don't buy that. I think America today is a better country than the one I left nearly six years ago," he wrote then.

Faith of My Fathers, in stark contrast, left national healing as an afterthought for the final five pages and set up the rest of the book as a semi-conventional redemption song of a rebel who found his cause behind bars. The inward-looking self-criticism and foreshadowing begin right from paragraph two: "I have spent much of my life choosing my own attitude, often carelessly, often for no better reason than to indulge a conceit. In those instances, my acts of self-determination were mistakes, some of which did no lasting harm, and serve now only to embarrass, and occasionally amuse, the old man who recalls them. Others I deeply regret." What a way to start a war story!

It wasn't only the structure of confession-sublimation-proselytizing that resembled 12-Step Recovery in McCain's first great literary expression; it was the language. In A.A., the primary villain (besides Demon Rum) is the character deficiency of selfishness. "The first requirement," teaches "The Big Blue Book" of *Alcoholics Anonymous*, "is that we be convinced that any life run on self-will can hardly be a success." *Faith of My Fathers* reaches the same conclusion after McCain breaks down under torture. "Ironically for someone who had so long asserted his own individuality as his first and best defense against insults of any kind, I discovered that faith in myself proved to be the least formidable strength I possessed when confronting alone organized inhumanity on a greater scale than I had conceived possible." In both tales, the moment of transcendence comes when the "egoist" finally realizes that there is greater strength in a supportive community, under God, devoted to the same cause.

For McCain and his fellow prisoners, that cause was more than just resisting their cruel captors. It was the exceptionalism of the country they ached to get back to. "I still shared the ideals of America," McCain wrote. "It was what freedom conferred on America that I loved most—the distinction of being the last, best hope of humanity; the advocate for all who believed in the Rights of Man. . . . In prison, where my cherished independence was mocked and assaulted, I found my self-respect in a shared fidelity to my country."

All of which would be a diverting character study, and not much more, if it weren't for the fact that at the moment McCain was articulating these notions for the first time, he was also taking this lesson and applying it to politics, using it as both policy navigation and campaign fuel.

On May 27, 1999, long after McCain decided to run for president but four months before he would officially declare, he gave a commencement address at Johns Hopkins University that David Brooks later described as "the core speech of the McCain campaign."[16] In it, the senator expressed anxiety that the same faith in country that helped save and give meaning to his life was now threatened by "pervasive public cynicism" in the U.S. government, "as dangerous in its way as war and depression have been in the past." What was once "healthy skepticism" springing from the ethos of "self-reliance" had now metastasized into alienation "that threatens our public institutions, our culture and, ultimately, our private happiness."

It was a remarkable statement coming from the mouth of a Republican, let alone one who held the Senate seat of limited-government hero Barry Goldwater and who had previously identified most closely with the ideology of Ronald "government is not the solution to our problem; government *is* the problem" Reagan. Instead of encouraging skepticism in government, McCain was warning that skepticism in government could lead to out-and-out chaos: "When the people come to believe that government is so dysfunctional or corrupt . . . basic civil consensus will deteriorate to the point that our culture might fragment beyond recognition." And it wasn't just the frothing anti-Clintonites of his own party that he was referencing; the apolitical rich also came under fire. "With every new Dow Jones record something gnaws at my conscience that we should not be lulled into unfeeling contentment," he said.

What was to be done? McCain asked the graduates to declare "war" on cynicism, and join "a cause greater than self-interest"—to "reform the practices of government and politics that threaten our freedom." Reforming U.S. government was central to "the new patriotic challenge; to recall Americans to the faith that has made us the greatest force for good on earth. Let it be the most important of your life's work to remind all Americans that we are part of a great experiment." For McCain, anything threatening that faith, whether justified or hysterical, became a legitimate target for government activism.

McCain was calling for a new nationalism, with a new and improved "federal bully pulpit" at its vanguard. "We Republicans have to acknowledge that there is a role for the federal government," he said. This sweeping new movement broke down a little on the details. Among the hodgepodge of initiatives he referenced were a slightly flatter tax, higher tolerance for U.S. casualties in Kosovo, taking Social Security "off budget" and having Republicans acknowledge "it is unconscionable that a bad politician is paid more than a good teacher." But that all could be worked out later; the important thing was that a new generation of patriots would reform the system so that Americans could renew their faith in government, and in U.S. exceptionalism.

"Many contemporary conservatives have let their healthy skepticism about government sink into something unhealthy, an embittered loathing of the federal government," he declared, expanding on the idea in *Worth the Fighting For*.[17] "Government should be restrained from unnecessarily aggregating power at the expense of individual liberty. But it must not shrink from its duty to be the highest expression of the national will and the last bulwark against all assaults on our founding ideals. . . . Our greatness depends upon our patriotism, and our patriotism is hardly encouraged when we cannot take pride in the highest public institutions, institutions that should transcend all sectarian, regional and commercial conflicts to fortify the public's allegiance to the national community."

If all this talk of fortifying "allegiance" to the "national will" sounds a tad on the militaristic side, it is. McCain, who had been giving lectures about public service since returning from Vietnam, was now talking more in terms of "obligations" than opportunities. "I believe it is every American's duty to contribute something to the common good," he told the Johns Hopkins graduates. "You don't have to wear a uniform or go to war to be a patriot. But you should, at some point in your life, seize an opportunity to put the country's interests before your own." In his book *Character Is Destiny*,

McCain states flatly that "we all have to be worthy of the sacrifices made on our behalf. We have to love our freedom, not
just for the ease or material benefits it provides, not just for
the autonomy it guarantees us, but for the goodness it makes
possible. We have to love it so much we won't let it be con-
strained by fear or selfishness." McCain's evolving concept of
freedom was one that carried specific duties.

With Barry Goldwater safely dead, and McCain leading a
sort of national self-help movement springing from his
efforts to impose retroactive meaning on his Vietnam experience, he was ready to freely admit that his ideas were "anathema
to the 'leave us alone' libertarian philosophy that dominated
Republican debates in the 1990s."[18] Neo-conservatives like
the *Weekly Standard*'s David Brooks and William Kristol,
who had always been skeptical about limited government,
cheered the concurrent development of McCain's "national
greatness" and George W. Bush's "compassionate conservatism," rightly declaring both to be a repudiation of the Reagan/
Goldwater tradition and the dawn of something new in the
GOP. Brooks, who was alternating between interpreting
McCain and suggesting new intellectual frames to present his
message, identified the "four pillars" of McCainism: using
government "to confront selfish interests," reforming government "to combat cynicism," reforming welfare and regulation "to keep America forever young" (by far the least
convincing of his pillars) and using "American might abroad
to champion democracy and freedom." It sounded more like
JFK than Ronald Reagan.

During this period McCain's legislative initiatives, unsurprisingly, drifted more toward regulation, taxation and
expanding government. He authored a $1.10-a-pack ciga-
rette tax, angrily denouncing the Republicans who voted it

down for not caring about children. He took on his party again with a "Patients' Bill of Rights," campaign-finance reform, and the war in Kosovo. Even while defending his party apostasy, McCain sounded themes that would be as familiar at an A.A. meeting as at a V.A. meeting. "I have no reluctance to subordinate my independence to a cause greater than my own self-interest," he wrote in *Worth the Fighting For*. "But that cause is my country, first and last. When my party serves my country, then my party deserves my loyalty. When I believe my party serves itself at the expense of my country, then it deserves my dissent. Were I to believe otherwise, the independence I have prized all my life will have been nothing more than egotism."

Where 12-steppers and recovery kibbitzers fall off the ladder is where the rubber hits the road: Step 6 ("Become entirely ready to have God remove all these defects of character") and Step 7 ("Humbly asked God to remove our shortcomings"). It's one thing to see the value in confessing your flaws, subscribing to a Greater Power, taking constant self-inventory; maybe even making amends. But to say you want chunks of your own personality *removed* . . . you really must be desperate. McCain doesn't draw the line at the defect, but how the defect is used. He acknowledges an occasionally fierce temper, but as he told the Johns Hopkins students, sometimes "We need to get riled up a bit." A worthy cause, he says, "could, if not excuse, at least compensate for a man's failings, no matter how many they numbered." Noble causes, he told the wild-eyed romantics in the crowd, "give even the most obscure lives historical importance. They offer us a form of immortality."

But even when trying to inspire people to enter public service, to serve a cause greater than their self-interest, McCain can't resist leaving bread crumbs that lead back to his own flaws and temptations. Crusades, he told the students, "are worth fighting for so long as we fight for principle and not personal advantage. It is easy to forget in politics where principle ends and selfishness begins." There are many trusted advisors around McCain in 2007 that worry that their candidate has forgotten precisely that.

FORGIVE THEM, FATHER, FOR I HAVE SINNED

Reform advocates suspect [Mitch] McConnell is less interested in the First Amendment than he is in lining his own pockets and swimming, Scrooge McDuck-style, through the gobs of cash he raises. But what if he's serious?

—Chris Suellentrop, *Slate.com*, March 29, 2002

I would rather have a clean government than one where quote First Amendment rights are being respected, that has become corrupt. If I had my choice, I'd rather have the clean government.

—John McCain, *Imus in the Morning*, MSNBC, April 28, 2006

George Stephanopoulos played John McCain a tape of Newt Gingrich. "Senator McCain carries both the burden of McCain/Feingold, and now the burden of the McCain/Kennedy bill," Gingrich said, referencing the old debate over campaign finance and the then-raging controversy over immigration reform. "He has the greatest challenge in the

Republican primary of explaining those positions." It was June 10, 2007; the immigration bill was being debated in the Senate and pummeled all over the talk radio dial, and McCain was busy fending off speculation that his recent decision to skip the Iowa straw poll was a sign that he was no longer a viable candidate in the Hawkeye State. "Well, I always respect Newt Gingrich," McCain said, sounding very much like the opposite was true, "but by the way, on McCain/Feingold, out here in Iowa, you go with me to all these town hall meetings, I never hear anybody ask about that. That's an inside the Beltway thing."[1]

With that comment, the inversion of the campaign-finance debate was nearly complete. Back when McCain's *raison d'etre* for seeking the presidency was to drive the "corrupting influence" of money out of politics, and "take our government back from the power brokers and special interests . . . so that Americans can believe once again that public service is a summons to duty and not a lifetime of privilege,"[2] the "Beltway" slur was the go-to term of derision for *opponents* of McCain's decade-long quest to pass new campaign finance rules. "It has no impact whatsoever on the average American. It's an inside-the-Beltway issue," antireform leader Mitch McConnell, R-Ky., told Jim Lehrer in April 2001, in a typical comment. "The interest groups that lobby here—which they have a right to do under the First amendment—will simply spend their money trying to influence elections in a different way than they do now."[3] McConnell's predictions came true, and six years later McCain was reduced to disparaging the place he'd lived for two-thirds of his life.

The greatest of the greater causes championed on the Straight Talk Express is almost nowhere to be found in 2007–8. Campaign finance is not part of his stump speech, barely visible on his Web site and didn't even merit a mention in McCain's hyped address on government reform given to the Oklahoma State Legislature in May 21, 2007. If asked about it at press conferences and debates, McCain quickly changes the subject. He has moved on to other "transcendent" issues—especially the War on Islamic Extremism—and focused his reduced bandwidth for reform on the process of scaling back congressional earmarks.

But the campaign finance crusade is where the modern McCain as we know him got his start. It combined all his best and worst character traits—noisy martyrdom for a hopeless cause, defiance in the face of hostile opposition, elitism, exaltation of the government at the expense of the individual, and a 12-Step sense of messianic fervor.

The Bipartisan Campaign Reform Act didn't start out as a grandiose tool to reignite American patriotism, but rather as a gesture to rejuvenate McCain's own demoralized career. The night John McCain won Barry Goldwater's seat in 1986, he immediately started picturing his pathway to the White House. "Even in the midst of my private revelry," he recalled later, "I felt an emotional need to envision some future goal, something that I could fix my gaze on and concentrate my energy to attaining."[4] His ambition was audacious and impatient, but at that point his political career had gone exactly as plotted. Soon the *New York Times* and *Washington Post* were taking turns gushing about what a "rising star" the white-haired "tornado" was. (One of the profiles was written by McCain's good pal, the late "Johnny" Apple of the *New York Times*, with nary a disclosing word about their relationship.[5]) By the 1988 Republican Convention, McCain's name made it to the shortlist of vice presidential candidates, and his future was as bright as any in the Senate.

But then came the Keating Five, an experience that the ex-POW torture victim would go on to call "the worst thing, the absolute worst thing that ever happened to me."[6] All bets were now off.

As biographer John Karaagac has pointed out, "The Keating scandal is a complicated tale. Such complications are often advantageous to the guilty party."[7] While this is true, the underlying story is actually not all that complex.

In 1987, just months after being sworn in to the Senate, McCain, along with four Democratic senators—Arizona's Dennis DeConcini, California's Alan Cranston, Michigan's Don Riegle, and Ohio's John Glenn—met with Ed Gray, the chairman of the Federal Home Loan Bank Board, to inquire about the regulatory agency's two-year investigation into Charles Keating's Lincoln Savings & Loan. Each senator's state had skin in the game (Lincoln's parent company American Continental employed more than 2,000 people in Arizona alone); each senator had taken bundles of campaign money from Keating in the past, totaling $1.4 million; and each was asked personally by the brash, 6 foot 5 former Navy flyer and anti-pornography crusader to make inquiries on his behalf. Cranston and Riegle were also on the Senate Banking Committee, which oversees the regulatory agency. Gray told the senators he didn't know much and suggested they talk directly to bank examiners. At that next meeting, after first testily voicing their concerns over the length of the inquiry, the five were informed that the investigation had uncovered serious wrongdoing and was being forwarded to the Justice Department. The meeting came to a close. Soon afterward, Gray accused the senators of improperly pressuring the regulators, which they hotly disputed.

There the story might have ended, except for the inconvenient fact that more than 1,000 Savings & Loan institutions were busy collapsing all around the country, none larger than Lincoln Savings & Loan, whose failure would eventually cost taxpayers northward of $3 billion. Keating's behavior would end in convictions for fraud, racketeering, and conspiracy, with the symbol of the 1980s spending much of the '90s behind bars. It was a slow trickle of a scandal, lacking details more sexy than a couple of bureaucratic encounters, until the *Arizona Republic* published a bombshell of a story on October 8, 1989. The paper revealed that McCain's wife Cindy and her father Jim had invested nearly $360,000 in a Keating-owned shopping center development in 1986, and that the McCains had taken "at least nine trips at Keating's expense, sometimes aboard the American Continental jet," while failing to reimburse more than $10,000 worth of tickets. A public already outraged by the S&L debacle now feasted on pictures of McCain yukking it up in the Bahamas with the banking industry's biggest villain. The Senate Ethics Committee soon decided to investigate whether the activity by the senators amounted to a quid pro quo for campaign contributions, and whether it delayed regulators' eventual takeover of Lincoln's assets, making a costly bailout that much more expensive.

Of the five, McCain had had by far the closest relationship with Keating, but it had ended abruptly just before the senators' meetings with the regulators in 1987, after Keating made the fatal mistake of calling McCain a "wimp" for not doing more to get the Board off his back. "Charlie, I am not a coward, and I didn't spend five and half years in a Vietnamese prison so that you could question my courage or my integrity," McCain seethed at him, and that was that. Though Keating was McCain's first main backer and had contributed more than $100,000 to his coffers in the past, that was mostly for his House races, and therefore outside the purview of the Senate investigations. For both McCain and John Glenn, there was enough distance between Keating's donations and the meetings with regulators to satisfy the committee's concerns, though that didn't excuse them from two months of excruciating daily televised hearings. Throughout, McCain expressed a mixture of tearful contrition over sullying the Senate's honor and angry defiance at what he thought was a political witch hunt. He offered constant access and document-dumps to the press (to the point that his fellow Arizona senator DeConcini became convinced that McCain was a serial and strategic leaker), and was eventually found guilty of nothing more serious than "poor judgment."

Still, he was crushed, nearly inconsolable. It was his first political failure, derailing what had been until then a charmed ascent up the ranks of power. Worst of all, his honor had been called into question. "I would very much like to think that I have never been a man whose favor could be bought," he wrote in *Worth the Fighting For*, "yet that is exactly how millions of Americans viewed me for a time, a time I will forever consider one of the worst experiences of my life." It placed a strain on his marriage since Cindy had been in charge of the family finances and thus failed to make sure that the Keating flights were paid, and his Senate offices were visibly drained of his usual high spirits. "I've seen the glow go out of him," Cindy told Robert Timberg after McCain's 1992 Senate re-election.

When McCain hit rock bottom in Vietnam, he had an enemy to focus his hatred on and his brothers there to support him. Now, even though, to his mind, the investigation had been unfair, the blame nevertheless fell on his own sagging shoulders. "I made the worst mistake of my life by attending two meetings," he wrote. McCain was haunted by what the *New York Times* called "a personal demon—a deep and seemingly unquenchable need to defend his honor."[8] So he took an unusual step. After having spent the 1980s as one of the most successful fundraisers on Capitol Hill, McCain consciously sought to make amends by trying to place federal limitations on the activity he so excelled at. It was the equivalent of an alcoholic using the federal government to lock up his own liquor cabinet, though mostly for appearances' sake, rather than a genuine desire to quit drinking. "Rightly or wrongly, the American people and the people of Arizona feel that the system has been corrupted," he said.[9]

The public outrage over campaign finance grew during the Clinton presidency, driven by a series of White House fundraising scandals, a new Republican majority in the House itching for reform, and a growing talk radio industry that feasted on distrust of the government. (From the beginning, McCain distanced himself from the Newt Gingriches and Rush Limbaughs of the world, finding their style too abrasive and partisan.) McCain's new reform agenda, built in part through an alliance he struck in 1994 with the principled and austere Wisconsin liberal Russell Feingold, at first comprised largely of self-imposed shackles on legislative behavior: A longer waiting period before ex-legislators could become lobbyists, a lower price limit on gifts they could receive, and a line-item veto (which passed in 1995) giving the executive branch the power to snip out legislative pork.

Some of these gestures were purely symbolic, meant not to improve government in any way, but to signal to the public that the Senate took reform seriously, even if the price of symbolism was reduced government performance. Such was the open intent of McCain's unsuccessful push to eliminate congressional parking privileges adjacent to the runway at Reagan National Airport. The rationale for the privilege was to allow representatives greater time flexibility to travel back and forth to their constituents, but McCain's explanation for the proposal provided a revealing glimpse into his base motivation for reform: "When the people perceive any distinction between their interests and ours—whether that distinction is apparent or real—then we will lose that most precious commodity—the hopefully given, but closely guarded trust of the people who sent us here," he said on the Senate floor. "Any effort to demonstrate how honored we are to be of the people—no matter how small or symbolic—has real value, and is a useful contribution to the preservation of this institution and the noble idea upon which it rests."

The focus was always more about alleviating popular suspicions and restoring citizens' faith in their country than actually improving the function of government. Such was the case in McCain's reform centerpiece, campaign finance. "My personal experience with scandal . . . taught me to recognize how much disproportionate campaign giving from what are euphemistically described as special interests caused the public to question the integrity of officeholders," he wrote in *Worth the Fighting For*. "Questions of honor are raised as much by appearances as by reality in politics, and because they incite public distrust, they need to be addressed no less directly than we would address evidence of expressly illegal corruption."

But there was one crucial difference from the other planks of his reform agenda: this time, the limitations wouldn't be slapped on legislators so much, but rather on the public that elects them. McCain and Feingold sought to ban "soft money," the euphemism for unlimited contributions that individuals and entities could make to political parties for general purposes. Such funds had more than doubled between 1992 and 2000, to more than $200 million. "Without soft money," he predicted before the bill's passage, "we'd go back to campaigns as we knew [them]."[10] But much more ominously for constitutional free speech, the McCain-Feingold bill in its final version as passed banned outside advocacy groups like the National Rifle Association or Planned Parenthood from running advertisements that even mentioned a candidate's name within 60 days of an election.

Since the original impetus and legal justification for campaign finance reform in the 1970s was to untangle the nexus of corruption between donors and candidates, what did the paid speech of independent political organizations have to do with anything? Plenty, if your emphasis was not actually on the corruption, but rather on the elements that bred public cynicism. Political ads from outside groups, McCain told the Supreme Court when it was first weighing the constitutionality of McCain-Feingold, "are direct, blatant attacks on the candidates. We don't think that's right." Elsewhere, he complained that the ads "do little to further beneficial debate," and are "disgusting and distasteful and should be rejected."[11] He clearly found the attack-ads of citizens to be repugnant. As syndicated columnist George Will, a longtime opponent of campaign-finance reform on constitutional grounds, put it, "McCain-Feingold's actual purpose is to protect politicians from speech that annoys them."[12]

These new restrictions empowered the Federal Elections Commission to maintain a database of all Americans who donate more than $200 to a political cause, and threw the weight of the Washington bureaucracy behind investigating such mundane citizen actions as NASCAR driver Kirk Shelmerdine putting a Bush-Cheney decal on his car, or four men in Texas making a homemade sign near a highway reading "Vote Republican: Not Al Gore Socialism."[13]

As then-FEC Chair Bradley Smith put it in 2005, "Right now . . . there is more protection for simulated child pornography, flag burning, tobacco advertising, or burning a cross in an African-American residential neighborhood than there is for running an advertisement that merely mentions a congressman's name within 60 days of an election." Smith, a conservative Republican, law professor, and outspoken critic of the law he was hired to enforce, argued that campaign finance reform was "an assault on the First Amendment and a transfer of power from citizens to incumbent politicians, one that doesn't address far more serious conflicts of interest, including those of politicians who bang the campaign finance drum the loudest. . . . I fear that the regulatory machinery set in motion by Sens. John McCain and Russ Feingold will be used to further grind down the free expression of individual citizens."[14]

Despite the clear constitutional implications of having the federal government dictate the boundaries of political speech, a funny thing happened during McCain-Feingold's long crawl through the legislative process: The professional beneficiaries of speech protection, journalists, not only cheered this suppression on, they sneered at Republicans for disingenuously wrapping their opposition in the First Amendment. "Opponents," wrote Elizabeth Drew in her book *Citizen McCain*, "made too much trouble over its alleged unconstitutionality—often using bogus, if somewhat effective, arguments."

Non-journalists have long puzzled over campaign-finance reform's popularity among the Fourth Estate, occasionally suggesting that it's a scheme to eliminate competition to editorial pages, or just a way to kneecap Republicans since the GOP was the party most hurt by the soft money ban. But there's a simpler explanation: Reporters, like soldiers and cops, have their noses rubbed on a daily basis in the problems of society, yet are trained to avoid using a set approach or ideology for solving them, aside from yelling "Something must be done!" Political reporters observe officeholders constantly raising money and accommodating the needs of donors more than those of everyday citizens, and they conclude something must be done. McCain-Feingold promised to be that something, and its backers encouraged those who agreed with its ends not to get too hung up on its means, since legislative sausage always has a little gristle. With McCain being one of the most sympathetic and media-flattering politicians in Washington, and Russ Feingold among its most attractively principled, it was easy, natural even, for journalists to line up on their side, especially when the opposition was represented by southern-fried smooth talkers like Mitch McConnell, or even bow-tied sophists like George Will; their very essences offended the sensibilities of most liberal reporters.

In choosing a side, journalists missed not only the story of McCain-Feingold's chilling effects on grassroots political activities, but also of McCain's flippant attitude toward the Constitution. Having buried Goldwater, taken aim at the libertarian wing of his own party, and decided that the federal government should be the focus of national greatness, McCain no longer held the Bill of Rights as such an immovable object. "I would rather have a clean government than one where quote First Amendment rights are being respected, that has become corrupt," he told syndicated radio host Don Imus. "If I had my choice, I'd rather have the clean government."

By the 2000 presidential campaign season, McCain's campaign finance reform had evolved from a face-saving gesture to the central policy plank of his greater cause of reform. It was, he said almost every day on the campaign trail, a "transcendent issue." But having whipped up the restoration of national greatness, he discovered it wasn't the only one.

Anything that contributed to the "pervasive public cynicism" that McCain had declared war against was now fair game. Steroids in baseball? Do something! "Are you and the players living in such a rarified atmosphere that you do not appreciate that this is a transcendent issue?" he growled at Players' Union representative Donald Fehr in 2005, while threatening Fourth Amendment-bending legislation to establish mandatory federal drug testing of both amateur and professional athletes, with zero-tolerance punishment. "Don't you get it? Don't you get it?"

McCain, a huge sports fan, is touchy about anything that might threaten the integrity of organized competition, or simply shock the sensibilities of gullible young fans. He has proposed a federal ban on college sports betting (even though he is an "avid gambler," according to a 2005 *New Yorker* profile,[15] and he hosted an NCAA championship bracket on his campaign website in 2007) because it "can have a terrible effect on young people."[16] He wants the federal government to regulate boxing, down to establishing a national commissioner. After seeing a tape of an Ultimate Fighting match, McCain sent letters to all 50 states urging them to ban the practice, calling it a "brutal and repugnant blood sport . . . that should not be allowed to take place anywhere in the U.S." Due in large part to his efforts, the sport was outlawed in more than 35 states and dropped from both TCI and Time Warner cable (McCain, as ranking Republican on the Senate

Commerce Committee, takes an active role in regulating cable and receives large donations from the industry). He also supports the ban on online gambling because "a lot of these outfits that do it are located outside the United States of America," and "there is no confidence that you're in a fair game, there are absolutely no rules, no regulation."

His restrictions on human activity in the name of combating cynicism are hardly limited to individuals. McCain wants broadcast companies to devote free airtime to political candidates, cable companies to offer their channels a la carte, all entertainment production companies (movies, video games, music) to use a single content-labeling system, and large online service providers to constantly check their user lists against a proposed federal database of sex offenders. Hollywood, the airline industry, and cable companies are constantly in his sights.

Depending on one's politics and interests, McCain's crusading interventionism is almost guaranteed to delight on one day and infuriate the next. Conservatives groaned when he worked to close the "gun-show loophole" that had allowed people to buy firearms without background checks, and when he plumped for a "Patients Bill of Rights." Liberals winced at his opposition to gay marriage and his vociferous support for the Iraq War. He has been the most convincing Republican voice both on closing down Guantanamo Bay and extending George Bush's troop surge. He thinks climate change is a priority and wants to build a new generation of nuclear power plants.

As a former soldier, an independent by temperament and a man who places high value on forming partnerships with his ideological foes, McCain was a natural at couching all of his initiatives in the high rhetoric of above-it-all patriotism. Because journalists are so accustomed to plotting politicians along a single axis from left to right, McCain's record looked like a mess of zigzagging contradictions, desperate for coherence and interpretation. Searching for "the real McCain" became a favored pastime of wish-casting reporters and analysts from coast to coast.

But the answer to his ideology was hiding in plain sight: The proper role of the federal government is to act as a beacon of faith for Americans and the world. Therefore, the state must be cleansed, then used as a tool to fix cynicism-breeding societal flaws, after which citizens will be inspired to serve, and the U.S. can go on robustly leading the world. "National greatness," he wrote in *Worth the Fighting For*, is "the proper object of every American's citizenship." Liberals, he argued, were too wed to "multiculturalism" to champion that cause, and conservatives were too hostile to Washington. "There are many things that only a federal government can do. Only the federal government can provide for the common defense and restrain powerful economic and social forces from pursuing their private or factional interests at the expense of the national interest." With his Reaganite support for limited government now waning, the last remnants of his libertarianism were channeled not into expanding personal freedom, but reforming and airing out the institutions of government—fighting wasteful spending, investigating the September 11 attacks, adhering to the Geneva Conventions. It's an intriguing, activist mix, but the calls for National Greatness especially had much more resonance as a response to the distracted and smallminded Clinton era, than as a successor to the grandiose failures of latter-day Bush.

But some details have gotten lost along the way in McCain's relentless pursuit of cleansing reform. Most notably, results. As it is for many legislators, the bulk of McCain's proposals have gone nowhere. Unlike his colleagues, though, he has an instinctive attraction to hopelessness and martyrdom. As Michael Lewis observed in 1996, "he is unlike most people who do what he does for a living in his taste for a losing or unpopular cause."[17] Such fatalism makes for great copy, but it doesn't exactly restore national pride. Even the reforms that McCain has managed to achieve—the line-item veto, McCain-Feingold—were so cavalier with the Constitution that the Supreme Court declared parts of them illegal. And the soft money ban, though he continues to laud it, has mostly served to rearrange the methods of campaign fundraising, not put a dent in the bottom line, and it has come at the expense of individual citizens who are faced with Byzantine regulations just to express their political will.

Perhaps most troubling at all, the candidate's own actions suggest that, for him, reform is a matter of "do as I say, not as I do." Yes, he opposes gambling on college sports while hosting a betting bracket; sure, he wanted to raise cigarette taxes even though he quit smoking only in his 40s; that kind of stuff is par for the political course. But more egregious is the fact that McCain has been gobbling up soft money ever since banning it.

After losing his 2000 presidential bid, McCain decided to keep the momentum of his reformist campaign alive by setting up two organizations—the Straight Talk America political action committee, designed to pay for McCain's travel and speeches while spreading money around to reform-minded pols; and the nonprofit Reform Institute, dedicated to advancing the cause of campaign finance and electoral reform. Straight Talk PAC was subject to the usual campaign finance restrictions (an individual can give up to $5,000 to a PAC per year; the PAC can dole out up to $5,000 to a politician per election); but the

Reform Institute, as a 501(c)3, was exempt, just so long as it didn't engage in express political activity.

The Reform Institute, which claims to be apolitical, operates as follows: The chairman of the advisory board was a politician named John McCain (until he resigned in 2005). McCain's accomplishments were touted on the press releases and his name went out on the fundraising letters, which were sent to mailing lists compiled by Straight Talk PAC and Friends of John McCain. The head of the Reform Institute for several years was Rick Davis, a cable/satellite lobbyist and McCain's campaign manager in his bid for president in 2000. (The Institute, in fact, was run out of Davis' lobbying office for a while.) The fundraising chief was Carla Eudy, who also held the same job in McCain's 2000 campaign. The legal counsel was Trevor Potter, who held that job for McCain 2000 as well. Same for communications chief Crystal Benton. And what did they all do in the apolitical, nonprofit world? According to a *New York Times* piece in March 2005, "In a small office a few miles from Capitol Hill, a handful of top advisers to Senator John McCain run a quiet campaign. They promote his crusade against special interest money in politics. They send out news releases promoting his initiatives. And they raise money—hundreds of thousands of dollars, tapping some McCain backers for more than $50,000 each."[18]

Not only did McCain's political hired guns essentially keep themselves fed and clothed while advancing his causes and raising unlimited money from donors who had extensive business in front of McCain's Senate Commerce Committee, they also adapted their mission statement as they went along to reflect . . . the same things that McCain was interested in: comprehensive immigration reform, climate change, homeland security, championing the "national interest." The donor list was impressive: more than $50,000 a pop from communications companies such as Cablevision Systems Corporation Holdings, Echosphere, and the Chartwell Foundation (which isn't a communications company, but is funded by Univision billionaire Jerrold Perenchio, who is a big McCain donor). "In fact," former FEC chair Bradley Smith wrote in December 2005, "Cablevision gave $200,000 to the Reform Institute around the same time its officials were testifying before the Senate Commerce Committee. Appearance of corruption, anyone?"

Meanwhile, the Reform Institute's Davis, Eudy, and Potter have since gone back to helping run McCain's presidential campaign.

McCain and his people deny any wrongdoing, insist his votes aren't for sale, and say that they're following the letter of the law. In other words, the exact same justifications used in the Keating Five scandal, minus any sense of shame. As McCain himself told CNN in 2002, "As long as the wealthiest Americans and richest organized interests can make the six- and seven-figure donations to political parties and gain the special access to power that such generosity confers on the donor, most Americans will dismiss the most virtuous politician's claim of patriotism." Cable and satellite companies might now be prohibited by McCain-Feingold from dumping unlimited soft money into the Republican Party, but they sure can spend their heart's content on organizations near and dear to John McCain.

And this just scratches the surface of McCain's dependence on the "iron triangle" of "lobbyists, big money and legislation" that he campaigned so furiously against in 2000. *U.S. News & World Report* in May 2007 investigated McCain's quarter-century of political fundraising, and concluded: "He has been an avid seeker of special-interest money to support his campaigns and initiatives. . . . Moreover, as the boss or No. 2 member of the Senate Commerce Committee, he has drawn heavy support from PACs and individuals associated with industries overseen by that committee—especially telecommunications, media, and technology firms. Between 1997 and June 2006, he collected nearly $2.6 million from such interests, according to the Center for Public Integrity, an independent watchdog group in Washington."[19]

The Web site Politico.com surveyed the personnel comings and goings of McCain's July campaign shake-up and observed that his new campaign manager and two chief fundraisers were all lobbyists, meaning that "lobbyists now both raise and spend McCain's campaign cash." Of all the major 2008 candidates, the site argued, "McCain could be most indebted to the lobbying and special-interest-money community that he has long sought to diminish."[20] And the *New York Times* kicked the reformer when he was down on July 12 when it reported that McCain's desperate phone call from Capitol Hill to assuage his panicked fundraisers may have been illegal. "Senate ethics rules expressly forbid lawmakers to engage in campaign activities inside Senate facilities," the paper reported. "If Mr. McCain solicited campaign contributions on a call from government property, that would be a violation of federal criminal law as well. . . . Mr. McCain was well aware of the rules. Ten years ago he led Republican calls for an independent prosecutor to investigate accusations of violations of the same rules by Vice President Al Gore. Mr. McCain went on to make the episode a cornerstone of both his 2000 Republican primary campaign and his argument for the McCain-Feingold campaign finance law."[21]

In these violations of the spirit, if not the letter, of campaign finance rules, was McCain acting any different than the average politician? Probably not. But other politicians don't make ethical virtue their selling point. Nor, as we shall see, do they blow a gasket when they get caught red-handed.

ANGER MANAGEMENT

*There's no temper. . . . I think it's been fabricated by [the] race
in 2000. I think that's what the then-Bush candidate was trying
to point out. But there's no temper. There is an extreme amount
of passion, yes. . . . I get a little frustrated when I hear that
because it's not temper. That's a concoction that they made up.
And I don't like that.*

—Cindy McCain, *New York Times*, June 29, 2007[1]

*During an otherwise tranquil early childhood, I had quite unex-
pectedly developed an outsized temper that I expressed in an
unusual way. At the smallest provocation, I would go off in a mad
frenzy, and then, suddenly, crash to the floor unconscious. . . .
When I got angry I held my breath until I blacked out.*

—John McCain, *Faith of My Fathers*[2]

At a Los Angeles press conference in June 2007, three weeks
before overhauling his senior campaign staff, John McCain
was asked the same question for the thousandth time: Did the
fact that he hired so many of the same people who had helped
savage him in South Carolina seven years ago on behalf of
George W. Bush indicate that the tenor of McCain 2008 was

going to be fundamentally different from the old Straight Talk Express? As is any candidate's wont when asked about going negative, McCain instead stressed that he was focused on "portraying our vision for the future of the country" and "taking important stances on issues." As for the 2000 unpleasantness, well, bygones were bygones, and he'd "had reconciliation with everybody, from the president on down." But then, out of left field, McCain became insistent on a character trait no one had brought up: "I'm not the type of person who holds grudges, nor will I ever."

By this time I had been living in McCain's world long enough to know that when he makes an unprovoked, absolutist statement about what he is *not*, chances are you're being tipped off about what he *is*. Contrary to his straight-talking image, McCain—like other politicians—will look you in the eye and lie, as he did repeatedly a month later when, with his candidacy on the verge of imploding, he insisted robotically day after day that he was "very happy with the campaign." (In fact, as several news organizations reported at the time, he was furious about its spectacular spending rate.[3]) During the 2000 campaign, he claimed he wasn't milking his Vietnam experience any more than usual, despite distributing a documentary on his war experiences to New Hampshire voters, releasing *Faith of My Fathers* the same month he announced his candidacy, leveraging his book tour to maximize free media, and letting his campaign manager slip in, for example, that "The story of John McCain is a powerful campaign tool. The more we tell the story, the more votes we get."[4] And in a telltale denialist tic, McCain told *Playboy* magazine in early 2000, "There's no chronicled event where I have even expressed anger, much less lost my temper." The article, written by the *Phoenix New Times*' Amy Silverman, went on to document four instances of McCain not only expressing anger and los-ing his temper, but holding a grudge for quite some time afterward.[5]

McCain's preemptive grudge denial also was suspect because I had just spent a week in Phoenix, where it's impos-sible to finish a cup of coffee before someone volunteers that, whether they love him or hate him, their senior senator sure does hold a grudge. The sentiment spans the spectrum from a random librarian, to a friend at lunch, to a retired judge. "McCain has always held a grudge; he's famous for holding grudges," longtime GOP activist Don Hesselbrock told me. Hesselbrock, the type of seasoned, behind-the-scenes GOP organizer who has long followed Reagan's 11th Command-ment ("Thou shalt not speak ill of a fellow Republican"), had never really gone public before with his decades-long con-cerns over John McCain's fitness for higher office. "That temper is not a small thing," he said. "I've been in his pres-ence when he's said other things . . . where that's just not the demeanor of somebody who should be in the oval office."

Outside of Arizona, McCain's legendary short fuse is often treated with an almost audible sigh, as if it were an irri-tating, exaggerated trope, ginned up periodically by his polit-ical opponents. "He has known since the start of the race that other campaigns have been waiting to portray him as a man with an uncontrollable temper," *Slate*'s John Dickerson wrote in July 2007.[6] Or maybe it's just the price of passion. "Looked at in the right light, Mr. McCain's weaknesses can also seem like strengths," *The Economist* magazine argued five weeks earlier. "The flip side of 'temper' is feistiness."[7]

Every new outburst leads to a perfunctory round of "McCain's temper back on campaign's front-burner" articles, where a few old blow-ups are trotted out, McCain's side defends their man as being merely passionate and frank, and a few experts debate how this might affect the presidential race.[8] What's almost always missing from these exercises is a root analysis of where and why the volcano erupts. As *Arizona Republic* columnist E. J. Montini put it during the high season of 1999 temper stories, "Once again, the media are getting it backward. It's not McCain's tantrums that matter; it's what sets him off."[9]

An instructive example was the incident that triggered the most recent batch of McCain temperament stories. In a May 17, 2007 meeting, Senate supporters of the comprehensive immigration bill and administration officials were busy trying to hammer out the final details of their "grand bargain" in time for an afternoon press conference. Sen. John Cornyn, R-Texas, who had co-authored a more enforcement-focused immigration bill the year before with Arizona Republican John Kyl, pushed hard to have the final language allow for easier deportation of illegal immigrants. Sen. Ted Kennedy, the leading proponent of the grand bargain, wouldn't budge, and the clock kept ticking. McCain, who had long been a co-architect of reform efforts with Kennedy, but hadn't been anywhere near the Senate for more than a month because he was out intensively fundraising, grew impatient, and then snapped. As recounted by the Powerline blog:

> "This is chickenshit," [McCain] told Senator Cornyn. "I think it would expedite things if you would just leave the room, Senator, so we can get along with finishing this up." Senator Cornyn responded: "Wait a minute. We've been meeting for three months on this in good faith, and now you parachute in here this morning and tell me to leave? I think you're out of line."
>
> Senator McCain responded: "F*** you! I know what is going on here. I know more about immigration than anybody in this room!"[10]

What this anecdote shares with so many of McCain's outbursts is that it came in response to criticism that was perfectly valid. McCain had indeed been largely AWOL from the immigration negotiations all year, after previously serving as the deal's lead Republican champion. (As the *Washington Post* reported the following week, McCain had missed half that year's Senate votes, "including all 45 votes held since first-quarter fundraising reports were released April 15 that showed McCain trailing all of the leading candidates in both parties."[11]) A couple of months earlier, Sen. Joseph Biden, D-Del., a friend of McCain's, said that he thought immigration reform was doomed for the year precisely because of McCain's missing leadership. For the Arizona senator it was the worst of all possible worlds: his effort to get something done about a pressing national problem was being held up on a what he considered to be a niggling detail; his absent leadership was (rightly) being called into question; and although he was no longer the Republican face on the deal—he'd sloughed that thankless duty off on his state-mate John Kyl, even though Kyl had recently won a close reelection by promising to be tough on immigration—he was still being hammered in the conservative media and the polls over the deeply unpopular "amnesty" bill. Plus, he had two fundraisers to get to later that night in New York.

In this case, McCain apologized, Cornyn pronounced himself satisfied, and the campaign staff went into full pooh-pooh mode. "If something is written every time members of Congress and leading politicians, behind closed doors, try to get the other's attention, and tempers flare, you'd run out of ink," McCain's then-chief strategist John Weaver told the *Los Angeles Times*.

But what happens when someone with less power crosses swords with the man *Washingtonian* magazine famously christened as "Senator Hothead" back in 1997?[12] Unlike past presidents such as Bill Clinton and Dwight Eisenhower, McCain does not direct his temper downward onto his own subordinates (his staff tends to be remarkably loyal and serve longer than those of just about any other senator). He has unloaded his wrath on public officials, bureaucratic henchmen, and journalists of lesser standing, who have made the mistake of criticizing him where it hurts. It is in these situations that McCain has held grudges, lashed back with criticism he knew (or should have known) to be false, and altered people's lives.

Take the case of Capitol Hill defense wonk Winslow Wheeler. For 30 years, Wheeler worked on defense issues for four different senators (two from each party) and the General Accounting Office. He helped write the War Powers Act, sounded alarms about military readiness under President Clinton, and above all else, targeted the pernicious defense pork in the yearly authorization and appropriations bills. In that fight he had no better Senate ally than John McCain, though the two never worked together. McCain for years has had his staff make exhaustive lists of senators' pet projects, many of them not remotely military-related, slipped into massive defense bills. He's gone after weapons systems the military branches don't need and sweetheart financing arrangements for companies like Boeing, all while steering clear of writing his own pork into legislation. Rhetorically, on both defense pork and run-of-the-mill earmarks, John McCain has been one of the best public servants in Washington.

But one day that just wasn't enough for Wheeler. It was December 7, 2001, Pearl Harbor Day, less than two months after the September 11 massacre. The 2002 defense appropriations bill was under discussion, and John McCain went up to the podium with his list of 245 gratuitous pork projects totaling more than $3.5 million in wasteful spending.[13] "This bill time and time again chooses to fund pork-barrel projects with little, if any, relationship to national defense at a time of scarce resources, budget deficits, and underfunded urgent defense priorities," McCain rightly noted.

"It was a great speech," recalled Wheeler, who was in the chamber at the time, working for Sen. Pete Domenici, R-N.M. "Then McCain sits down, and so I sort of gave him—we were too far away to talk to each other—I gave this body motion of like, 'Ok, what are you going to do now?' And his body motion response was, 'That's it. The speech.'" Two weeks and hundreds of more items of pork later, the bill passed 94-2, with only McCain and Sen. Phil Gramm, R-Texas, voting no.

Wheeler was livid. He thought McCain should have filibustered, which the senator had threatened to do on a similar bill earlier in the year. "The United States Senate is a place very specifically designed to help the minority, even when it's just one guy or a woman, tie that place up in knots unless he or she gets his way," he said. "A golden opportunity for McCain to say 'I'm going to be a parliamentary pain in the ass until you guys start taking some of this garbage out of here.'"

At the time, Wheeler was sending copies of his dense and oftentimes unread staff reports to an online mailing list under the pseudonym of Spartacus. (He started using the pseudonym after writing the first one under his own name and then getting chewed out by Domenici when the memo was referenced in the *Washington Times* without mentioning that it came from Domenici's office.) Spartacus built up a small following among defense geeks and journalists, including staff in McCain's office, which after all was doing similar work.

But Wheeler was so angry at what he felt was McCain's empty words on Pearl Harbor Day that he titled his next Spartacus missive "Mr. Smith Is Dead," detailing at length the sausage-making of the 2002 defense bill, then wrapping it up with a swipe at the bill's biggest critic. "When it comes to action—meaningful action—McCain is only a paper press release tiger," he wrote. "Knowing at least as well as any other just what is going on, he finds it somehow going too far to put an end to it with the many tools at his disposal. By assuming this role—i.e. the self-anointed, but also self-disarmed, crusader against 'pork'—McCain has made himself not the Senate's 'pork buster' but its 'pork enabler.'"[14]

Strong words; quite possibly unfair. But not as unfair as what came next. McCain, outraged at the attack, and clearly not seeing it as the "kick in the pants" that Wheeler intended, decided to reveal Wheeler's identity—which was an open secret in defense circles—to the *Washington Post*'s Howard Kurtz. Kurtz then assisted the senator by framing the issue as a question of pseudonymity and journalism ethics. "If I want to respond and out him, there's no reason I should be restrained. I don't think that's correct journalism," McCain told Kurtz.[15] The result was predictable: Wheeler was fired within the week (though he was later able to structure it as a resignation), and that was the last of the soft-on-pork critique.

Perhaps worse, McCain made it sound like Wheeler/Spartacus was carrying water for the appropriators by attacking the great reformer, when in fact McCain's own staff knew the opposite to be true. "I just don't quite understand why we can't say he's the staffer of an Appropriations Committee member," he told Kurtz. "Why should we be forbidden from doing that? I think it puts it in some perspective." Despite the "demonstrably false" implication that he was corrupt, Wheeler retains a soft spot for McCain. "I like his anger; he gets angry at the right things. But he has this fatal senator's flaw that he thinks talk is action. . . . These false reformers are going to be the death of us."

The tales of McCain butting heads with Washington big-wigs have been retold enough to sound leathery at the edges, almost comical. One time he went nose-to-nose with Iowa senator Chuck Grassley and called him a "fucking jerk."[16] Another time, he informed Domenici that "Only an asshole would put together a budget like this," adding helpfully, "I wouldn't call you an asshole unless you really were an ass-hole."[17] He screamed "You are finished!" to then-Navy Secretary John Dalton for failing to promote a commander McCain liked.[18] Former Sen. Rick Santorum, R-Penn., told the *Weekly Standard*'s Fred Barnes that "Everybody in the Senate has had a McCain moment—when John jumped down your throat for some reason or other."[19] He even scuf-fled with an ancient Strom Thurmond once for interrupting him on the Senate floor.[20] Depending on one's opinion of the politicians on the receiving end, this behavior can seem quite sympathetic. Who hasn't wanted, at least once, to call some Senate blowhard a "jerk"?

But it's the lesser-told stories of thin-skinned retribution, like that against Wheeler, that indicate something far more troubling about the way McCain wields power and reacts to even legitimate criticism. When the *Arizona Republic* called McCain for comment about his wife's business ties to Charles Keating, he called the reporter a "liar" and an "idiot," and then asked: "You do understand English, don't you?"[21] Years later, he exploded at Robert Timberg when the sympathetic biographer suggested that his wife's investment in Keating's shopping center was a legitimate news story.[22] (McCain blames the original incident on the *Arizona Republic* continually playing the temper card, and he insists he's never been as nasty to reporters again.[23]) However, he threatened to get *Arizona Republic* columnist E. J. Montini fired after Montini criticized him for preemptively dismissing the as-yet undelivered testimony of Anita Hill.[24] When his hometown paper in 1999 editorialized that his "volcanic temper" was a reason "to seriously question whether McCain has the temperament and the political approach and skills we want in the next president of the United States," he accused George W. Bush of planting the stories.

This tic extends much further than the usual skirmishes with local reporters. After a man named Tom Gosinksi filed a $250,000 wrongful termination lawsuit in 1993 against Cindy McCain—who had taken out prescriptions for painkillers in Gosinki's name without telling him—the McCains brought in high-powered Washington, D.C., lawyer/fixer John Dowd to convince the Maricopa County district attorney to investigate Gosinski for extortion.[25] Gosinksi dropped the suit, then left the state when the criminal investigation turned up nothing. The *Phoenix New Times'* Amy Silverman co-authored a devastating September 1994 account of the whole shady tale, including a stage-managed Cindy McCain confession of her drug use that was embargoed to come out on the same day that the first court documents were being released corroborating her illegal activities. McCain was furious; he cornered Amy Silverman's father Richard, then director of an Arizona utility called the Salt River Project, and reportedly "berated" him.[26] The McCains also refused to speak with other reporters who followed up on the drug story.

"McCain is a man who carries get-even grudges," former *Arizona Republic* publisher Pat Murphy, a onetime close friend of McCain's, wrote in 2000.[27] "He cannot endure criticism. He threatens. He controls by fear. He's consumed with self-importance. He shifts blame. . . . McCain is a man obsessed with political ambitions but plagued by self-destructive petty impulses." Murphy had his own falling out with the senator after the *Arizona Republic*, in his words, "exposed McCain as a liar." Murphy told his story:

> McCain boasted to my wife and me over lunch in Washington that he had planted complex questions with the Senate Interior Committee chairman to sabotage the testimony of Arizona Gov. Rose Mofford, a Democrat, about the Central Arizona Project, the multibillion-dollar Colorado River water delivery system for Arizona urban areas. . . . "I'm duty bound to embarrass a Democrat whenever I can."
>
> When reporters later asked McCain about planted questions, he feigned insult and injury and denied any such ploy. Editors in Phoenix were informed of McCain's deceit. After a news story and editorial appeared, McCain went into meltdown, shrieking on the phone: "I know you're out to get me!"

After Murphy's exposé, Murphy claims McCain then went to "war" against him, which contributed to his being fired both from the *Arizona Republic* and the Phoenix talk radio station KTAR.

As befits a man torn between defiant martial aggression and ambitious Beltway climbing, between selfish pride and selfishness-hating penitence, McCain is known almost as much for his apologies as his outbursts. There's even a name for them on Capitol Hill: "McCain Notes," which frequently come with flowers or other gifts, and "fill his friends' and enemies' drawers like souvenirs."[28] It is a curious mix of behaviors for a man in his 70s. Some of the disaffected Arizonans who gave testimony to his temper back in 1999 are now actively working for McCain 2008.

Depending on his mood or the political necessities of the day, McCain has denied having much of a temper, acknowledged occasional flashes while defending his passion, or identified anger management in almost 12-Step-style terms. "When I ran in 2000, that was an issue that was raised and attempted to be raised," he told the *Houston Chronicle* in May 2007. "Didn't work then, won't work now."[29] A full decade earlier, he confessed to *USA Today* that he had "spent the last 10 years doing everything I can to control my temper," and in 1999 he told the *L.A. Times*: "I do everything I can to keep my anger under control. I wake up daily and tell myself, 'You must do everything possible to stay cool, calm and collected today.'"[30]

One of the lazier myths about McCain is that this hair-trigger is somehow the result of his captivity in Vietnam. People who have read his medical records say otherwise, and besides, McCain's own books are filled with examples of a pre-Vietnam John blowing his stack at real or imagined slights. In the first autobiographical chapter of *Faith of My Fathers*, we learn that a two-year-old McCain would become so furious that he'd hold his breath until he passed out, a condition which his parents treated by dunking him in ice water. At new schools, his first order of business was "to impress upon my classmates that I was not a person to suffer slights lightly." And as already mentioned (chapter 3), he was especially set off by any suggestion that he'd received favorable treatment because of his family. In *Worth the Fighting For*, he explains how in his very first congressional primary campaign, after learning that his opponent had called his ex-wife looking for dirt, he told him after a debate: "If you ever try to hurt anyone in my family again, I will personally beat the shit out of you."[31]

As in that example, it's clear that McCain remains ambivalent about his most-cited character flaw, showing contrition for its excesses one moment, pride in its deployment the next. "Over the years," he waxes philosophically, "my temper has become one of my most frequently discussed attributes. I have one, of course, and its exercise, usually when I am very tired, has caused me to make most of the more serious mistakes of my career. It is fair to say that my temper has now become legendary. But like most legends, it is exaggerated far beyond reality. I have used it for effect as often as I have lost it involuntarily. Also, I have in recent years managed to control it better than I ever could earlier in life."

Later in the same book, he's much more defiant. "I have a temper, to state the obvious, which I have tried to control with varying degrees of success because it does not always serve my interest or the public's. I have regretted losing my temper on many occasions. But there are things worth getting angry about in politics, and I have at times tried to use my anger to incite public outrage. I make no apologies for that."[32]

As in his national greatness-inspired yen for government interventionism in the name of reducing public cynicism, McCain's flashes of anger can be righteous or appalling, depending on where you line up on the underlying issue. Conservatives have been passing around YouTube clips of his thunderous C-SPAN condemnations of Democratic criticism of the war. Liberals have cheered his withering indictments of Bush's torture policies. And as his supporters never get tired of pointing out, there have been presidents with tempers before, and many of them (unlike McCain) showed cruelty to their underlings. He may be prickly and proud, but he's not a sadist.

Perhaps the most intriguing and suggestive display of McCain's anger was unleashed at the unlikeliest of targets— families of missing POWs in Vietnam and the people who believe there were more soldiers left behind. It's hard to imagine that America's most famous former POW wouldn't be more sensitive to his ex-comrades' loved ones; but his anger is easily triggered by impatience, and there was no single policy McCain was more impatient about than restoring close relations with the communist country that locked him up.

HEALING VIETNAM

In the case of Vietnam, obviously it was a tragic failure in many respects, but also it impacted the conduct of our national security policy in a very negative way for at least 20 years, that I know of. And the specter of Vietnam still haunts us. I've got to tell you, my friends, I spent the last 30 years trying to heal the wounds of the Vietnam War and help many of our veterans come all the way home. I was astonished at what a poor job that I, working with John Kerry, had done, because we spent five weeks of the last presidential campaign arguing over a war that was over 30 years ago. I've become tragically convinced that my generation may have to die off before the wounds of that conflict are finally healed.

—John McCain, BBC, July 4, 2005[1]

In Congress, colleagues and staffers who have seen him erupt—in the open and, more often, in closed meetings—profess themselves confounded by his behavior. Insisting upon anonymity so as not to invite one of his verbal assaults, they say they have no easy way to explain why a former POW would work so hard and so persistently to keep POW/MIA information from coming out. Typical is the comment of one congressional veteran who has watched McCain over many years: "This is a man not at peace with himself."

—Sydney Schanberg, APBNews.com, April 25, 2000[2]

William Bader, chief of staff of the Senate Foreign Relations Committee during the Carter presidency, had never seen anything like it. It was 1979, and Bader was accompanying a Senate delegation to China, along with Navy liaison John McCain. In Robert Timberg's telling, "During the trip no fewer than five senators, all antiwar Democrats, wandered separately to the rear of the plane where McCain was seated and invited him to join them up front. After watching the parade for several hours, the perplexed Bader puzzled it out. The senators, he decided, were making their peace with John McCain."[3]

After five and a half years of deprivation, torture, and illness, John McCain came back not to vent his well-earned bitterness, but to heal the national divisions over Vietnam. In his essay for *U.S. News & World Report* two months after returning, though he took some mild swipes at the "peaceniks" who had visited North Vietnam and said that "antiwar quotes from people in high places back in Washington" amounted to "the most effective propaganda" his captors used, McCain exuded a remarkably generous spirit of reconciliation. "I think America is a better country now because we have been through a sort of purging process, a reevaluation of ourselves," he wrote. "Now I see more of an appreciation of our way of life. There is more patriotism. The flag is all over the place. I hear new values being stressed—the concern for environment is a case in point."

But first, he had a lot of catching up to do. As a history and pop-culture omnivore—in the latter days of Hanoi, when prisoners were allowed to spend the day in a communal space, McCain would reenact entire movies for his comrades, and he taught a class called "A History of the World From the Beginning"—the thing about America he missed the most was "the free, uncensored, abundant flow of information." As he wrote in the forward to a new edition of David Halberstam's classic Vietnam-policy opus *The Best and the Brightest*, upon touching down to Clark Air Force base, "I was as hungry for information as I was for food. As I sat down to enjoy my first decent meal in a long while, I asked a steward if he would also provide me with any newspapers and magazines he could find. I was desperate to fill in the blanks about what I knew was going on in the world."

At the time McCain was shot down, *The Jungle Book* was America's most popular movie, Andy Griffith had the number-one TV show, and *Sgt. Pepper's Lonely Hearts Club Band* was dominating the pop charts. He came back to a country of *The Poseidon Adventure*, *All in the Family*, and *The World is a Ghetto* by a band called War. The AFL and NFL had merged, the Beach Boys were making experimental stoner music, and his beloved Marlon Brando had taken to sending Native Americans to give political speeches on his behalf at the Oscars. It's little wonder that McCain's favorite new movie became George Lucas' 1950s nostalgia exercise *American Graffiti*. The United States since he'd been gone had put a man on the moon, buried Bobby Kennedy and Martin Luther King Jr., elected Richard Nixon twice, and squandered public confidence in the prosecution of the Vietnam War.

The returning POWs, the bulk of whom were officers and pilots, held a unique position in the domestic politics of Vietnam. Lyndon Johnson had chosen not to publicize their plight, but Richard Nixon let the first gravely injured returnees give extensive testimony about their appalling treatment. Antiwar liberals like Jane Fonda had scoffed at reports of their torture and focused sympathy instead on the luckless lower-class teens drafted into the war machine. Pro-war conservatives, who didn't want to hear too much about the embittered rank and file coming home to protest the war, instead turned their attentions on McCain and his repatriated brothers. "By focusing on the POW, the model vet," wrote John Karaagac in *John McCain: An Essay in Military and Political History*, "the right could altogether ignore the breakdown of morale and discipline in the U.S. armed forces."[4] Ross Perot had been the main civilian champion of the POW cause, and Ronald Reagan made sure they were welcomed home with the parades and national gratitude that non-POWs almost never received. McCain gravitated easily to the Reaganite message of national healing and military restoration, giving inspirational speeches about his fellow prisoners' acts of patriotic courage, and encouraging young people to enter public service.

McCain's snap take on events, as captured in his *U.S. News* essay, contained plenty of analysis and depictions that went missing in his subsequent statements about Vietnam. Among the more trivial of these were his observations that "a lot" of his captors "were homosexual, although never toward us"; that "the Oriental, as you may know, likes to beat around the bush quite a bit"; and that "you never can fathom the 'gooks.'" More substantively, he gave hawkish testament to the "caliber" and "courage" of President Nixon in mining Hanoi Harbor and bombing Cambodia, acts he credited with ending the war. "He has a long background in dealing with these people. He knows how to use the carrot and the stick," he wrote. "We're stronger than the Communists, so they were willing to negotiate. Force is what they understand. And that's why it is difficult for me to understand now, when everybody knows bombing finally got a cease-fire agreement, why people are still criticizing his foreign policy."

The most interesting of the details McCain left out of all subsequent interviews and books was his anecdotal evidence lending support to the controversial domino theory—the notion that once Vietnam fell, the communists would sweep through the rest of southeast Asia. It was one of the main justifications for the war, and especially for staying in it long after success seemed unlikely. In the essay, McCain claimed that two separate Vietnamese generals in May 1968 told him following: "After we liberate South Vietnam we're going to liberate Cambodia. And after Cambodia we're going to Laos and after we liberate Laos we're going to liberate Thailand and after we liberate Thailand we're going to liberate Malaysia, and then Burma. We're going to liberate all east Asia." What was McCain's interpretation of these politically convenient quotes? "Some people's favorite game is to refute the 'domino theory,' but the North Vietnamese themselves never tried to refute it. They believe it. . . . This is what Communism is all about—armed struggle to overthrow capitalist countries."

Perhaps one reason McCain stopped repeating this story is that he enrolled in the Naval War College soon after returning to the United States and immediately set about a nine-month, self-designed course in how America "entered and lost" Vietnam. He read histories of French colonialism; Halberstam's *The Best and the Brightest*; realistic novels like Graham Greene's *The Quiet American*; and the Pentagon Papers, a damning, 7,000-page top secret Defense Department internal analysis covering in detail the cynicism and dishonesty of U.S. decision-making in Vietnam from 1945–71. The Pentagon Papers were leaked by Daniel Ellsberg, who had helped work on them, and then published by the *New York Times*. As President Nixon's Chief of Staff H. R. Haldeman told his boss at the time, they had a "very clear" message: "You can't trust the government; you can't believe what they say; and you can't rely on their judgment. And the implicit infallibility of presidents, which has been an accepted thing in America, is badly hurt by this, because it shows that people do things the President wants to do even though it's wrong, and the President can be wrong." Though McCain took great educational sustenance from the Pentagon Papers, that didn't stop him from agreeing to testify for the state in Ellsberg's treason trial, which was dismissed before McCain had his chance.

For such a momentous bout of intellectual discovery, with potentially devastating ramifications for his bedrock faith in country, McCain seems disinterested in talking about his War College conclusions. The course gets all of one paragraph in just one of his books, *Worth the Fighting For*. "I had satisfied my curiosity," he wrote. "The experience did not cause me to conclude that the war was wrong, but it did help me understand how wrongly it had been fought and led. I was not an embittered veteran before I entered the War College, nor am I now. But I did resent how badly civilian leaders had mismanaged the war and how ineffectually our senior military commanders had resisted their mistakes." He thought the war should have been fought with maximum force and that all of the military's senior leaders—including his own father—should have resigned in protest because it was not.

The thing that made him maddest of all had very little to do with the bigger questions of foreign policy and everything to do with personal honor and service. McCain found it "appalling" that the war was fought disproportionately by minorities and poor people, while the privileged white kids found a way to avoid the line of fire. "No national endeavor requires as much unshakeable resolve as war. Before we enter one, we ought to know that most Americans share the commitment and are prepared to make the personal sacrifice it entails," he wrote. If there were any other applicable insights from the War College besides "fight to win," the most famous POW has not shared them. When National Public Radio's Terry Gross asked McCain in 2000 whether what he learned shook his faith in Washington, he said no, then stressed that one of his chief motivations in entering politics was embarking on a "healing process" between the American people, veterans and the Vietnamese.[5] "Curiously," Karaagac wrote, with some understatement, "McCain has not worked the lessons of Vietnam, what he concluded from his year of reading and reflection, into his foreign-policy discourse."

From observing events on Capitol Hill, McCain did take away one critical lesson of governance—that Congress should honor the president's foreign-policy promises instead of micromanaging wars. And he did feel some resentment toward the new generation of antiwar Democrats and "elites who mistook fashion for wisdom," though not enough to avoid becoming close personal friends with many of them, especially George McGovern's former campaign manager Gary Hart. He thought his new liberal pals were naive but well-intentioned and smart, and he was sensitive to the fact that he might be the only military man—let alone a highly decorated veteran and POW—that many of them knew well. Approval from McCain was a way of absolving the excesses of their radical youth; and their embrace of him showed the military ideal that, as he told Robert Timberg, "the freedom they were exercising was what I was fighting for."

Tales of McCain's absolution became legend. He refused to bash draft-dodgers, telling Timberg: "They have to judge whether they conducted their lives in the best fashion, not me." The same applied to Jane Fonda, who aside from taking that famous picture in Hanoi with the gun, recorded propaganda for the North Vietnamese directed at Americans, and declared that the captive POWs she met with were "all in good health" and would "go home better citizens than when they left." (Explained McCain to Wolf Blitzer: "She said she was sorry. . . . I'm a great believer in redemption. All the things I've done wrong in my life and all the times I've failed, I'm a great believer in redemption."[6]) Perhaps the most moving tale of rapprochement was between McCain and another anti-war visitor to Hanoi who, at age 22, showed up on the cover of *Life* magazine with Jane Fonda.

David Ifshin, as president of the National Student Association, had led a group of antiwar activists to North Vietnam, where he recorded anti-American propaganda that was likely broadcast into McCain's prison camp. He went to Israel to work on a kibbutz, then came back home, became a lawyer, worked on the presidential campaigns of Walter Mondale and Bill Clinton, and served as general counsel to the American Israel Public Affairs Committee. Despite his mainstream success, he was haunted by his past and irregularly hounded by veterans groups when he got too close to the levers of power. "I had always wanted to apologize," Ifshin told journalist Michael Lewis in 1996, "but did not know who to apologize to." By chance, he found John McCain, who said to him, "Look, I accept your apology. We'll be friends. But more importantly I want you to forget it. Go on with your life. You cannot look back."[7] The two former adversaries became friends. McCain defended Ifshin on the Senate floor against his persistent critics, encouraged him to join the Clinton administration, and together they helped cofound the Institute for Democracy in Vietnam. When Ifshin died prematurely of cancer in 1996 at age 47, McCain spoke at his funeral. "David Ifshin was my friend. His friendship honored me and honors me still," he said.[8]

President Clinton was so moved by McCain's eulogy that he asked him for a copy of it. "It is what he said about David—and how he said it—that I'll always remember," Clinton told the *National Journal*.[9] Clinton had good cause to praise a man who in other circumstances had called him a "liar." From the beginning of Clinton's first term, McCain had given the draft-dodging president all the political cover he wanted on issues pertaining to Vietnam. Before Clinton's first Memorial Day as president, when veterans were threatening to harass him if he showed up at the Vietnam Memorial in Washington, D.C., McCain urged him to go and carry out his presidential duty, and offered to tag along if he wanted. As the United States thawed its diplomatic relationship with Vietnam in the 1990s—from lifting the trade embargo to fully normalizing relations with the former enemy—McCain bent the president's ear at each benchmark, assuring him that the majority of veterans would support him. During a meeting with Clinton at the White House over re-establishing diplomatic relations, McCain said he "decided to address only one issue, whether his own past and all the old arguments about the war really were an obstacle to moving forward. . . . I told him that it didn't matter to me anymore who had been for the war and who had been against it. 'I don't give a shit about that anymore. I'm tired of looking back in anger. I'm tired of America looking back in anger. It's time to put the past behind us, Mr. President, and do what's right for both countries.'"[10]

What has motivated McCain to be such a relentless force for putting Vietnam in the past? As often as he uses the "don't look back in anger" formulation, it's hard not to jump to the easy psychological conclusion that he's just trying to find his own personal cloture and using his influence on the federal government to do likewise for his fellow vets. After all, when he quotes George Washington's famous line "The nation which indulges toward another an habitual hatred or an habitual fondness is in some degree a slave," it begs the question of who really bears "hatred" toward Vietnam in the twenty-first century. It could even be argued—if you believe that Vietnam was the source of McCain's occasionally flaring temper—that he's trying to finally put to rest the very source of his nagging demons.

But any explanation resting on McCain's instability or psychological weakness has to overcome the inconvenient fact that by all accounts and extensive public record, he's a happy, wisecracking, hyper-productive and energetic public servant and father of seven, one who is convincing when he says, as he does in the final sentence of *Faith of My Fathers*, "I held on to the memory, left the bad behind, and moved on."

No, there's something else going on here, and as usual with McCain it's hiding in plain sight. The single-worst thing about the Vietnam War, he has said repeatedly, is the list of 58,000 dead American soldiers, commemorated at the Vietnam Wall he visits so often and praises for its power of "reconciliation." But runner-up is what Vietnam did to the country he loves. "A lost war is a terrible calamity and, in this instance, all the more so for its last casualty, America's faith in herself," he wrote in *Worth the Fighting For*. Restoring that faith—the same faith that helped sustain him in Vietnam—became the object of his post-Vietnam reconciliation project, made all the more urgent by what he felt was the dangerously pessimistic drift of the 1970s Democratic Party. "It had become an antiwar party, and opposition to the Vietnam War was growing inexorably into a general suspicion of the military, of an assertive foreign policy, even of that sense of American exceptionalism that had been the transcendent faith of American leaders since our founding."

But Democrats were hardly the only people who'd grown gun-shy about the use of force as a result of America's only twentieth-century defeat. McCain himself was largely considered a Vietnam Syndrome politician until the late 1990s, when he rediscovered his inner exceptionalist with the Kosovo War and his new doctrine of "rogue state rollback." Before that he'd been cautious about deploying U.S. troops abroad, whether in Central America, Lebanon, or Somalia, and warned his Capitol Hill colleagues about murky missions, unintended quagmires, and the folly of taking sides in a civil war. His sigh of relief was almost visible after the prosecution of first Gulf War, which he had been very anxious and unsure about beforehand. At the 1992 Republican National Convention in Houston, McCain framed the war almost as an extension of Operation Homecoming: "Our victory in the Gulf also provided the president and the American people an opportunity to say to the veterans of another war, for whom there were no parades, 'welcome home, job well done.' Those of us who fought in Vietnam will be forever grateful."

But as much as the Gulf War had served to boost confidence in the American pysche, the road toward final Vietnam reconciliation still faced one giant roadblock: normalized relations with still-communist Vietnam. And before that was even conceivable, McCain and his new ally John Kerry (yet another former antiwar activist turned close personal friend) had to settle once and for all one of the most contentious and long-simmering disputes in the United States: whether there were still American POWs being held in Southeast Asia.

Sorting out the competing claims of the POW saga, separating wishful activist hyperbole from arrogant government malfeasance, is a task beyond our purview here. The recently published *An Enormous Crime* includes a notes section alone that is probably longer than this entire book. However, a few contextual comments can be stated confidently:

- John McCain and John Kerry, two of the most decorated Vietnam Vets in the Senate, were dead set on normalizing relations with Vietnam as part of the reconciliation process. (President George H. W. Bush, late in his term, praised them for "writing the last chapter of the Vietnam War.")
- McCain, as has been previously noted, is famously impatient and does not suffer criticism of his honor gladly, especially when it has some validity.
- McCain is also drawn to quixotic causes and unlikely partnerships with onetime enemies, especially concerning Vietnam.
- The people who believe there are still POWs in Vietnam and Laos *hate* John McCain.
- The feeling is often mutual.

The thaw between Hanoi and Washington began in earnest in the late 1980s, when Vietnam pulled its forces out of Cambodia, sent the remains of more than 100 U.S. soldiers home, and allowed joint U.S.-Vietnamese field investigations at crash sites. While these confidence-building steps down the road map toward normalization were taking place (with the active participation of McCain), something unexpected happened back in Washington.

Army Col. Millard Peck, director of the Defense Intelligence Agency's Office for POW/MIA Affairs, noisily resigned after a brief tenure of heavily pursuing POW leads, charging in his resignation letter that a "mindset to 'debunk' is alive and well. It is held at all levels, and continues to pervade the POW/MIA Office. . . . Practically all analysis is directed to finding fault with the source." Outraged New Hampshire Senator Bob Smith, a Republican POW advocate, called for a Senate Select Committee on POW/MIAs. Kerry was selected as co-chair, and McCain reluctantly signed up as well.

For years, the most audacious activists had claimed that there were hundreds of soldiers left behind in Vietnamese-controlled territory after Operation Homecoming, used as chits for reparations that never came, and then abandoned by a U.S. government that thwarted any attempt to investigate their whereabouts. Others just thought one of their family members might be one of the American-looking men occasionally spotted by human intelligence or photographs.

Despite being an important member of a 12-senator committee statutorily tasked with investigating all leads on POWs in good faith, McCain never really believed there were many or even any Americans left behind. As he explained with some defensiveness in *Worth the Fighting For*, "During our captivity, we had worked hard and taken considerable risks to make sure we had pretty thorough knowledge of every American who was a prisoner in North Vietnam." (The presumption of the left-behind argument is that there were prisons McCain & Co. weren't aware of, especially in Laos.) Nor could McCain figure out what was in it for the Vietnamese. "I pledged to keep an open mind and share the government's official 'assumption of survival,'" he wrote. "But in truth, I though it very unlikely that the Vietnamese had kept any American prisoner after the war. And if I was wrong . . . I found it hard to imagine how the victims could have survived in captivity for eighteen more years."

Such words didn't soothe the nerves of POW/MIA families, who even McCain acknowledges have been treated shabbily by a secrecy-obsessed government. Insincere pledges of open mindedness from officials with a mindset to debunk were what they'd been up against for 15 years. McCain also didn't exactly breed confidence with his open hostility toward the "small cottage industry made up of swindlers, dime-store Rambos, and just plain old conspiracy nuts who preyed on the emotions of the families and on the attention of officials who were dedicated to the search."

The results were predictable, if a bit unsettling. The Arizona senator spent much of the Select Committee hearings badgering witnesses, flipping off citizens in the gallery and making surviving family members cry. "McCain stood out because he always showed up for the committee hearings where witnesses were going to talk about specific pieces of evidence," wrote *Killing Fields* author Sydney Schanberg, who covered the hearings. "He would belittle and berate these witnesses, questioning their patriotism and otherwise scoffing at their credibility." When witness Dolores Apodaca Alfond, chairwoman of the National Alliance of Families and sister of MIA Air Force Capt. Victor Apodaca, criticized McCain and Kerry for dismissing some overhead satellite imagery indicating possible distress signals, McCain "suddenly rushed into the room to confront her. His face angry and his voice very loud, he accused her of making 'allegations . . . that are patently and totally false and deceptive.' Making a fist, he shook his index finger at her and said she had insulted an emissary to Vietnam sent by President Bush. He said she had insulted other MIA families with her remarks. And then he said, through clenched teeth: 'And I am sick and tired of you insulting mine and other people's [patriotism] who happen to have different views than yours.'" Alfond wept openly.

In the end, the unanimous 1,223-page committee report released in January 1993 concluded there was "no compelling evidence" that any Americans were still alive and that the government didn't cover up any such information. McCain was elated; he immediately moved on to the business of lifting the trade embargo and marching toward normalized relations. He had some regrets about the heated exchanges, but justified them as a legitimate defense of the government's honor against the groundless charges of petitioning citizens.

"Many of the families came to resent me as well, which I regret, but I didn't let their disapproval prevent me from speaking what I believed was the truth about the missing and the efforts of government officials to account for them," he wrote later. "I would become quite angry at times over the unfair charges hurled at hardworking officials who, although they made mistakes from time to time, had done their best to find the answers we all sought."

With relations to Hanoi finally reestablished, and the trifecta of victories in the Cold War, Gulf War, and Yugoslavia (even if McCain thought the latter to be messy and poorly executed), America in the late 1990s was finally on the verge of ridding itself once and for all of the crippling insecurities of Vietnam Syndrome. The act of writing his first book and imposing meaning on his war experiences had already led McCain to embrace the greater cause of government reform; now was the time to formulate a bold, confident post-Vietnam foreign policy to match. With a feckless, casualties-shy president in the White House, one who lacked consistent geopolitical convictions, the moment seemed ripe for a new McCainite internationalism, especially since his main GOP rival, George W. Bush, was campaigning on a "humble" foreign policy that eschewed nation-building.

"Surely, for a time, our loss in Vietnam afflicted America with a kind of identity crisis," McCain wrote in *Faith of My Fathers*. "For a while we made our way in the world less sure of ourselves than we had been before Vietnam. . . . We should never have let this one mistake, terrible though it was, color our perceptions forever of our country's purpose. We were a good country before Vietnam, and we are a good country after Vietnam. In all of history, you cannot find a better one."

THEODORE REDUX

I found as much virtue in his ceaseless activity as I have in his purposes. His was the most important presidency since Lincoln's. He invented the modern presidency by liberally interpreting the constitutional authority of the office to redress the imbalance of power between the executive and legislative branches that had tilted decisively toward Congress in the half century since the Civil War. He was an extraordinarily accomplished president.

—John McCain, *Worth the Fighting For*[1]

Theodore Roosevelt believed that if only politicians had enough power, they could solve the world's problems.

—Jim Powell, *Bully Boy: The Truth About Theodore Roosevelt's Legacy*[2]

On September 15, 1997, the *Wall Street Journal* ran an op-ed co-authored by *Weekly Standard* Editor William Kristol and his star writer David Brooks lamenting that "something is missing at conservatism's core."[3] The *Weekly Standard*, a political magazine launched in 1995 with Rupert Murdoch's money, is the highbrow home for neoconservatism, a minority strain within the Republican big tent. The neocon movement, launched in

the 1950s by Kristol's father Irving and former Trotskyite
Norman Podhoretz, was a place where New York liberals
who'd been mugged by the Cold War could experiment with
their mixture of literary criticism, social tolerance, and anti-
communist hawkishness in magazines such as *Commentary*,
The Public Interest, and the CIA-funded *Encounter*. Its stal-
warts shuttled back and forth between Manhattan and Washington, government and publishing, churning out manifestos
and launching grandiose think tanks whose missions were to
keep the world safe for democracy. They had influence far
greater than their numbers, but by the 1990s they were getting gray around the temples, bypassed by GOP Young Turks
more interested in Rush Limbaugh than Lionel Trilling.
William Kristol aimed to update this philosophy for a new
generation—literally (one of his cofounders was Podhoretz's
son John). After a brief initial embrace of Newt Gingrich, the
Weekly Standard soon found its niche championing a more
activist form of Republicanism, particularly in the application
of foreign policy.

At the time of the Kristol/Brooks op-ed, Republicans had
controlled both houses of Congress for more than two years,
yet found themselves in a dispiriting game of triangulatory
cat-and-mouse with the politically more gifted President
Clinton. The GOP had squandered its revolutionary momentum of 1994 and seemed philosophically adrift. That's where
the *Weekly Standard* team aimed to help. "The era of big government may be over," the column started, with dubious
accuracy, "but a new era of conservative governance hasn't yet
begun." For that the duo blamed the libertarian wing of the
Republican coalition, warning that the tendencies found there
posed a danger to the republic. "Wishing to be left alone isn't
a governing doctrine. And an American political movement's

highest goal can't be protecting citizens from their own govern-ment. Indeed, in recent years some conservatives' sensible con-tempt for the nanny state has at times spilled over into a foolish, and politically suicidal, contempt for the American state."

What Kristol/Brooks proposed instead was something they called "national-greatness conservatism," an intention-ally vague but nonetheless inspirational stew of free trade, "moral assertiveness abroad," reduction of the welfare state, semi-open borders, rejection of multiculturalism, increased spending on national parks and monuments, and above all, a confident, unabashed patriotism directed from the White House. It would be a program, they vowed, in the tradition of the twentieth century's most energetic president, Theodore Roosevelt. "National-greatness conservatism does not despise government," they wrote. "How could it? How can Americans love their nation if they hate its government?"

The new manifesto was greeted by the chattering classes with a chorus of groans. Libertarian Virginia Postrel and free-market conservative James Glassman, responding in the *Wall Street Journal*, called it "a kind of wistful nationalism in search of a big project," and cheekily suggested some possi-bilities: "It could go looking for the next war, hope for another Great Depression, or sponsor a trip to Neptune."[4] Prince of Darkness columnist Robert Novak dismissed it out of hand as "big government conservatism."[5] Conservatives Laura Ingraham and Stephen Vaughn asked, "Do we really need a federal initiative to tell us what national greatness is?"[6] The *Washington Post*'s E. J. Dionne pointed out that "there is absolutely no mass base" for the idea.[7] Tellingly, the few pos-itive reviews came from liberals: *Slate*'s Jacob Weisberg hailed the piece as a bit of "glasnost" from the GOP politburo,[8] and columnist Garry Wills pronounced it "one of the more promising and unexpected developments in the Republican Party."[9] But on the whole, as *Commentary* magazine's Adam Wolfson would point out a few years later, "Most Republicans simply yawned."[10]

Not John McCain. In the spring of 1998, McCain was a great national story, a man who'd long been on everyone's shortlist of presidential candidates, but lacking anything like a recognizable political ideology. He still considered himself a Reaganite, with default sympathies for capitalism and social conservatism, but the campaign-finance crusade and his tenure on the Senate Commerce Committee was turning him into a more enthusiastic regulator. His life's work of healing Vietnam was largely finished with the opening of the U.S. embassy in Hanoi (headed up by McCain friend and former POW Pete Peterson); he was in the process of writing a book-length interpretation of his life, and his staff was looking for a catchy mission statement for the long-planned run at the White House.

It was at this time that Marshall Wittmann, one of Bill Kristol's best friends, handed McCain a stack of David Brooks essays on national-greatness conservatism, supplementing it with a little light reading on McCain's old hero Teddy Roosevelt. From that day forward, until well into 2001, it became difficult to determine where the *Weekly Standard*'s imagination ended and McCain's stump speech began. As *The New Republic*'s John Judis later reported, the candidate began staffing up with people from Kristol's orbit: "When McCain wanted to hire a new legislative aide, his chief of staff, Mark Salter—himself a former aide to neoconservative Jeane Kirkpatrick—consulted with Kristol, who recommended a young protégé named Daniel McKivergan. . . . Randy Scheunemann, who had drafted the Iraq Liberation Act and was on the board of

Kristol's Project for a New American Century, became McCain's foreign policy adviser."[11]

McCain and Kristol talked frequently on the phone, Wittmann and Scheunemann helped write McCain's defining "rogue-state rollback speech," the *Weekly Standard* sent Tucker Carlson to cover the Straight Talk Express, and both Kristol and Brooks provided regular (and presumably impartial) primary-campaign analysis to PBS, National Public Radio, the *Washington Post*, *Los Angeles Times*, and other outlets. Kristol, Wittmann, and campaign manager John Weaver told *The New Republic*, were "the home breeding ground for the legislative and strategic concepts that ultimately emanate from McCain."[12]

The foundational document for the *Standard*-McCain fusion project was an April 1999 cover story by David Brooks entitled "Politics and Patriotism: From Teddy Roosevelt to John McCain." Reading it now is like opening a time capsule from the late Clinton era, when Washington was good mostly for pointless partisan bickering, and Americans seemed more interested in riding the dot-com wave to a twenty-first century of innovation and the pursuit of happiness. "Affluence," Brooks warned chastely in the piece, "carries its corruptions. When a people turn toward the easy comforts of private life, they inadvertently lose connection with higher, more demanding principles and virtues." The "antidote" to these alleged "temptations of affluence" was a new if vaguely defined "patriotism," which aimed to "act as a counter-vailing force to excessive individualism, reminding people of their common bonds and reengaging Americans in national life."

McCain, too, sounded the warning against cultural Balkanization. "The spirit of America is dissipating," he told Brooks. "People are not proud any more of their institutions. They are not eager for public service, or willing to work for a cause greater than themselves." In case it wasn't clear enough, Brooks hammered home the point that individuals would have to bend in the same direction under the guidance of a virtuous state: "Citizenship implies a set of habits and obligations that counteracts the decentralizing tendencies of American life, the impulses to autonomy and self-expression."

Brooks, who has a gift for thinking out loud about politics and society, lets slip throughout the essay the sense that McCain's agenda was a piece of clay in the *Weekly Standard*'s capable, intellectual hands. "Right now his sentiments are vague," wrote the same man who, when introducing national-greatness conservatism, argued that laying out "some sort of 10-point program" would be "silly" because "particular policies are less important than getting Americans to begin to think differently about politics." You could almost see Brooks rubbing his hands together at the prospect of marrying his opaque national greatness with McCain's lofty greater cause: "In fact," he wrote, "if you look at his policies, you can begin to imagine a national narrative and a public philosophy that might be erected around them." They had the man; all they needed was the theory.

Aggressive foreign policy was a key component to the McCain/*Standard* greatness formula, and Teddy Roosevelt was nothing if not aggressively interventionist in his foreign policy. But Brooks' main point in harkening back to T. R. was that the Bull Moose dared to challenge and unify Americans with his "pioneer spirit," creating a "national narrative" and a "public philosophy of what might be called muscular progressivism." Specific details were always less important than the sheer inspirational enterprise of it all.

McCain's arms needed no twisting to read more about Teddy Roosevelt. He had been reared in the military traditions that Roosevelt, more than any other American president helped create. McCain's grandfather Slew served in Roosevelt's Navy; sailed on Roosevelt's globe-trotting Great White Fleet; participated in Roosevelt's Philippine Insurrection; and passed down to his son Jack an appreciation of T. R.'s favorite military theorist, Alfred Thayer Mahan, which Jack in turn passed down to John. McCain says reading Roosevelt biographies has shaped his own sense of patriotism "more than any other influence except the navy." Though he made a self-conscious show in *Character Is Destiny*, of repeating that "There was only one TR, and there will never be another,"[13] McCain has made it clear that the one historical figure he would most like to emulate, if lucky enough to serve as president, is the rough-riding, trust-busting T-Rex of yore.

On the surface McCain and his political idol share quite a bit in common. There is a palpable sense of projection in the senator's writings on the man. T. R. was the child of a well-to-do family with a good name, an "eastern swell" who eventually moved out west to "become a man of the people." He "could be impetuous, intemperate, egotistical, and entirely too self-confident for such a young man." Sound familiar? He had six kids (McCain has seven), married twice, and was noted in his time for nurturing a close relationship with the media. He was short and bull-necked, and wrote best-selling books. He boxed, took punishing hikes in the interior West, and had a "romantic temperament." If only he had lived long enough, he would certainly have loved *For Whom the Bell Tolls*.

But what, besides some personal affinities, does McCain see in Roosevelt? How does that model translate into his ideas of governance and his designs on the White House? McCain has written and spoken of T. R. more extensively, and with more rhetorical enthusiasm, than he has about any other historical figure not in his immediate family. The ideas he conveys in the process are among the most explicit and disturbing that come out of his mouth; the Roosevelt chapters in *Worth the Fighting For* and *Character Is Destiny* contain the most salient points of his ideas and are worth scrutiny. Contained in these pages are four main Rooseveltian traits and principles that the modern-day maverick most admires, each with its own troubling implications for a McCain presidency. These are: personal vigor and courage, preference for national unity over multiculturalism and individualism, preference for the common good over materialism, and embrace of superpower interventionism. Taken in order:

McCain, like Roosevelt, is famous for his boundless, restless, productive energy. "His entire life," McCain wrote, "before and after the Battle of San Juan Heights, was as crowded with breathtaking activity and stunning accomplishments as any life it has ever been my pleasure to admire." Before turning 30, an age at which McCain had managed to learn how to fly and not get kicked out of the Navy, Roosevelt had already graduated from Harvard and attended law school at Columbia, written the first three of what would be nearly two dozen books (including the widely respected history *The Naval War of 1812*), married and buried a first wife and then married a second, served three terms on the New York State Assembly, and ran unsuccessfully for mayor of New York City. Along the way he traveled extensively through the west, lived as an outdoorsman, and found time to build a reputation as a reformer in New York machine politics. Not long after, he transformed the Navy as its assistant secretary, resigned so he could go fight in Cuba with a regiment of irregulars, ran and won for New York governor, ran again for vice president on William McKinley's ticket, and then became the youngest commander in chief in history when McKinley was assassinated. He boxed and fenced in the White House, swam in the Potomoc, and promoted the virtues of the "strenuous life." What's not to like?

For starters, one has to be driven to the point of mania to crowd an otherwise busy life with that much testosterone-fueled skirmishing. Roosevelt had been sickly as a child, stricken by asthma, and his manly exploits were certainly a way of overcompensating and proving his vigor to a skeptical audience. As McCain writes, "I have never entirely lost my adolescent admiration for that kind of pugnacious vitality, and Roosevelt's extraordinary zest for combat, both the physical and rhetorical varieties, remains the source of much of his appeal to me." Extraordinary zest for combat is, indeed, an adolescent virtue; it's also inappropriate and potentially dangerous in the hands of the most powerful man in the country. "Roosevelt believed fighting was essential to a happy life. I know what he meant," McCain wrote. Most voters, however, don't need to fight to be happy and might be skeptical about a president who does.

Roosevelt's self-created mythology and sizeable ego eventually degenerated into a predictable megalomania in which he almost dared voters to have the courage to vote for him. "It would be a mistake to nominate me unless the country has in its mood something of the heroic," he famously said before the 1916 election. "Unless it feels not only devotion to ideals but the purpose measurably to realize those ideals in action." Unfortunately for T. R., the nation was just not brave enough.

McCain also acknowledges little in the way of Roosevelt's ulterior motives or the unintended consequences of his ostentatious displays of courage. He delights in retelling T. R.'s career-making charge up Cuba's San Juan Hill in the bloodiest battle of the Spanish-American War, but he doesn't mention that Roosevelt was so hungry for military glory that he begged Sen. Henry Cabot Lodge prior to the fight, "Do not make peace until we get Puerto Rico."[14] When he was assistant secretary of the Navy, prior to the Spanish-American War, Roosevelt had blatantly disobeyed orders by commanding Commodore George Dewey to steam on to the Philippines and prepare for "offensive operations," a rebellious act McCain describes merely as "an extraordinary arrogation of authority." Such excesses are excusable, he writes, as long as they are channeled toward "the well-being and elevation" of the United States. Trust in the man, and there's no reason to distrust his considerable excesses of power.

Teddy Roosevelt was a racist whose energies and expansionist policies were motivated, in part, by completing the victory of the white Anglos over the New World's "savages." This is no less true for being unpleasant to read. In his *The Winning of the West* anthology, T. R. gets right down to the heart of the matter: "During the past three centuries the spread of the English-speaking peoples over the world's waste spaces has been not only the most striking feature in the world's history, but also the event of all others most far-reaching in its effects and its importance," he begins. "There have been many other races that at one time or another had their great periods of race expansion—as distinguished from mere conquest,—but there has never been another whose expansion has been either so broad or so rapid."[15]

This fact was uncomfortable enough that David Brooks had to spend several paragraphs grappling with its implications for his McCain/T. R. national-greatness fusionism. After quoting a particularly egregious chunk of Roosevelt's exterminationist rhetoric—"The most ultimately righteous of all wars is a war with savages, though it is apt to be also the most terrible and inhuman. . . . It is of incalculable importance that America, Australia, and Siberia should pass out of the hands of their red, black, and yellow aboriginal owners, and become the heritage of the dominant world races"—Brooks declared that "the public philosophy based on the pioneer experience is obsolete." Then he called for a new one to replace it rather than explore the possible correlation between federally driven "greatness" and the darker angels of our nature.

McCain doesn't even go that far. While grudgingly admitting that "there is no denying" T. R.'s racialist foundation for American greatness, the senator flat-out denies any Rooseveltian "race hatred," and suggests hopefully that at least the Bull Moose didn't "consider racial inferiority to be a permanent biological condition." In fact, his views were "moderately progressive in his day" and stressed the civilizing virtues of the Melting Pot, McCain maintains. Then, instead of stepping gingerly away from Roosevelt's race-fueled nationalism, McCain instead offers a full-throated defense. "TR denounced what he called 'hyphenated Americanism,' immigrants who gave greater importance to political and cultural affinities with the nation of their origin than to the values, responsibilities, and customs of their American citizenship," he wrote. "His insistence that every citizen owed primary allegiance to American ideals, and to the symbols, habits, and consciousness of American citizenship, is as right then as it is now."

McCain is not a racist; far from it. He has always exuded a natural personal tolerance. He adopted a Bangladeshi girl, fights hard for Native American affairs, praises the Civil Rights movement and believes comprehensive immigration reform is so important partly because he fears the nativism in his own political party (yet another reason why the GOP base doesn't trust him). But it's striking that the racial underpinnings of a previous president's call for a nearly militaristic sense of citizenship has not dulled his appetite for more of the same. Now that we're no longer racist, the implication seems to be, what's wrong with the federal government expecting a little loyalty from its citizens?

"In the Roosevelt code," McCain writes approvingly, "the authentic meaning of freedom gave equal respect to self-interest and common purpose, to rights and duties. And it absolutely required that every loyal citizen take risks for the country's sake." McCain has long been the leading proponent for drastically expanding national service, warning frequently about the "growing gap" between military and civilian life. As he wrote in the liberal *Washington Monthly* just after the September 11 massacre, "Americans did not fight and win World War II as discrete individuals. Their brave and determined energies were mobilized and empowered by a national government headed by democratically elected leaders. That is how a free society remains free and achieves greatness."[16]

Roosevelt was just as famous for his trust-busting as he was for his Big Stick of gunboat diplomacy. McCain, who was gorging on T. R. while fighting Big Tobacco and trying to drive corporate money out of politics, has gravitated toward a more activist approach toward regulation. He continues to warn of the emptiness of materialism for its own sake, a non-Reaganite suspicion of capitalism that colors all his writings on Roosevelt:

"He distrusted leading financiers of his day who put profit before patriotism. . . . He respected the role business conglomerates played in America's emergence as a great economic power, but he also understood that unrestrained laissez-faire capitalism would crush competition from smaller businesses. . . . He fought the spirit of 'unrestricted individualism' that claimed the right 'to injure the future of all of us for his own temporary and immediate profit.' . . . He sought not to destroy the great wealth-creating institutions of capitalism, but to save them from their own excesses."

All of these tendencies share a single element in common—distrust of the individual to make choices sufficiently beneficial to the common good. "Freedom," McCain writes, not only "empowered individuals to decide their destiny for themselves, [but] empowered them to choose a common destiny. And for Roosevelt, that common destiny surpassed material gain and self-interest. Our freedom and our industry must aspire to more than acquisition and luxury."

Not to put too fine a point on it, but this is the definition of authoritarianism. National politicians (let alone presidents) deciding whether private transactions are sufficiently oriented toward a "common destiny" is the kind of thing found in collectivist or totalitarian countries, not the nation that made "the pursuit of happiness" a foundational aspiration. To throw around a word like "must" after "our freedom" is to claim unique authority, backed by the power of the federal government, to judge how best a private individual can conduct his or her own legal affairs. Ask not what you can do for your country, but whether what you're doing is enough to keep the president off your back. As H. L. Mencken once said of Roosevelt, "He didn't believe in democracy; he believed simply in government."

Once a politician crosses that threshold, there's no private activity off-limits to government scrutiny. And you can bet that the common destiny will be mobilized for a reason. "Base materialism, Roosevelt believed," wrote McCain, "tempted people to indolence and greed and tempted nations to 'shrink like cowards' from the duty of playing 'a great part in the world' and seek shelter in 'the cloistered life which saps the hardy virtues of a nation, as it saps them in the individual.'" Put in plainer English, how can you fight a proper war if all the people aren't pulling in the same direction?

There is literally no Roosevelt military action that McCain finds deserving of retrospective criticism. Building a great fleet to "make possible the expansion of American power in our hemisphere and beyond"? Check. Driving Spain out of the Caribbean and the Philippines, regardless of any legitimate *causus belli*? Check. Asserting "the right to intervene militarily in Latin American countries where disorder might attract the unwelcome attention of other great powers"? Check. Fomenting insurrection in Panama to dig and control a canal? Check. Can't make an omelet without breaking some eggs.

McCain's reflection on these momentous Roosevelt acts is largely limited to two sentences in *Worth the Fighting For*: "But his purpose was not to seek war and conquest for personal or even national glory. He sought to preserve peace and order by confronting potential adversaries with America's resolve and readiness to fight if necessary to protect its interests." Well that settles it, then.

Teddy Roosevelt was the architect of America's empire, a not-insubstantial legacy that the world, and especially Latin America, lives with to this day. McCain sees this as a great accomplishment, a flowering of "our messianic belief in ourselves as the New Jerusalem," otherwise not requiring further review. Just as Roosevelt's racism does not invalidate his strident nationalism, neither do the Monroe Doctrine's excesses—military governance of Haiti, the CIA overthrow of Guatemala's government, the invasion of the Dominican Republic—give McCain cause to reexamine the assumption of U.S. military supremacy in the Caribbean and beyond. In fact, these events don't merit mention at all, save for the invasion of the Dominican Republic, and only then because it was McCain's father who did the invading. ("Critics judged it, with good reason, to be an unlawful intervention in the affairs of a sovereign nation," McCain wrote in *Faith of My Fathers*, before relating this rough-and-ready quote from Jack McCain: "People may not love you for being strong when you have to be, but they respect you for it and learn to behave themselves when you are.")[17]

Teddy Roosevelt wouldn't have been able to pursue such a robust foreign policy without concentrating power in the executive branch to a degree not seen since Abraham Lincoln, and matched thereafter only by Woodrow Wilson, Franklin Roosevelt, Richard Nixon, and George W. Bush. Theodore Roosevelt was the first president to govern extensively through executive orders. Perhaps only Dick Cheney—"as capable and sensible a public servant as I've known," McCain has said—has done more to expand the legal boundaries of the executive office than Teddy Roosevelt. Which wins nothing but praise from John McCain: "He invented the modern presidency by liberally interpreting the constitutional authority of the office to redress the imbalance of power between the executive and legislative branches."

The other thing T-Rex was famous for, of course, was his political independence—abandoning the inadequately interventionist Republican Party in 1912 to run for president on his new Bull Moose ticket. By the time McCain, Kristol, and Wittmann were digesting the lessons of Roosevelt, they found themselves in the midst of an insurgent campaign running against the Republican establishment, picking fights with camps the neocons had always distrusted, particularly the Religious Right. When McCain unloaded on Jerry Falwell and Pat Robertson in February 2000, calling them "agents of intolerance," Wittmann helped craft the speech, while Brooks and Kristol went into overdrive in the national media, arguing that the "McCain Insurrection" was changing the shape of the Republican Party for good. "Leaderless, rudderless and issueless, the conservative movement, which accomplished great things over the past quarter-century, is finished," Kristol declared, wrongly, in the *Washington Post*.[18] "The rebels believe the conservative movement has cracked up, the Republican establishment has ossified, and the Goldwater-Reagan ideological message needs to be overhauled," Brooks added in the *New York Times*.[19]

With every primary defeat, the McCain juggernaut made more incendiary comments against their fellow Republicans and more open hints about converting the energy of their campaign into a Bull Moose movement somewhere down the road. Other conservatives viewed these developments with a mixture of amusement and alarm. "An anarchic passion to smash is not a conservative impulse," the *National Review* archly editorialized.[20] "But the good news is," added *National Review* Editor Rich Lowry, "that America doesn't necessarily need a new Roosevelt now, doesn't need a vigorous executive or a national cause. Sometimes there are no great crises, no Cold War to win, no civil-rights revolution to effect. . . . McCain often says he wants to give our country back to us. What he doesn't understand is that it isn't his to give."[21] Fellow political journalists couldn't resist the chance to poke fun at what was, after all, a tiny philosophical grouping. "The McCain campaign has inadvertently revealed a shocking fact about neoconservatism," wrote *The New Republic*'s Franklin Foer. "It lives."[22]

After McCain dropped out of the primaries and Brooks' prediction that Bush would lose the general election failed to pan out, the only thing remaining of national greatness conservatism was a T. R.-style temptation to bolt from the Republican Party and create something new. Marshall Wittmann cofounded with Kristol a short-lived conservative reform think tank, launched a Bull Moose blog, and eventually left the GOP to work for hawkish Democratic Senator Joe Lieberman. McCain campaign manager John Weaver worked for Democrats for a while, after complaining that Karl Rove had queered his prospects of working for Republican Washington. With the Senate deadlocked 50-50, there was intense lobbying on McCain to leave the Republican caucus, but Vermont Senator Jim Jeffords took the plunge first. McCain instead busied himself with such GOP-infuriating issues as campaign finance reform and the Patients' Bill of Rights. Kristol, meanwhile, was still catching heat for his performance during the McCain insurgency and responding by calling the conservative movement "sick."

By May 2001, the smart money was on the McCain/ *Standard* project leaving the GOP for good, perhaps becoming what the Reform Party was for Ross Perot—a shell for an irascible personality who liked to run for president.

"Kristol and Brooks have come a long way in the past three years," Franklin Foer wrote in *The New Republic* at the time. "These days they champion campaign finance reform and environmental protection. They oppose the Bush administration's proposed repeal of the estate tax because, as Brooks puts it, 'We should be concerned with the widening income gap.' They attack corporate power with Naderesque ferocity. No one can accuse them of being mere libertarians in Bull Moose garb anymore. National-greatness conservatism, to the surprise of many, has come to mean something. It's a real ideology now. It's just not a conservative one."[23]

The *National Review*'s Jonah Goldberg was crueler: "National greatness as an idea is at a crossroads. It can resurface as a serious idea for conservatives to debate and refine through debate, which one day might be a 'movement' with more than four or five members. Or, it can be the slogan for a havoc-wreaking politician whose only allegiance is to a movement that has his name above the title. It cannot be both."[24]

And then four months later, the world changed forever. Neoconservatism was dusted off at the National Security Council, Kristol and the *Weekly Standard* became the in-flight magazine of Air Force I, and John McCain's theory of rogue-state rollback was finally ready to be put to the test. The era of speaking softly was over; it was time for the Big Stick.

10

BOMB BOMB BOMB, BOMB BOMB IRAN

The American people and Congress now appreciate that we are neither omniscient nor omnipotent, and they are not prepared to commit U.S. troops to combat unless there is a clear U.S. national security interest involved. . . . If we do become involved in combat, that involvement must be of relatively short duration and must be readily explained to the man in the street in one or two sentences.

—John McCain, *Los Angeles Times*, April 28, 1985[1]

The key is turning the military and law enforcement responsibilities over to the Iraqis, and I don't know when they are going to be capable. An exit strategy is when the Iraqis can take over those responsibilities. That's it. We've been in South Korea for 50 years. Is anybody asking for an exit strategy out of Korea?

—John McCain, interview in *Men's Journal*, June 2005

In June 2007, the nonprofit Taxpayers for Common Sense examined the Defense Authorization bill then making its way out of the Senate Armed Services Committee and found 309 earmarks worth $5.6 billion tacked on by senators creating pork as they tried to bring jobs back home to their states. John McCain, as usual, was responsible for none of them. Even better for his campaign, the second-porkiest senator was Democratic front-runner Hillary Clinton, with a whopping 26 projects. At a press conference criticizing his putative presidential opponent, the Senate's ranking pork-buster said, "We can't do this earmarking and pork-barreling if we're ever going to be careful and serious stewards of the taxpayers' dollars."

Pork is one issue that bedevils defense budgeting, but the proper stewardship of the taxpayers' dollars also depends on the overall size and strategic priorities of the defense bill itself. So I asked McCain a follow-up question: "We now spend about roughly the same amount on defense as the rest of the world combined. Is that a healthy ratio, and if it's not, what would be a healthy ratio?" I figured since he'd spent much oxygen in the past blasting Western Europe for a pacifism sewn by inadequate defense spending, he might take the opportunity to encourage U.S. allies to play a more active role. No dice.

"Oh, it's healthy," he responded. "We need a bigger Army, we need a bigger Marine corps. You look around the world—Iran, North Korea, Afghanistan—it's not going to be over for a long time."

John McCain envisions a more militaristic foreign policy than any U.S. president in a century. He wants to continue the surge in Iraq, wishes it could have been much bigger, and has refused to publicly contemplate any kind of future withdrawal aside from warning at every opportunity that the "consequences of failure" would be genocide in Iraq and Al Qaeda inside America. He imagines U.S. forces in Baghdad and beyond for at least another half-century, arguing that "we've had troops in South Korea for 60 years, and Americans are . . . very satisfied with that situation."[2] He famously sang "Bomb Iran" to the tune of the Beach Boys' "Barbara Ann" at a campaign event (and thereafter had his staff play "Barbara Ann" before his appearances); continues to call that country's nuclear program the "single greatest" threat to the United States besides the War on Terror, and has urged the president keep preemptive military strikes on the table.[3] He has advocated threatening North Korea with "extinction,"[4] agitated for military intervention in Darfur,[5] and rattled many a saber in the direction of Vladimir Putin's Russia, which he calls a "KGB oligarchy."[6] (In one of the funnier McCain videos making the rounds on YouTube, the candidate sends up George Bush's famous friendship with the Russian president by saying, "*I* looked into Putin's eyes; I saw three letters: K-G-B.") And what about China? "We have to keep a careful eye on how they behave themselves, particularly in the neighborhood. That's another argument for America maintaining a military presence in Asia."[7]

It hasn't always been this way.

In September 1983, as a freshman congressman and loyal foot soldier of the Reagan revolution, John McCain voted against a successful measure to extend the deployment of U.S. Marines in war-torn Lebanon. Though McCain didn't necessarily believe in the constitutionality of the War Powers Act, the law was the law, and he couldn't shake the nagging feeling that sending troops to sit in barracks in the middle of a Middle Eastern civil war was even more of a confused mission than what he and his comrades had been asked to fight in Vietnam. His speech on the House floor was a splash of post-Vietnam realism, one that would have eerie echoes to debates two decades later:

> The fundamental question is "What is the United States' interest in Lebanon?" It is said we are there to keep the peace. I ask, what peace? It is said we are there to aid the government. I ask, what government? It is said we are there to stabilize the region. I ask, how can the U.S. presence stabilize the region? . . .
>
> The longer we stay in Lebanon, the harder it will be for us to leave. We will be trapped by the case we make for having our troops there in the first place.
>
> What can we expect if we withdraw from Lebanon? The same as will happen if we stay. I acknowledge that the level of fighting will increase if we leave. I regretfully acknowledge that many innocent civilians will be hurt. But I firmly believe this will happen in any event.
>
> What about our allies and worldwide prestige? We should consult with our allies and withdraw with them in concert if possible, unilaterally if necessary. I also recognize that our prestige may suffer in the short term, but I am more concerned with our long-term national interests. . . .
>
> I do not foresee obtainable objectives in Lebanon. I believe the longer we stay, the more difficult it will be to leave, and I am prepared to accept the consequences of our withdrawal.

Less than one month later, 241 Marines were killed by suicide bombers in Lebanon, marking the deadliest attack on U.S. soldiers during the Reagan presidency. The House tried to cut off funding for the deployment, but the measure failed, with McCain voting against it.

The brash young congressman would cross swords with the Reagan administration yet again over Central America. In April 1985, to commemorate the 10th anniversary of the U.S. withdrawal from Vietnam, Secretary of State George Schulz launched a broadside against the Democratic-controlled Congress, which had just rejected a $14 million aid package to Nicaragua's rebel *contras*. "Do we want another Cuba in this hemisphere? How many times must we learn the same lesson?" Schulz seethed. "Broken promises. Communist dictatorship. Refugees. Widened Soviet influence, this time near our very borders: Here is your parallel between Vietnam and Central America."

Not so fast, said Vietnam vet McCain. "There are similarities and differences between Vietnam and Central America," he told the *Los Angeles Times*. "The biggest difference is that there were 500,000 American boys in Vietnam and there are only about 50 American advisers in Central America. We have to make sure we don't get into a situation where we have American boys in Central America. . . . One of the lessons of the Vietnam War is that we can't fight these wars for them. . . . We have to provide military, moral and economic support."[8]

McCain had staked clear ground—don't fight other people's civil wars, and think twice before taking sides between two potential belligerents. When President Reagan in 1987 moved to reflag 11 Kuwaiti oil tankers in the Persian Gulf and offer them U.S. Navy protection against a threatening Iran, McCain was livid. The move was "a dangerous overreaction in perhaps the most violent and unpredictable region in the world," he wrote in the *Arizona Republic*. "American citizens are again being asked to place themselves between warring Middle East factions, with no tangible allied support and no real plan on how to respond if the situation escalates."[9]

That didn't mean the congressman and future senator was opposed to meddling in other countries' affairs—to the contrary. He was an active supporter of Reagan's Monroe

Doctrine, just not if it involved U.S. troops fighting a civil war. He bucked the administration in supporting economic sanctions against apartheid South Africa. And after observing Panama's fraudulent elections in May 1989, he encouraged and supported President George H. W. Bush's eventual unseating of Manuel Noriega by force from the country where McCain was born. "Frankly, I think the situation had reached such an untenable point with the murder of an American military officer that clearly this action was appropriate," he told *USA Today* at the time.[10]

Still, he remained wary of spilling American blood overseas. When Saddam Hussein invaded Kuwait in the summer of 1990, McCain oscillated between hawkishness and reluctance, denouncing the Iraqi dictator and then the U.S. government for having cozied up too closely to Hussein during the Iran-Iraq war, but at the same time warning against a protracted land battle. "I think the biggest mistake we could make is getting into a ground war," he told Larry King.[11] "We should not be trading American boys for Iraqi boys," he told the *Boston Globe*.[12] He even went so far as telling *U.S. News & World Report* that "We have to weigh the risk of the continued existence of Saudi Arabia versus the risk of the U.S. becoming entangled."[13]

Nevertheless, he was a strong supporter of the troop buildup in Saudi Arabia, held extensive hearings on the Senate Armed Services Committee, tilted uncommon vitriol at Japan and West Germany for not chipping in with enough money ("The contemptible tokenism of the actions of the Japanese government to date merit nothing but the world's contempt and American hostility," was one of his milder quotes[14]), and when push came to shove, supported the war in a stirring speech on the Senate floor:

We determine at this moment whether we, in the first crisis of the post-Cold War era, whether we, along with the United Nations and every other civilized nation in the world, will act together to prevent international, naked aggression of the most heinous and disgraceful kind.

In this new world order it is clear to me that if we fail to act that there will be inevitably a succession of dictators, of Saddam Husseins, of which around this globe there are an abundance, either in reality or would-be. And those dictators will see a green light, a green light for aggression, a green light for annexation of its weaker neighbors, and indeed, over time a threat to the stability of this entire globe. And it is unfortunate that at this time in history that the United States has to bear the majority of this burden. And I believe that over time we can rightfully expect other nations to provide the kind of coordination and assistance that will be necessary in the next crisis. But let us not shirk from our duty and obligation.

So the United States would be a global cop this time, at the head of a large coalition, but hopefully the New World Order would involve allied countries taking more responsibility for the world's affairs. The ensuing six-week Gulf War, with its lightning-fast 100-hour ground campaign, exorcised the operational ghosts of Vietnam, proving to a battle-scarred country that the U.S. military was back with dazzling new weaponry, professional competence, and charismatic leadership in the guise of generals like Colin Powell and Norman Schwarzkopf. As McCain's brother Joe told *The New Republic*'s John Judis in 2006, the victory restored the ex-POW's confidence as well. "Once the chess pieces were back on the board, then he thought he would play chess."[15]

The other shot in McCain's arm was the victorious end of the Cold War, proving anew that the American principles and ideals he had suffered for and took sustenance from in prison in Vietnam still served as a powerful beacon to the rest of the world. He never gets tired of telling the story of a Czech student who during the Velvet Revolution began a speech in front of a million protesters by saying, "We hold these truths to be self-evident: that all men are created equal and endowed by their Creator with certain unalienable rights, that among these are life, liberty and the pursuit of happiness." As McCain reflected in a Boston College commencement speech in 2006, "For all the terrible problems that still afflict humanity, for all the mistakes America has made in the past, and the imperfections we must still confess, I cannot imagine another nation's history will ever so profoundly affect the progress of the human race. That is not a boast, but an expression of faith in the American creed, and in the men and women who understood what history expected of us."

In 1993 McCain became chairman of the International Republican Institute (IRI), a creation of the National Endowment for Democracy, aimed at supporting democrats and dissidents worldwide. While fellow Republican senators like Jesse Helms were threatening to secede from the United Nations and thundering against the expansion of NATO, McCain through his work in the IRI and elsewhere was meeting with heroic dissidents such as Russia's Natan Sharanksy, and especially Aung San Suu Kyi, the rightfully elected prime minister of Burma who has been under house arrest at the hands of a ruthless military junta for much of the last two decades. His ears were filling with the whispers of democracy activists looking for the "shining city on a hill" to weigh in on their side against the dictators keeping them down. "We were all intoxicated by the fall of the Soviet Union and the collapse of its empire," McCain told Judis.

But that doesn't mean he was ready to jump on Bill Clinton's foreign policy bandwagon just yet. McCain found the new president's approach to international relations "spasmodic, vacillating and reactive," a product of a "mystifying uncertainty about how to act in a world where we are the only superpower."[16] McCain was withering in his criticism of Clinton when he broached the question of gays serving in the military, making pointed reference to the former Arkansas governor's lack of martial experience, and charging that he had lost the "respect" of the soldiers at his command.[17] The president careened from one crisis to the next in his first term, with his experienced but hapless secretary of state, Warren Christopher, always stepping on or off a plane somewhere looking baffled; in the heat of the partisan moment, McCain began to lose his long-held faith in the primacy of the executive to carry out foreign policy.

He became a frequent and pointed critic of the Clinton administration's waffling and drift. Eleven days after two Black Hawk helicopters were shot down over Mogadishu, killing 18 and creating the gruesome spectacle of warlords dragging American soldiers through the streets, McCain, who had already been agitating for the troops to come home, did just what he'd criticized Democrats for doing two decades earlier—tried to cut off funding to precipitate a withdrawal. The U.S. troop presence, which began under President George H. W. Bush, was initially sent to alleviate an acute starvation crisis brought on by political chaos. But under Clinton the mission had crept to rooting out warlords and providing security. McCain was having none of it: "Mr. President, our mission in Somali is over," he said on the Senate floor. "It is time to come home. Our mission in Somali was to feed a million starving Somali who needed to be fed.

It was not an open-ended commitment. It was not a commission of nation building, not warlord hunting, or any of the other extraneous activities which we seem to have been engaged in. If the President of the United States cannot say, 'Here is what we are fighting for in Somalia, that more Americans may perish in service to the goals, and here is why it is worth that price,' then, Mr. President, we have no right—no right—to ask Americans to risk their lives in any further misadventures in Somalia."

The same went for Haiti, where Clinton won United Nations approval to drive out the country's rulers and restore exiled President Jean-Bertrand Aristide in September 1994. The next month John McCain not only called for withdrawal, but he got riled up about it, too. "First, the President should have sought congressional approval before employing United States Armed Forces to Haiti. Second, the resolution offers support for the withdrawal of United States Armed Forces as soon as possible. In my view that does not mean as soon as order is restored to Haiti. It does not mean as soon as democracy is flourishing in Haiti. It does not mean as soon as we have established a viable nation in Haiti. As soon as possible means as soon we can get out of Haiti without losing any American lives."

McCain also became one of the Senate's most stubborn opponents to U.S. military intervention against Serbs, who were then making target practice out of Bosnian Muslim residents of Sarajevo and committing ethnic-based atrocities on a scale not seen on European soil in nearly a half-century. "The aspect of the future of this nation that bothers me more than anything else," he said during the January 1993 confirmation hearings for Les Aspin as defense secretary, "is the prospect of sending American troops on the ground into

Bosnia. I have yet to meet a single military expert who tells me how we can get in, what we do when we get in, and how we can get out." It's not that he wasn't outraged by Serb President Solobodan Milosevic, or unsympathetic to the outgunned Bosnians; McCain just thought the military task looked daunting and should be handled by the Western Europeans for once.

In July 1995, three sets of foreign policies were forever altered at once—Bill Clinton's, the international community's toward Yugoslavia, and John McCain's. When Serbs drove out ineffective United Nations peacekeepers from the "safe" enclave of Srebrenica and slaughtered thousands of Muslims with impunity, the era of deferring to Europeans, even on European security matters, was effectively over. President Clinton, who had been urged to intervene for years by the morally persuasive heads of state in Central Europe (particularly Czech President Vaclav Havel), became convinced that the "lessons of Munich"—the haunting memory of the 1938 conference in which British Prime Minister Neville Chamberlain effectively allowed Adolf Hitler Czechoslovakia and Poland— demanded U.S. military leadership, not more appeasement. From that point onward his foreign policy team was dominated by Munichites such as Madeleine Albright, the Czech-born U.N. ambassador who later became secretary of state, and the Polish-born Chairman of the Joint Chiefs of Staff John Shalikashvili.

The muddling, ineffective-by-design approach to Yugoslavia by the West was now ditched. Croatia was given the silent go-ahead to drive occupying Serbian forces out of Croatian territory. The next time Serbs opened up serious mortar fire from the hills of Sarajevo, they were pounded by NATO warplanes. The three main sides to Yugoslavia's war of dissolution were bombed to the bargaining table at Dayton, Ohio, and they signed peace accords to end the war. As part of the agreement, Clinton pledged 20,000 U.S. troops to keep the peace. The worry, based on experience, was that he'd get rebuffed by a restive and increasingly isolationist Republican-run Congress. And that's where John McCain, under the guidance of Senate Majority Leader (and presidential candidate) Bob Dole, came in.

After years of opposing Clinton's approach to Yugoslavia and rejecting the notion of American troops in the Balkans, McCain rallied support for the president in a speech that showed the conflicting impulses of a man changing his own foreign policy views in real time. The stated justification for his seeming about-face was deference to the executive. "By supporting the deployment, I do not confer any approval of the decision to deploy," he said. "As I have already stated, I would not have committed American ground forces to this mission, had that decision been mine to make. But the decision has been made, by the only American elected to make such decisions." It was also crucial for U.S. and NATO credibility that a president be able to keep his word.

But the old worries about spilling American blood for undefined missions still gnawed at him: "This may be the hardest vote I have cast as a member of Congress. It may be the hardest vote I will ever cast. To send young men and women into such evident danger is an awful responsibility," he said. "If I have any private oath that I have tried to abide by in my public service it is that I would never ask Americans to serve in missions where success was not defined, the commitment to achieve it uncertain, and its object of less value than its price. I pray today that I have kept my oath."

But there were new worries, too, about the consequences of America not fulfilling its commitment and the resulting resumption of hostilities. "We will then watch Bosnians suffer again the mass murder and atrocities that have repulsed all people of decency and compassion."

After hemming and hawing further, McCain ended with a remarkable anti-isolationist flourish that hinted at what his international philosophy would be for the years to come:

> But I want to make one last point to those Americans . . . who oppose this deployment and this resolution because they resent the costs or America's leadership in the world. The burdens that are imposed on the United States are greater than the burdens borne by any other nation. There is no use bemoaning that fact or vainly trying to avoid its reality. This reality will be so for as long as we remain the greatest nation on earth. When we arrive at the moment when less is expected from our leadership by the rest of the world, then we will have arrived at the moment of our decline. We should accept that burden with courage. We cannot withdraw from the world into our prosperity and comfort and hope to keep those blessings. We cannot leave the world alone. For the world will not leave us alone. So I will support this mission, with grave concern and more than a little sadness.

McCain would later see the events of 1995 as the turning point in his foreign policy evolution, as indeed it was for many liberal hawks newly convinced that only America could stand in the power vacuum left by the end of the Cold War.

"I was wrong about Bosnia, and that is something I reproach myself for," McCain told the *Los Angeles Times'* Gregg Easterbrook in 1999. "Learning about the atrocity at Srebrenica had a deep effect on me."[18]

During the second Clinton term, McCain was like the neoconservative yang to the Clintonites' Wilsonian yin. Clinton's new defense secretary, Republican William Cohen, was one of McCain's best friends; and Secretary of State Madeleine Albright, with her articulation of the United States as the "indispensable nation," was sounding themes indistinguishable from McCain's stump speech. The success of the Dayton Peace Accords—no U.S. casualties, a lasting cease-fire, and the beginnings of political reconciliation— only emboldened both camps further. By the time Milosevic was putting the lash on the predominantly Albanian Yugoslav province of Kosovo, the question was no longer whether McCain and the administration would support intervention, but rather how far they'd be willing to go.

McCain became the leading Republican hawk on Kosovo, and he railed at the White House night and day for not having the resolve to send in ground troops and accept casualties. The Vietnam Syndrome no longer described his own reluctance to deploy troops, but the White House's unforgivable tentativeness in prosecuting war. "I am not haunted by memories of Vietnam," he said in an April 1999 speech to the Center for Strategic and International Studies, "but I must admit I never thought we would again witness in my lifetime the specter of politicians picking targets and ruling out offensive measures in the absurd hope that the enemy would respond to our restraint by yielding to our demands."

McCain predicted that air power alone wouldn't bring Milosevic to the bargaining table; concerns of a land-war quagmire, which he himself had voiced a few years earlier, he now considered "overstated," because "we are a vastly superior power." Lacking boots on the ground, the subsequent defeat would "devastate our credibility everywhere in the world," jeopardizing the NATO alliance. Though none of his fears came to fruition, he was nevertheless hailed throughout the bombing campaign as a welcome and mature Republican voice on foreign policy, an antidote to the Pat Buchanans of the party. "I guess I began falling for McCain's foreign policy during the Kosovo crisis," confessed *The New Republic*'s Charles Lane later that year.[19]

What started with Srebrenica came to full fruition over Kosovo. McCain's Vietnam Syndrome had been swept away by the Cold War, Gulf War, and normalization with Hanoi; and his appetite had been whetted by watching a feckless president radiate doubt where bold American confidence was called for. Boning up on Teddy Roosevelt and conferring with the *Weekly Standard* crew in preparing for a White House run finally produced the inevitable: A new McCain Doctrine.

Unveiled over two speeches in the spring of 1999, the McCain Doctrine remains the template of the senator's foreign policy approach in the twenty-first century. The central notion, even more radical for its time than it is now, is his policy of "rogue state rollback."

"Nowhere is the threat more worrisome than in rogue states such as Iraq, North Korea and others," he said at Kansas State University in March 1999. "The United States should formulate a policy, in many ways similar to the Reagan Doctrine, of supporting indigenous and outside forces that desire to overthrow the odious regimes that rule these states." This preemptive warfare, even when conducted covertly and without any American soldiers, would still be backed by the full force of the U.S. military. "If you commit to supporting these forces, accept the seriousness of the obligation. Don't abandon them to the mercies of tyrants whenever they meet with reversals as the administration did in the north of Iraq. Character counts, my friends, at home and abroad."

That issue of credibility is central to the McCain Doctrine: If the president makes an interventionist promise, that promise must be kept. If the U.S. issues a threat, that threat must be backed by action if the conditions aren't met. "The world's only superpower should never give its word insincerely. We should never make idle threats," he said. "Friend and foe alike perceive a gap between a great power's rhetoric and its actions as weakness."[20]

Underlying the whole project is the assumption that America should hit the accelerator on the drive to further global dominance. When the *National Review*'s Ramesh Ponnuru asked McCain in March 2007 if he thought U.S. diplomatic relations could be improved with Europe, the candidate said: "I think we probably could improve our image a great deal, I don't think there's any doubt about that. But the United States leads. The United States is the world's superpower. We lead. There are many benefits of being the world's superpower, and there's also occasionally great sacrifices [that] have to be made. If the United States militarily were in the same situation as our European friends are, we'd probably be much more diplomatically inclined."

This approach borders on expanding U.S. power for its own sake, which is perfectly in keeping with the deeply held traditions of McCain's own family. His grandfather Slew was an intellectual disciple and participating executioner of Teddy Roosevelt's Naval imperialism. His father Jack's favorite poem was Oscar Wilde's paean to the British Empire, "Ave Imperatrix," which he would quote in his lectures about why the United States needed to control the world's sea lanes. Doubt about this approach, or even guilt about its excesses, was for suckers, or at least Vietnam vets on the mend. With the success of even a handcuffed U.S. military in Kosovo, the quarter-century of Vietnam-inspired realism had given way to something that felt more natural: embrace of global supremacy.

But this is an aggressive, far-reaching posture for an isolated superpower with an already overstretched military. So McCain proposes putting the country on much more of a war footing than President Bush has ever contemplated. For instance, he would boost the standing Army and Marine troop levels from 750,000 to 900,000, create a 20,000-strong "Army Advisor Corps" to "work with friendly militaries abroad," increase spending on weapons systems, and drastically ramp up language instruction in the military. These initiatives would cost real money, "But we can also afford to spend more on our defense," he argued when unveiling some of these plans in New Hampshire this past July. "Our defense budget currently consumes less than 4 cents of every dollar that our booming economy generates—far less than we spent during the Cold War."

Of course, the booming private economy generates many more dollars than it did in 1968; and the defense budget, despite amounting to only a little more than half of total defense-related outlays,[21] still manages to soak up more than 50 percent of federal discretionary spending. But that doesn't at all change McCain's basic point—the country as a whole needs to shoulder more of the defense burden. "We should . . . be concerned by the growing gap between our nation's military and civilian cultures," McCain wrote in the *Washington Monthly* in October 2001. "While the volunteer military has been successful, fewer Americans know and appreciate the sacrifices and contributions of their fellow citizens who serve in uniform. The military is suffering severe recruitment problems. . . . The decline of the citizen-soldier is not healthy for a democracy. While it is not currently politically practical to revive the draft, it is important to find better incentives and opportunities for more young Americans to choose service in the military, if not for a career, then at least for a limited period of time."[22]

To narrow that gap between citizen and soldier, McCain has some ideas, too: Greatly expand the AmeriCorps national service program (which he has called "the best assurance that the cynicism about public causes . . . does not threaten the continued progress of this nation"[23]); withdraw federal financial aid from colleges that don't allow the Reserve Office Training Corps (ROTC) to operate on campus ("It is truly outrageous that some colleges receive federal aid while forbidding access to an organization that promotes the defense of our freedoms"[24]); and have civil servants and soldiers "train and work together in peacetime so that they can cooperate effectively in wartime and in postwar reconstruction."[25]

Among his most ambitious and curious ideas is to create a "new civil-military agency patterned after the Office of Strategic Services in World War II." The OSS, which processed intelligence data and covertly fomented rebellions abroad, did not exactly die after World War II; its duties and personnel were largely reconstituted in 1947 under the brand new Central Intelligence Agency. Still, McCain is attracted to the idea of bringing more private citizens into the fight against Islamic extremism. "A modern-day OSS could draw together unconventional warfare, civil-affairs, paramilitary and psychological-warfare specialists from the military together with covert-action operators from our intelligence agencies and experts in anthropology, advertising, foreign cultures, and numerous other disciplines from inside and outside government," he said in New Hampshire in 2007. "In the spirit of the original OSS, this would be a small, nimble, can-do organization that would fight terrorist subversion across the world and in cyberspace."

In McCain's journey from skeptical interventionist to rogue-state rollbacker, he has exposed himself to charges of hypocrisy, and more importantly, painted himself into some rhetorical corners. Nowhere is this more true than in his stance regarding Iraq. In January 2007, he made the absurd argument on the Senate floor that if you don't support the U.S. mission in Iraq, you don't support the troops (a standard which McCain failed to live up to when he did not support sending troops into Lebanon, Haiti, Somalia, and perhaps even Bosnia, at minimum). He has ruled out a regional peace settlement, dismissing the James Baker/Lee Hamilton Iraq Study Group suggestions for multiparty talks with a wave of his hand: "Well in war, my dear friends, there is no such thing as compromise; you either win or you lose."

Long before the administration adopted a version of the troop-escalation and counterinsurgency strategy that McCain had been advocating for years, the senator indicated that there were basically no scenarios under which he thought the troops could leave. When the *Arizona Daily Star* asked him in August 2005 why he supported the continued presence of U.S. troops if he thought the White House had done such a poor job managing the war, he said: "Because we cannot afford to lose. I'd be glad to have a debate with you but we cannot afford to lose. I debate this all the time. I'd be glad to have another one with you. But the fact is we cannot afford to lose. We must win. We must prevail. And it may require additional service and sacrifice, tragically."[26]

His strategy, if you can call it that, is to remind Americans constantly about the consequences of failure. There is no Plan B. "It's just so hard for me to contemplate failure that I can't make the next step," he told *Vanity Fair* in a February 2007 profile. "Do I know it would be a tremendous strain on the army and Marine Corps? Absolutely. But I saw the kind of impact of a broken army, a defeated army and Marine Corps, after Vietnam. And I'd much rather have 'em take a strain and have some success than be defeated."

Even though the Iraq War is hugely unpopular among the press (as it is with the rest of the population), the man with no backup plan is still treated as a foreign policy sage. "McCain is a warrior," MSNBC.com's Howard Fineman wrote in May 2007. "He knows the world, its dangers and wonders; he knows the military, its powers and its limitations."[27]

But if there is anything McCain *doesn't* know, or at least stubbornly refuses to recognize, it's the limitations on the exercise of U.S. power abroad. After a presidency made infamous by preemptive war and military overstretch, the third-generation Navy man is ordering up double helpings of the same. After all, if we've learned anything about Vietnam, it's that a superpower can't lose. It just can't.

THE CROOKED TALK EXPRESS

Everywhere he goes, McCain takes on all comers, all questions. A rolling no-holds-barred political free-for-all, unlike most other American campaigns these days. . . . That's pure John McCain. Blunt, unyielding, deploying his principles as political weapons. . . . Play[ing] it as straight as possible. A directness that still startles.

—Terry Moran, *Nightline*, ABC, March 26, 2007

I ran a campaign saying I always tell the truth, and then on a key issue, I didn't tell the truth.

—John McCain, *Larry King Live*, CNN, Oct. 12, 2002

Terry Moran seemed tickled. It was March 2007, the presidential campaign was just getting underway, and the *Nightline* anchor was in the political reporter's version of paradise: riding along on the Straight Talk Express. "John McCain is back on the bus," Moran intoned, almost triumphantly. "Back in his element, talking."

Few political campaigns have ever been blessed with such an effective, all-purpose metaphor as John McCain's metallic blue six-wheeler of 1999–2000. It was a daily reminder that this candidate, at least, knew the meaning of the word *is*. As a blunt-speaking ex-soldier with a mile-wide streak of rebelliousness, he seemed to hold almost as much disdain for the dull pieties of political-party discipline as did the national press that was busy firing questions at him all day long. His ragtag staff was a good-time Rebel Alliance, fighting the Dark Lord of establishment conservatism, wolfing down cheeseburgers and booze, yukking it up like athletes in a locker room after the big game. And oh, the access! It was almost like Hunter Thompson interviewing George McGovern in the urinal every day, except without the drugs (and the great writing). As Tucker Carlson put it in the *Weekly Standard*, in the best of the hundreds of giddy journalistic diary entries from the first Straight Talk Express, "It takes only a day or two of this sort of thing for the average political reporter to decide that John McCain is about the coolest guy who ever ran for president."[1] Underlying it all was a postulate so worn into the campaign's fabric that it was presumed to be beyond further question: John McCain was a straight-talking loose cannon who, between Irish-bar jokes, told the God's honest truth.

In 2007, there is a palpable sense of journalistic nostalgia for those wacky, hopeful days of yore. "You almost feel as if it could be 2000 again," Moran narrated. "When he was the maverick outsider, riding a lightning bolt connection to the American political psyche. When it all seemed so natural. So much fun." But then comes the obligatory list of post-September 11 downers: McCain's taking a beating on Iraq, the immigration bill is killing him with the base, he looks pretty old and haggard this time around, and there's that long, awkward suck-up to the Right.

It's that last suggestion that raises the hair on McCain's neck. "If you look at my positions on literally every issue, I haven't changed," he insisted to Moran. "I'm no different from what I was. And that's a tiny bit frustrating to me that this portrayal, well, he's pandered to this or done that."

Forget the pandering charge, which, once the tape recorder's turned off, McCain's own closest advisers freely admit (and, depending on their point of view, bitterly lament). Focus instead on his rigid insistence that his policies are the same on *literally every issue*. We have already seen McCain's tic of issuing unprompted absolutist denials—he would never hold a grudge, "ever"; there is "no chronicled event" of his so much as expressing anger; he would never overhype his Vietnam story for political gain—all of which are a classic tell, indicating that the opposite, in fact, is worthy of investigation. (They also amount to a mildly effective tough-guy tactic to get the people in his face to change the subject, though in the age of YouTube such misdirection has its limitations.) Recall, too that the candidate's counterpunches come quickest after critiques that question his honor and contain uncomfortable truths. With his words, McCain is asking us to take it on faith that his aim is still true and his positions haven't moved one inch in eight years. With his testy reaction he's almost begging us to conduct a fact-check.

Start with that old primary-season favorite: ethanol. In the 2000 campaign, McCain, who had a limited budget with which to pick his battles, decided to skip the conservative-heavy Iowa caucus and focus instead on independent-rich New Hampshire. He had also long been opposed to federal subsidies for the production of ethanol, the fuel derived from fermenting the sugars produced by Iowa's abundant corn. This combination of facts allowed the straight-talker to claim the moral high road in avoiding one of the key early primary states. As he recalled to Tim Russert in June 2005, "My opposition to ethanol has, obviously, hurt me. But you know what I've found out? That every time I've done something for what may have been influenced by political reasons, I've regretted it."[2] Just over a year later, McCain did something for what may have been influenced by political reasons—announce his "support for ethanol," while traveling through Iowa.[3]

What changed? McCain claims it was the price of oil. "When oil is $10 a barrel, ethanol doesn't make much sense," he told Russert in November 2006. "When it's $40 a barrel, it does make sense. I do not support subsidies for ethanol and I have not supported it and I will not. But ethanol makes a lot of sense, particularly [given] our dependence on foreign oil, and my belief that . . . climate change is real and is part of the solution to this climate greenhouse gas emissions problem."[4]

The only problem with McCain's analysis is that it directly contradicts his own words on the Senate floor just three years earlier: "Ethanol does nothing to reduce fuel consumption, nothing to increase our energy independence, nothing to improve air quality." Not only that, McCain's office sent out a press release condemning ethanol when oil was as high as $60 a barrel, according to a devastating October 2006 piece in *Fortune* magazine for which McCain refused to be interviewed.[5] When Russert confronted him with these contradictions, McCain said "No, I, I, I don't, I don't think I said that at $60 a barrel," and quickly changed the subject.

Claiming to "support ethanol" while opposing subsidies for it begs the question of what "support" from the federal government then could possibly mean? An internal campaign memo from mid-July 2007 explaining how McCain planned to compete in Iowa offers a hint of what that interventionism would look like: "creating new markets for farmers by providing incentives to create low carbon auto fuels like ethanol and other energy sources from corn." So instead of handing out cash to Iowa ethanol producers, a McCain presidency would tell Iowa ethanol producers they don't have to pay as much cash to Uncle Sam. And "creating new markets"? McCain was against it before he was for it. "Ethanol is a product that would not exist if Congress didn't create an artificial market for it," he told the Senate in November 2003.

What else has changed? His stance on gay marriage famously changed within 15 minutes of the same 2006 broadcast. At first he told MSNBC's Chris Matthews, "I think that gay marriage should be allowed, if there's a ceremony kind of thing, if you want to call it that. . . . But I do believe in preserving the sanctity of a union between man and woman." Then, after getting some whispered political advice from campaign strategist John Weaver,[6] McCain clarified his position in the middle of answering a totally unrelated question: "Could I just mention one other thing? On the issue of the gay marriage, I believe that people want to have private ceremonies, that's fine. I do not believe that gay marriages should be legal."[7] The crowd of college students booed.

That wasn't the only time McCain gave a little nationally televised crooked talk on the subject. In November 2006, on ABC's *This Week*, he had the following exchange with George Stephanopoulus:

STEPHANOPOULOS: You say you believe that marriage should be reserved for between a man—
MCCAIN: Yes.

STEPHANOPOULOS:—and a woman. You voted for an initiative in Arizona that went beyond that and actually denied any government benefits to civil unions or domestic partnerships. Are you against civil unions for gay couples?

MCCAIN: No, I'm not. But the—that initiative I think was misinterpreted. I think that initiative did allow for people to join in legal agreements such as power of attorney and others. I think there was a—I think that there was a difference of opinion on the interpretation of that constitutional amendment in Arizona.

STEPHANOPOULOS: So you're for civil unions?

MCCAIN: No. I am for ability of two—I do not believe gay marriage should be legal. I do not believe gay marriage should be legal. But I do believe that people ought to be able to enter into contracts, exchange powers of attorney, other ways that people who have relationships can enter into.[8]

There was no "difference of opinion on the interpretation" about whether Arizona's failed Proposition 107 of 2006 banned civil unions. The text of the initiative said: "The State of Arizona and its cities, towns, counties or districts shall not create or recognize a legal status for unmarried persons that is similar to marriage." The official Web site in support of the proposition bragged that it "restricts all levels of government from using taxpayers' dollars to undermine the state's marriage policy by giving recognition or benefits to marriage counterfeits, like 'civil unions' or 'domestic partnerships.'"

More relevant to his prospective job as president, McCain has long led the minority caucus within the GOP that is *opposed* to a constitutional amendment banning gay marriage. In 2004, he called the idea "antithetical in every way to the core philosophy of Republicans," because it "usurps from the states a fundamental authority they have always possessed and imposes a federal remedy for a problem that most states do not believe confronts them." McCain's sternly articulated federalist principles do not extend to the constitutional prohibition of flag-burning, which he has enthusiastically supported. But his record on the federal marriage amendment has been clear—until, as on the issue of ethanol, the pre-campaign year of 2006.

In February 2000, on the eve of the South Carolina primary, McCain famously called Republican televangelists Jerry Falwell and Pat Robertson "evil," "agents of intolerance," who have been "corrupting influences on religion and politics," and who "shame our faith, our party and our country." In November 2005, he began mending fences with Falwell, a process he has repeated since then with other Christian conservative leaders he had so memorably trashed. He spoke at Falwell's Liberty University in May 2006, and in the telephone conversations negotiating that appearance, Falwell told ABC News, McCain "reconfirmed" that he would reverse his position and support a federal constitutional amendment if some federal court struck down a state's constitutional ban of the type he supported in Arizona.[9] In March 2007 he went further: When a reporter from Politico.com asked McCain if he would sign a federal marriage amendment into law, he said "of course." (His campaign then sent a follow-up clarification that this would only apply in the case of the federal judiciary prohibiting states from defining marriage how they see fit.)[10]

But this condition for constitutional intervention set the bar far lower than what McCain had sketched out on the Senate floor in 2004: "If the Supreme Court of the United States rejects the Defense of Marriage Act as unconstitutional; if state legislatures are frustrated by the decisions of jurists in more states than one, and if state remedies to such judicial activism fail; and finally, if a large majority of Americans come to perceive that their communities' values are being ignored and other standards concerning marriage are being imposed on them against their will, and that elections and state legislatures can provide no remedy then, and only then, should we consider, quite appropriately, amending the Constitution."

There are more position-changes in the direction of social conservatism where that came from. In March 2007, as he re-launched the Straight-Talk Express, McCain was asked a question any tenth grader knows the answer to. The full exchange:

> Q: Do you think contraceptives help stop the spread of HIV?
>
> MCCAIN: *(Long pause)* You've stumped me.
>
> Q: I mean, I think you'd probably agree it probably does help stop it?
>
> MR. MCCAIN: *(Laughs)* Are we on the Straight Talk express? I'm not informed enough on it. Let me find out. You know, I'm sure I've taken a position on it on the past. I have to find out what my position was. Brian, would you find out what my position is on contraception—I'm sure I'm opposed to government spending on it, I'm sure I support the president's policies on it.
>
> Q: But you would agree that condoms do stop the spread of sexually transmitted diseases. Would you say: 'No, we're not going to distribute them,' knowing that?
>
> MR. MCCAIN: *(Twelve-second pause)* Get me [Sen. Tom] Coburn's thing, ask [John] Weaver to get me Coburn's paper that he just gave me in the last couple of days. I've never gotten into these issues before.[11]

McCain *had* gotten into those issues before, acknowledging the link between contraception and HIV prevention, and supporting federal money to purchase condoms. In 2004, as the Democratic National Committee has gleefully pointed out, McCain answered yes to a question posed by Project Vote

Smart: "Should aid to African nations for AIDS prevention programs fund distribution of contraceptives?" And on *Meet the Press*, on February 17, 2002, when asked what he thought of Colin Powell encouraging sexually active young people to use condoms, McCain said: "Oh, I agree with him. I think that he established the priorities correctly. We should emphasize, first of all, abstinence, faithfulness, but there are people in American society who are sexually active, and in the world. And when HIV/AIDS has reached an epidemic proportion, I think we need to use every means possible to try to eradicate this epidemic that has affected particularly Third World countries. But I do believe it's appropriate to emphasize abstinence and other ways, as well, and give them priority."

Then there is abortion. McCain staffers say their candidate has made only one verbal gaffe in an otherwise unblemished quarter-century record opposing abortion—a comment to the *San Francisco Chronicle* in 1999 that "I'd love to see a point where [*Roe v. Wade*] is irrelevant, and could be repealed because abortion is no longer necessary. But certainly in the short term, or even the long term, I would not support repeal of *Roe v. Wade*, which would then force X number of women in America to [undergo] illegal and dangerous operations."[12] Explained McCain campaign staffer and social conservative Patrick Hynes on his personal blog in December 2006: "Okay, so what of that quote from 1999? The one about not supporting repeal [of] Roe v. Wade? It was a mistake, plain and simple. And it was immediately clarified. His spokespeople 'said he was trying to explain that efforts to repeal Roe v. Wade would have to come in conjunction with efforts to reduce abortion through other means, including adoptions and counseling.'"[13]

In fact, the comment wasn't "immediately clarified" at all. Several days later, when the *Washington Post* asked the campaign whether McCain had misspoken, they said no.[14] But a few days before the *Post* story ran, McCain said on CNN that he would work for the long-term repeal of *Roe v. Wade*, that he rejected a "litmus" test for Supreme Court nominees, and that "we all know, and it's obvious, that if we *repeal Roe v. Wade* tomorrow, thousands of young American women would be performing illegal and dangerous operations."

Meanwhile, however, McCain was actively seeking to rewrite the national Republican platform to make abortion acceptable in cases of rape and incest, or where the life of the mother was in danger. He told Tim Russert just before the New Hampshire primary that he "would not prosecute" a woman who had an abortion,[15] and on the Straight Talk Express he said that, despite wanting to make abortions illegal, if his daughter were pregnant, he'd leave that decision up to her.

Has his position on abortion literally stayed the same since then? No. Now, instead of supporting the repeal of *Roe v. Wade* only in the "long term," he wants an immediate overhaul. He has even on at least one occasion (ABC's *This Week*, Nov. 19, 2006) said he supports a constitutional amendment banning abortion, though on others he has stated his preference for letting states decide. What's more, he said in March 2006 that he would have signed into law South Dakota's strict (and eventually repealed) abortion ban, prohibiting the procedure even in cases of rape and incest. Trying to have it all ways, his spokesman told the *National Journal* at the time that McCain "would also take the appropriate steps under state law—in whatever state—to ensure that the exceptions of rape, incest or life of the mother were included," even though the law specifically stated otherwise.

On taxes, too, McCain has flip-flopped. He voted against President Bush's 2001 and 2003 tax cuts on grounds of fiscal "sanity," warning as recently as 2004 against the folly of providing "tax cuts for the wealthiest citizens" at the expense of the "American taxpayer," but is now in favor of extending them indefinitely.[16] As he tried to explain to George Stephanopoulos in June 2007, "The tax cuts were enacted. I was for tax cuts. I wasn't for those. But to be against maintaining them, of course, would be the effect tax increases."

These policy shifts have three things in common: (1) contra John McCain, they exist; (2) with the exception of the tax cuts, they all involve government restricting the freedom of the individual; and (3) they represent red meat to the GOP base that McCain has transparently been trying to kiss and make up with for the last several years. All of which is standard behavior for politicians ambitious enough to run for president, but McCain has based his entire last 10 years on the proposition that he, uniquely in the field, is not like other candidates. "Neither party," McCain said in his famous Virginia Beach speech in February 2000, "should be defined by pandering to the outer reaches of American politics and the agents of intolerance, whether they be Louis Farrakan or Al Sharpton on the left or Pat Robertson or Jerry Falwell on the right." Yet he's been pandering to precisely those "reaches" of the Right since Bush's second term.

Consider his 2005 book, *Character Is Destiny*. This was his fourth book, so a certain writing style and set of emphases had already been clearly established, in addition to a career full of speechmaking and public policy. Throughout his life, at least until this book, McCain was the type of Christian who refused to be showy about his faith, limiting discussion to a few heart-warming anecdotes from Vietnam (for example, when one of his captors silently stood next to him and drew a cross in the dirt, signifying religious solidarity, and when that same guard loosened the ropes on him during one of his overnight torture sessions). Faith was important in his memoir, *Faith of My Fathers* (1999), but the religious element was only one of four objects of that faith, and discussed much, much less than faith in his country, his family traditions, and his brothers in arms. In fact, much of the first half of the book is devoted to raucous tales of his boozing, rule-breaking, and carousing with strippers.

But suddenly, with *Character Is Destiny*, the man once known as "McNasty" couldn't stop yammering about God. "God has given us . . . life, shown us how to use it, but left it to us dispose of as we choose," he wrote in the book's very first paragraph. The first subject of his 31 character sketches is, of all people, Sir Thomas More, a man who history remembers for (among other accomplishments) being put to death by Henry VIII because he refused to publicly endorse his king's heretical marriage to Anne Boleyn and the creation of the Church of England. Here's how the chapter ends: "In his last address, spoken moments earlier, he had asked the crowd of witnesses to pray for his soul and for the king, for he died 'the King's good servant, but God's first.' One swift stroke and the king's will was done. The life on earth of honest Thomas More was ended. His glory had just begun."

Besides McCain's unprecedented onset of religiosity, his reverence for "honest" Thomas More is curious because More sentenced an untold number of Lutherans to death for heresy. Here's how McCain handles the "to be sure" paragraph: "More defended the Church out of religious principle, and because he and the king feared the uncontrollable social disorder that a permanent split among the faithful would

surely cause. But his hatred, if it could be called that in such
a mild man, was for the heresy and not the heretics."

In chapter 2, devoted to Mahatma Gandhi, McCain says:
"I can't offer you an informed explanation of Gandhian philosophy; it is too rooted in his religious devotion, derived
mostly from Hindu beliefs, for me to fully comprehend,
much less explain, even though his beliefs were influenced by
the traditions of all major religions, including mine."

In chapter 3, about Joan of Arc, the writing again veers
toward Jonathan Edwards territory. "God's messenger went
bravely to her death, forgiving her accusers and asking only
that a priest hold high a crucifix for her to see it above the
flames. She raised her voice to heaven, calling out to her
saints and her Savior. Even her enemies wept at the sight.
Her executioner was shaken with remorse, and an anguished
English soldier who witnessed the crime feared for his soul.
'God forgive us,' he cried, 'we have burned a saint.'"

The book goes on and on like that, praising various Puri-
tans, chaplains, Mother Antonia, and Mother Theresa. Just
when you think he's about to leaven the sermon with a chapter celebrating Charles Darwin, McCain squares the circle of
his pro-God and pro-evolution fusion by lamenting the sci-
entist's lack of fervor: "Regrettably, although he never
rejected the existence of God, he did admit to having become
an agnostic on the subject," he wrote. "Is not our conscience
and its effect upon our will enough confirmation for the
believer that God, the Creator, has endowed us with the divine
spark of His love to improve, if we so choose, our second
nature in service to Him?"

The change in rhetorical style (and especially capitaliza-
tion) is as dramatic as it would be if McCain's good friend Warren Beatty decided overnight to become a priest. It beggars

belief. And it trickles down to the meaningless social-policy gestures of the type McCain used to savage on the campaign trail—the senator now, for, instance, endorses the teaching of intelligent design in public schools, even though the chances of a president having any effect on school curricula are as remote as dinosaurs coming back to life.

Despite all this crooked talk, and pandering while denying the pander, McCain still continues to receive the media benefit of the doubt. "To be sure," *Washington Post* media columnist Howard Kurtz wrote in April 2007, "no one can accuse McCain of pandering."[17] When McCain issued some criticism of President Bush's handling of the Iraq War (which McCain has done since 2003, with varying levels of vehemence, though not much during the 2004 presidential campaign), *Post* political columnist David Broder declared that the straight-talker was back: "There must be at least some relief now in being able to speak his own mind—whatever the consequences. Candor, even belatedly, becomes him."[18] CNN's William Schneider contributed, too: "The straight talker is back. And he's hoping to turn into the comeback kid."[19]

Journalists have announced the return of the maverick almost every time he makes news—supporting the Iraq surge policy in January 2007, falling on his sword in the immigration fiasco, performing well at the third GOP debate, firing most of his campaign team, and starting over. Even though the lack of excitement is striking compared to his 2000 campaign, and the majority of stories have been of the horse-race and death-watch variety, there is still a ready "base" (as McCain's own people have called the national press) laying in wait for any sign of good news. As of this writing, they are preparing their anguished obituaries.

"You know, if you look at it on paper, here's a guy who's more seasoned than the current president, President Bush," Chris Matthews said on MSNBC July 10. "He's got more military experience. He's been around a long time in terms of national responsibility. He's been a patriot, of course. He served his country brutally as a POW. He's always been honest and respected in the media. He has all the pluses in the world of a sort of a, you know, an Audie Murphy, if you will, a real war hero. It's not working." Imagining a GOP race without McCain, Matthews said, is "really the worst part of my job."

The Straight Talk Express has been mostly dormant this campaign season, as the candidate eschewed face-to-face town halls for behind-closed-gates private fundraising sessions. The *Washington Post* reported on May 23, 2007 that "the candidate who rode the Straight Talk Express for 71 days and 15,000 miles in 2000 has spent eight days on the bus so far in the 2008 campaign, aides said." For months, the most common message on the bus calendar at john mccain.com has been "there are currently no Straight Talk Express Events scheduled." The greatest metaphor in presidential politics may have slowed to a crawl, but it's not done yet. Not as long as the candidate can continue looking at himself in the mirror every morning.

THE THIRTEENTH STEP

I knew a man who slept through the night, when everything hung in the balance. He would accept whatever the day brought, whether it be joy or sorrow. He had done his best and had taken his rest. And that, my friends, is all that is required of any of us.

—John McCain, *Hard Call*[1]

This time McCain has been gradually sliding in the polls, and he has responded not by panicking or by changing, but by surrendering himself to the fates. He's had a wonderful life, he feels, and if he is not president, it will be no tragedy. At first I thought he was making pre-emptive excuses for a possible defeat, but after observing him closely I concluded this is a fatalism that Navy fliers must often adopt as they go into combat.

—David Brooks, *New York Times*, April 12, 2007[2]

When I wrote my first essay about John McCain's tendencies toward intrusive big government, hyper-aggressive foreign policy, and a 12-Step-style approach to the "greater cause" of American nationalism,[3] the negative reaction was, as always, the most instructive. On the Ankle Biting Pundits Web site, in a blog run by Patrick Hynes, who has been doing Web-consulting work for McCain's campaign, blogger B. T.

weighed in with: "Let's be honest: when push comes to shove, the [L.A.] Times isn't going to give the nod to any Republican no matter how far left they lean from the core of the party." A nice attempt at base-rallying, but (1) I don't speak for the *Times*, much as I might like to; (2) I don't know who *I* will endorse, let alone the editorial board, and I personally have not ruled out a Republican; (3) the editorial board had backed three of seven GOP candidates running for statewide office earlier that month; and (4) I sure as hell ain't no Democrat. (Hynes, in case you were wondering, said my piece was "remarkably petty and childish," filled with "name calling and puerile armchair psychoanalyzing.")[4]

There were also various iterations of, "If you like Hillary so much, why don't you marry her?" (Answer: I like McCain better than Clinton; this isn't about her.) Or, as Dave G over at Race 4 2008 wrote, "It's clear from the tone of the article that there's no love lost between Welch and McCain."[5] This line of thinking has always struck me as queer. I happen to be quite fond of McCain; it's why I rooted for him in 2000 and started reading his books in the first place. But why anyone's personal sympathies should get in the way of trying to figure out what kind of a president a candidate would make, I'll never know.

Has there been a recent politician *more* conspicuously liked by journalists than John McCain? As Tucker Carlson put it in his amusing *Weekly Standard* piece from March 2000, "The Bush campaign complains that McCain's style and personality have caused many reporters to lose their objectivity about him. The Bush campaign is onto something. . . . There are reporters who call McCain 'John,' sometimes even to his face and in public. And then there are the employees of major news organizations who, usually at night in the hotel bar, slip into the habit of referring to the McCain campaign as 'we'— as in, 'I hope we kill Bush.'"[6] I'm an opinion journalist, not an objective campaign reporter, but the day I'm part of a political "we" is the day I'm moving to the baseball beat.

More illuminating than these responses to that first column was how people charged me with being unfair for calling McCain a "carpetbagger," mentioning that his father had been a "drunk," and that his second wife battled addiction to pain pills. In a similar vein, after I wrote a much longer version for *Reason* magazine,[7] a man who had known McCain since his days as a plebe in the Naval Academy wrote in to say he was "surprised to read about [McCain's] 'binge drinking' . . . since it was against the rules then to drink within seven and a half miles of the Chapel Dome," and that "given the emotional stress of his time as a POW, I believe it was not family ties that prompted orders to the Navy War College for a year but a compassionate detailer, who was giving him an opportunity to decompress."[8]

What these last critiques shared in common was a lack of knowledge or concern that John McCain has freely admitted to all of the above charges in his extensive autobiographical writings. As a serial self-confessor, a man with a rich and colorful life, who is constantly struggling to keep his egotism focused on the country's greater good, McCain evidently finds it useful to be a witness to his own prosecution, gambling that by volunteering the information the court will show mercy. That ethic of forgiving confessed sins is the moral of a story he tells at some length in his newest book *Hard Call: Great Decisions and the Extraordinary People Who Made Them*, about a teammate who faced expulsion for skipping practice from his J.V. football team at Episcopal High

School. The coach, William Ravenel, who was one of McCain's first father figures outside of his immediate family, sat back and let the boys on the team decide the scofflaw's fate. Young John, in the style of *Twelve Angry Men*, went against the prevailing wisdom of the locker room and eventually rallied the others to his way of thinking, based in part on the fact that the kid had preemptively turned himself in. "Our teammate had broken training but hadn't been discovered doing so by anyone," he wrote. "He had confessed his transgression himself, without coercion or even questioning. He had felt bad and owned up, and I thought this was a mitigating factor." And so McCain hopes we do with him.

John McCain has lain on the table personality flaws and interior struggles that go far beyond what the journalistic observer might ever be able to guess from the outside. He's given us a remarkable map with which to navigate his political career and presidential future. And most people have ignored it.

Arguably, the most valuable lesson McCain learned during the Keating Five scandal was not the necessity for campaign-finance reform, but the practical benefits of media over-exposure. By answering hostile questioning for nearly two full hours, until the reporters had exhausted their lines of inquiry, McCain found himself praised by his hometown paper for manfully owning up to his misdeeds. By making himself available to almost any reporter at any hour, he found that he had sown some useful empathy. "McCain grimly marched about the country, struggling to clear his name," the *Arizona Republic* recounted of the Keating days, in its massive October 1999 mini-biography of the senator. "McCain's hobnobbing with the press had an unexpected side effect. Reporters started to like him. McCain always returned phone calls. He showed up for his television appearances. He was willing to go off the record to help reporters unearth certain stories. He answered questions bluntly, without much political tap dancing. For Beltway reporters bored with bureaucrats, McCain was fresh, new and different."[9]

Parrying verbally with a skilled politician is like playing defense in basketball: The advantage, by far, goes to the guy with the ball, particularly if he's skilled at throwing elbows that the refs don't see. For a banal, everyday example, note this exchange from a June 2007 press conference in Los Angeles:

> Q: You've been sinking in the polls just a little bit, how are you going to reverse that pattern when it seems to be based on your views of war and torture and immigration?
>
> A: Actually none of those are true. There's a poll out today where I think we have . . . mayor Giuliani at 24, and me at 20. I think that's pretty much the same where it's always been; a majority of polls showing that we're ahead in the early states. And I'm very happy with where our campaign is. And *I will always stand up for what I believe in, and I will not be driven by polling numbers, I will be driven by principle.*

Next question please.

There are maybe four untruths in this one small passage that went unchallenged:

1. *Actually none of those are true.* In fact, three out of the four things the reporter said were demonstrably true. McCain's national poll numbers had been moving downward from the high 20s to around 15 percent by mid-June, and the trend lines held in the early-primary states, too. Polls, and McCain's own campaign staff, indicated that his support, especially for immigration reform but also the war, was hurting his popularity.

2. *There's a poll out today where I think we have . . . mayor Giuliani at 24, and me at 20.* That poll was conducted by American Research Group (ARG), which compared to all the major presidential polling firms, has consistently reported higher numbers for McCain than other polling firms by a wide margin. At the time of McCain's statement, other polls had him losing in national match-up numbers with Giuliani by 30–18 percent (Harris Interactive), 27–15 percent (Quinnipiac), 24–11 percent (Rasmussen), 27–12 percent (*L.A. Times*/Bloomberg), and 27–19 percent (AP-Ipsos).

3. *I think that's pretty much the same where it's always been; a majority of polls showing that we're ahead in the early states.* At the time of his statement, McCain was behind—and trending downward—in every major poll of Iowa and New Hampshire, with the exception of ARG.

4. *I will always stand up for what I believe in, and I will not be driven by polling numbers, I will be driven by principle.* To cite one of dozens of examples to the contrary supplied by McCain himself, in *Worth the Fighting For* he talked about his 2000 campaign platform in which he supported using the budget surplus mostly to pay down the debt, rather than offer a huge tax cut (an issue on which he has since flip-flopped): "Lest anyone think my positions were brave, if self-defeating, honesty obliges me to note that every poll my campaign conducted (and we took as many as we could afford) found greater support for paying down the debt than cutting taxes for upper-bracket incomes, among Republican voters as well as Democrats and independents."[10]

Again, this is not to make the claim that McCain is any different from other politicians in spinning his campaign performance, but rather to illustrate that the press-conference approach to politicking has tremendous built-in advantages for the assertively glib candidate. It takes skill and preparation to catch a dissembler in real time, and the few who have done so this campaign cycle have reduced McCain to a sad, stammering man, hoisted on the petard of his thousands of previous on-the-record statements.

On Mother's Day 2007, McCain appeared for the entirety of *Meet the Press*.[11] If Tim Russert does one thing very well, it's dig up old statements that contradict new positions. With McCain, that's now a long list—ethanol, progress in Iraq, abortion, tax cuts. It was one of the most excruciating hours of network television this side of *Fear Factor*. A sample:

> MR. RUSSERT: On tax cuts. You were on this program back in '03, and I asked you this.
> SEN. MCCAIN: Mm-hmm.
> MR. RUSSERT: "Do you believe the president, because of the war, should be asking Americans for more sacrifice, should . . . hold off any future tax cuts until we have a sense of the costs of the war and the state of our economy?"
> "Yes, I do. I believe that until we find out the costs of this war and the reconstruction that we should hold off."
> SEN. MCCAIN: Mm-hmm.
> MR. RUSSERT: " . . . on tax cuts." You came back the next year, I again asked you about opposing the Bush tax cuts.
> SEN. MCCAIN: Mm-hmm.
> MR. RUSSERT: . . . and this is what you said.
> SEN. MCCAIN: Mm-hmm.
> [Videotape from April 11, 2004]
> SEN. MCCAIN: I voted against the tax cuts because of the disproportional amount that went to the wealthiest Americans. I would clearly support not extending those tax cuts in order to help address the deficit.
> [End videotape]
> MR. RUSSERT: Disproportionate to the wealthiest Americans.
> SEN. MCCAIN: Mm-hmm.
> MR. RUSSERT: And you didn't—wouldn't extend them because it would hurt the deficit. You voted to extend them.
> SEN. MCCAIN: I voted to extend them because it would have the effect of having a tax increase. I also had a proposal, and also stated time after time, that we needed to restrain spending. The tax cuts have increased revenues enormously. I mean, they've been very beneficial. The

problem is that spending has lurched completely out of control. My proposal was to restrain spending. And now, if you don't make them, those tax cuts, permanent, businesses, families, farms all over America will have to experience what, for all intents and purposes, the impact on them would be a tax increase. Would I have like to have seen more tax cuts to middle income Americans? Did I have a different proposal? Yes. But I supported tax cuts, and I have never supported—I have—I do not support tax increases. And the effect of not making them permanent would have the effect of a tax increase.

Such encounters have become more frequent in 2007—George Stephanopoulos, Jon Stewart of *The Daily Show*, and Scott Pelley of *60 Minutes* have all grilled the senator in revelatory exchanges. But as in 1999, McCain has an ace in the hole: A book that happens to be coming out in the fall, guaranteeing a free round of friendlier book-tour interviews, in which he'll get to discuss the qualities of leadership that produce the "hard call" of courageous decision-making, from Abraham Lincoln to Winston Churchill to Ronald Reagan. If viewers and listeners want to draw any parallels to McCain's lonely stances on Iraq and immigration, well, that's up to them.

The promotional material for *Hard Call* is almost hilariously disingenuous: "Well before John McCain began his quest for the 2008 Republican nomination for president, he and his long-time collaborator, Mark Salter, began to write their most ambitious work to date. . . . Their publisher asked them to write this book in 2005, on the assumption that McCain's insights on decision-making would provide a useful perspective on difficult issues, both national and personal. No one knew for certain that McCain would again be a presidential candidate, nor did anyone have any idea that McCain's own hard calls on Iraq and immigration would figure so prominently (and controversially) in his campaign." Perhaps it was a mere coincidence that at the time McCain's publisher was tapping him for a new book, he has already said that he "absolutely" wanted to be president, because he was "qualified to help make the world a better place" (in an interview that was printed in the June 2005 issue of *Men's Journal*).

For a candidate looking for good press, the companion piece to the softball interview and rolling press conference is the document-dump. When McCain was beginning to be buried under an avalanche of temper-tantrum stories in the fall of 1999, complete with the unfair whispers that maybe *something funny* happened to him over there in Vietnam, his campaign smothered the story by releasing hundreds of pages of regular psychiatric evaluations from the Robert E. Mitchell Center for Prisoner of War Studies, showing that if anything, the ex-POW learned to *harness* his temper in Vietnam.

A similar cycle played out in January 2000, when the *Boston Globe* reported that—as in the Keating Five scandal—McCain lobbied federal regulators on behalf of a major campaign contributor that just so happened to have also allowed him to use their corporate jets. Paxson Communications, whose executives had donated $20,000 to the Straight Talk Express, was waiting for approval of its application for a television license from the Federal Communications Commission, which McCain's Senate Commerce Committee has oversight responsibility. McCain, the *Boston Globe* reported, had flown on a Paxson jet to a Florida fundraiser one day, then sent a letter to the FCC at the suggestion of Paxson's lobbying firm the next. And just as in the Keating scandal, the regulators squawked, with FCC Chairman William Kennard complaining that McCain's intervention was "highly unusual."

In the days to come, reports came out that McCain also had prodded the FCC on behalf of another campaign contributor,

Ameritech. As Paul Alexander would put it later in his book, *Man of the People*, "McCain made the decision to do what he had done to stop the whisper campaign [about his temper]: release a mountain of information to make the unwanted story disappear."[12] The release of 500 letters to various regulators muted the scandal by placing it in a messier, fact-intensive context of McCain's oversight history, and after one more round of articles, the story basically died.

But the biggest document-dump of all has been his five books, released over the past eight years, each with its own timely and useful purpose. *Faith of My Fathers*, the classic, highlighted the senator's most winning personal story, while imposing an interpretation of redemption that cleared the decks for concentrating on the greater cause of erasing public cynicism and embracing our nation's destiny. *Worth the Fighting For*, in many ways the most interesting book (and most telling, in terms of his politics), is a paean to irascible political independence and cross-partisan cooperation, showing the burn scars of the 2000 primary fight, while further developing McCain's ideas for "national greatness." *Why Courage Matters*, from 2004, is the sore thumb of the bunch, a perfunctory and unsatisfying attempt to answer his publisher's question of how Americans could go about finding their courage after September 11. *Character Is Destiny*, as detailed in chapter 11, is perfectly in keeping with McCain's rapprochement with the Religious Right; and now *Hard Call* provides an opportunity to associate McCain with courageous decision-makers.

But mild political intent aside, it's awfully hard to hide inside a million words worth of original text, especially when you're one of the great preemptive self-deprecators in politics. (Such is the extent of McCain's flagellation that he managed to call his own character into question in the dedication of *Hard Call*: "For Roberta McCain and Lauralie Salter, assured and intelligent decision makers, whose example their sons have, with mixed success, tried to emulate.") As he wrote in the introduction of his newest book, "My life has been blessed with the good company of many people of exemplary character and sound reason, who made hard calls with courage and humility. I have learned from their examples. If I fail to heed those lessons when making an important decision, the fault doesn't lie with the stars, but with my own deficiencies." Before deciding to elect anyone president, it's best to look at the deficiencies he (or she) chooses to reveal up-front.

John McCain is haunted by his father's honor; it is one of the things that make him so compelling as a public figure. Though Jack McCain was an alcoholic, and there haven't been many alcoholics who don't lie, his son is nevertheless convinced that his father never told one. "He believed dishonesty was a personal disgrace, and the very thought of being deceitful, even in small, inconsequential matters, upset him," he wrote in *Character Is Destiny*. "Once, my mother jokingly accused him of cheating at cards. He shot up from the table, in great distress, and begged her never, ever to doubt or even pretend to doubt his honesty. . . . He simply couldn't bear the idea of being deceitful or being accused, wrongly, of deceiving anyone." That anecdote might send off warning flags about Jack's defensiveness to cynical readers, but the message it tells us about John is unmistakable: Having a father with a sense of absolute rectitude, coupled with a lifetime of honor codes ranging from Episcopal High to the U.S. Navy to the oath of federal office, has given John McCain a powerful northern star by which to guide his service to the country. It's why he campaigns on always telling the truth, never wavering or pandering, always putting principle and the country's interest first, sublimating all to the greater cause. "Happiness," he wrote in *Hard Call*, "lasting happiness, is found in the possession of virtues required to serve a cause greater than oneself. It took me years to learn that lesson, and even now I cannot claim to heed it faithfully as [my family and the Naval Academy] did. But they helped to embed in my conscience a sense of self-worth that was measured by how close I approached or how far I fell from the standard they set."

But coming into conflict with that conscience, and knocking McCain off that straight and narrow path, is the hyperambitious, temperamentally impatient and combative political climber, eager to (in the words of his father's hero Admiral Nelson), place "his ship alongside that of the enemy." The headstrong and attractive young narcissist he portrayed in the first half of *Faith of My Fathers* is still with us, for good and ill, still committing the grave sins of arrogance and "selfishness," still occasionally placing his own interests above that of his country. The guy who forgave Emiliano Zapata's sins of cruelty, Billy Mitchell's excesses of bravado, and Ted Williams' lifelong surliness, all because they were channeled into a greater cause, is also still with us, trying to figure out the lines between ego and public service. "It is easy to forget in politics where principle ends and selfishness begins," McCain warned Johns Hopkins students in 2006.

As a senator, he wrote in *Hard Call*, decisions "are not supposed to be made to benefit me personally or, if they do, only inasmuch as I am a citizen of the state I represent and the nation I serve. But in truth, it is asking too much of human nature to expect that exclusively personal considerations will never influence a politician's decisions. . . . But I can say that while I have made sound and not-so-sound decisions as a member of Congress—and have made the latter even when I sincerely believed them to be in the public interest— the worst decisions I have made, not just in politics but over the course of my entire life, have been those I made to seek an advantage primarily or solely for myself."

For the first time in print, in his latest book, McCain confessed the true nature of his culpability in the Keating Five scandal. Earlier, in *Worth the Fighting For* he copped to "poor judgment," but was harsh toward the Senate Democrats who investigated him, and he justified his intervention with regulators as being for the sake of looking after his constituents' jobs. Remarkably, 20 years after the original sin, McCain tells us that "I did so for no other reason than I valued [Charles Keating's] support. . . . Had I weighed the question of honor it occasioned and the public interest more than my personal interest to render a small service to an important supporter, I would not have attended the meeting. . . . I lacked humility and an inspiration to some purpose higher than self-interest."

Should McCain be penalized for his candor? That's the wrong question to ask. The right question is: Are the faults and tendencies he describes still present, and if so what might that mean under a McCain presidency?

People in the candidate's inner circle will say what's been obvious from the outside for years: the Arizona senator really really really wants to be president. He thinks that his becoming president is vital for the future health of the country. By McCain's standards, U.S. nationalism is the greater cause, and the only way to assure its progress is with him at the helm; by this token, the same flaws that made so many of his heroes endearing can be forgiven, if channeled toward that goal. This has produced, in this election cycle, two distinct John McCains.

The McCain haunted by his father's conscience does his best not to lie and makes stirring invocations to high principle. The McCain desperate to be president bends his positions for political considerations, spins furiously when caught out on his contradictions, and makes absurd declarations about how none of his policy positions have changed. Honest John tries to rally bipartisan support for his unpopular support of the war; opportunist John puts himself into a rhetorical straightjacket by accusing his opponents of "surrendering" and not supporting the troops—charges that by the same logic could have been applied several times in the past to Sen. John McCain.

But the tension is visible, even to his supporters. He's trying to mend fences with a GOP grassroots he's never felt any affinity with (one of his favorite jokes in 2000 was the old saw about how the Christian Right is neither). He's trying to run as a Beltway outsider even though he's worked on Capitol Hill for three decades, and his party has controlled most of the government for the past eight years, following many of the policies he supports (if not quite aggressively enough in the foreign arena). After being a deficit hawk through the years of surplus, he's become a supply-sider in a time of great debt; but the supply-siders believe his convictions even less than the Christian conservatives.

Part of the attraction to men of principle is that they have some. The only throughline of McCain's political philosophy, aside from his presidential aspirations, is that he wants to use the powers of the federal government to restore the public's faith in American exceptionalism. No private individual, concern, or company will be exempt from this common struggle under a McCain White House.

If he wins the presidency it will have been on a platform that says the United States can never retreat from any war zone, for reasons of "credibility," and because the "consequences of failure" include a repeat of what he saw as a depressing spectacle upon his return from Vietnam: a nation no longer aggressively confident in its righteousness, and suddenly gun-shy about using the military that helped win two world wars. He has invested what remains of his political career in the singular goal of avoiding that failure, by any means necessary.

McCain wants to overthrow the governments of rogue states, back all U.S. threats and covert activities with force, and greatly increase the size of the military and its defense budget. He has consistently called for drastically more boots on the ground in every intervention of the past decade and is a firm believer in the Powell Doctrine of using overwhelming force. He thinks the United States should account for at least half of the world's defense spending, embrace its role as global cop, and try to squeeze out more support from its too-grudging allies.

To support this expansive foreign policy, McCain wants to narrow the gap between civilians and military, create more opportunities for civilians to join the struggle, and increase opportunities for immigrants to gain citizenship through war. He'll save money by vetoing bills laden with pork, create maneuvering room by further expanding the executive powers of the presidency, and use the bully pulpit to remind Americans that a life dedicated to merely private pursuits, instead of the national common good, is a life half-lived. It was a provocative vision in the happy and distracted late '90s, but will it play in the glum first decade of the new century?

One suspects the hand of beautiful fatalism has not yet finished its work. When McCain was asked by the *Wall Street Journal* in May 2007 to name his five favorite books about war, each one listed—including Gibbon's *The History of the Decline and Fall of the Roman Empire*, which McCain continues to reread—was about the side that lost. ("This peerless imperial power," McCain writes, "had a hand in its own decay, done in by decadence, corruption and war. The soldiers of Rome's legions could not make up for the negligence of their leaders.") The introduction to *Hard Call* begins with the story of his POW comrade Bud Day, who made a "hard call" while on the lam in Vietnam that ended in failure. "The proof," McCain writes, "isn't always in the pudding." And his favorite fatalistic war book of them all, *For Whom the Bell Tolls*, ends with the romantic hero, near-dead from injury, preparing to go out in a hail of gunfire. Life is indeed "worth the fighting for," he says, and then he dies.

In the six months between the hardcover publication of this book, in October 2007, and the deadline for this paperback edition afterword, John McCain went from dead meat to top dog in the Republican presidential primaries. Political scientists and campaign strategists will be scratching their heads for years to figure out exactly how this wisdom-rattling series of events went down (Mike Huckabee? *What*?), but preliminarily we can say one thing for certain:

John McCain won the Republican nomination because voters did not understand who they were voting for.

Sound extreme? Consider the following five points, in order:

1. *McCain effectively sewed up the nomination by January 29, when he beat Mitt Romney and Rudolph Giuliani in the Florida primary.* (Former front-runner Giuliani immediately dropped out and backed his "hero" from Arizona; chief rival Romney hung around another week, until Super Tuesday failed to reverse his fortunes.) Thus, McCain earned the top slot by winning the three early primaries of New Hampshire, South Carolina, and Florida.

2. *In not a single early primary or caucus did McCain win even a plurality of voters who described themselves to exit pollsters as "Republican."* That's a sentence worth re-reading. In early-state elections, MSNBC asked voters "do you usually think of

yourself" as either a "Republican," "Democrat," or "Independent or something else." New Hampshire and South Carolina, luckily for McCain, were open to non-Republicans; but even in the "closed" primary of Florida he didn't win the self-described GOP vote. Here's how the eventual Republican nominee fared among voters who usually think of themselves as belonging to the party he now heads. (The actual winner of the primary is in bold.)

IA:	**36% Huckabee**	12% McCain (behind two others)
NH:	35% Romney	**34% McCain**
MI:	**41% Romney**	27% McCain
SC:	32% Huckabee,	**31% McCain**
FL:	33% Romney	**33% McCain**

(Note: I could find no such polls for Wyoming, Nevada, and Louisiana.)

3. *Lacking Republican enthusiasm, McCain won the three early primaries due to overwhelming support from five overlapping groups of voters: independents, liberals, moderates, those who "strongly disapprove" of the Iraq war, and those who are "angry" at the Bush administration.* A table, with McCain's percentage totals in bold, the runners up in parenthesis, and Michigan added for flavor:

State	Independents	Liberals	Moderates	Anti-War	Anti-Bush
NH	**40** (27 MR)	**45** (16 RP)	**37** (23 RP)	**38** (26 RP)	**37** (27 RP)
SC	**42** (25 MH)	**47** (20 MH)	**51** (21 MH)	—·	**44** (22 RP)
FL	**44** (23 MR)	**49** (24 MR)	**43** (21 (MR)	—	**48** (18 RP)
MI	**35** (29 MR)	**30** (33 MR)	**40** (34 MR)	**35** (22 MR)	**39** (23 MR)

(Note: MR = Mitt Romney; MH = Mike Huckabee; RP = Ron Paul. In Michigan, where Democrats did not compete in the primary, there was a low-level campaign among liberals to vote for Romney in order to thwart McCain.)

4. *If there's one issue that unites independents, Democrats, anti-war voters, and Bush-haters, it's vehement opposition to the very Iraq War McCain plans on extending indefinitely.* According to a February

Gallup poll, 81 percent of Democrats and 61 percent of independents favored a specific timetable for withdrawal from Iraq, the opposite of McCain's stay-until-we-get-the-job-done strategy. Which, according to an April CBS/*New York Times* poll, only 35 percent of *all* Americans support any more. Just 34 percent from that second poll still say going into Iraq was the right thing to do (McCain's position); 62 percent said we should have stayed out. In March, Harris Interactive asked independents what they thought of McCain's concept of stationing troops in Iraq *a la* Korea, except twice as long, and 67 percent said they "disagreed," 42 percent "strongly."

How is it that the same people who most vociferously oppose McCain's Middle East strategy—the centerpiece of his presidential campaign—not only turn around and vote for him by margins of two to one over the Republican competition, but also remain in play for the general election? Aside from some nutty Nixon-in-China fantasia, in which a President McCain would somehow top off two years of never-surrender campaigning and a full decade of agitating for pre-emptive war by announcing upon inauguration that he's bringing our boys home, the best explanation is that (A) people give McCain an enormous benefit of the doubt; and (B) they do so largely in ignorance of just how radical his foreign policy would be.

On both of those counts, McCain's indie fans are encouraged and reinforced daily by a national press corps that, with sporadic exceptions, has done a laughably poor job of examining the candidate's foreign policy and interpreting his daily remarks on the hustings. Which brings us to:

5. *The media continues to misrepresent McCain as less interventionist than George W. Bush, which is a direct function of believing*

*that, no matter how much they disagree with him, his heart is still
in the right place.* Since this pathology has continued on long
past the March 14 Texas primary, when McCain wrapped up
the Republican nomination in deed, it's worth examining at
some length.

On March 26, in front of the Los Angeles World Affairs
Council, McCain delivered what his advisers had for days
been talking up to the press as a major foreign policy address
distancing himself from the deeply unpopular President Bush.
Though the political context didn't get much play in the next-
day coverage, the nominee was in a peculiar bind. To have any
chance at all in November he needed to retain his popularity among independents, moderate Democrats, and anti-war
types, even while advocating concrete policies that are a con-
tinuation of the same foreign policy that has made George
W. Bush so despised. The McCain camp had understood
for weeks that its biggest enduring irritant on this front was
the candidate's oft-repeated comment that the United States
could be in Iraq for "maybe 100" years.

McCain had to distance himself both from that comment—
which he had defended in scores of follow-ups with journalists, usually with a sense of bewilderment that anyone would
even *consider* the drawbacks of a permanent U.S. garrison in
Iraq if no casualties were being taken. At the same time, he
had to distance himself from the president's foreign policy,
even though on all substantive issues, save for Guantanamo
Bay and torture, McCain was either on the same page as
Bush (Iraq) or even more belligerent (Iran, Russia, China,
North Korea).

Sounds like a tough rhetorical nut to crack. How'd he do?

"An implicit rebuke to the mindset of the current White
House," raved the *Washington Post*'s David Broder, "dean" of

the national press corps, after the speech. "A vastly different approach from President Bush's . . . that might heal the wounds left here at home and abroad by the past seven years."[1]

National Greatness Conservative co-creator David Brooks, writing on the *New York Times* op-ed page (where, improbably, the *other* National Greatness Conservative co-creator, William Kristol, *also* has a regular column), sniffed that "Anybody who thinks McCain is merely continuing the Bush agenda is not paying attention."[2]

More telling than the easily won enthusiasms of Washington's chief establishmentarian and McCain's most reliable major-media supporter was how the speech was greeted on the nation's news pages. The *Washington Post* began its story like this: "Sen. John McCain on Wednesday promised a collaborative foreign policy that would seek the input of allies abroad and would contrast sharply with the go-it-alone approach of the Bush administration."[3]

Remarkably, that same article went on to blatantly contradict its own thesis by pointing out that McCain was "a vocal advocate for unilateral U.S. action in Kosovo and the Middle East," that he "would push to eject [Russia] from the Group of Eight club of industrial powers" while treating China as a "central challenge" to American ambitions, and that he has "hinted at an eagerness to take military action" against Iran. Despite all that, the article framed these definitionally go-it-alone approaches thusly:

McCain is often portrayed in the news media as a global John Wayne who would tread on the world stage with a Navy veteran's swagger and talk tough toward unfriendly governments in Iran and North Korea.

But his record on foreign policy during two decades in the Senate is more nuanced. . . .

Since becoming the presumptive Republican nominee, McCain has rarely used the language of the neoconservatives in Washington who pushed Bush to adopt a policy of preemptive strikes against foreign enemies.

Instead, McCain has sounded more like the foreign policy "realists" who advised Bush's father, President George H. W. Bush.[4]

Note the lack of citations on that "often portrayed" bit. And stow that "realists" line for later, because it will keep coming up as a buffer against charges of neoconservatism until Election Day and perhaps even beyond.

How did McCain prove to the journalistic world that his foreign policy marked a less interventionist, more multilateral departure from that of George W. Bush?

1. *He mouthed the magical three-syllable phrase: "I hate war."* As "only a man who has experienced its horrors can do," gushed Broder. It was due to such grave-sounding yet cheaply uttered pieties (which he also used to great effect in his March 1999 speech introducing his radical philosophy of "rogue-state rollback") that McCain was able to convince editorial boards nationwide that, in the words of the *Des Moines Register*, "He knows war, something we believe would make him reluctant to start one."[5]

Two weeks later, after the applause for McCain's alleged war-reluctance had died down, a young man at a Westport, Connecticut campaign stop asked the candidate: "If you're elected president, will you reject the Bush doctrine of pre-emptive war?" McCain replied: "I don't think you could make a blanket statement about pre-emptive war, because obviously, it depends on the threat that the United States of America faces." The quip was reported by the *Hartford Courant*, picked up by a blog or two, and then died.

2. *He said "the United States cannot lead by virtue of its power alone," and that "when we believe international action is necessary, whether military, economic, or diplomatic, we will try to persuade our friends that we are right. But we, in return, must be willing to be persuaded by them."*[6]

It's true: This is a rhetorical departure from the kind of to-hell-with-France rhetoric that marked, for example, the Republican National Convention in 2004. In speeches from people like, um, John McCain.

"Only the most deluded of us could doubt the necessity of this war," he snarled then. "And, as we've been a good friend to other countries in moments of shared perils, so we have good reason to expect their solidarity with us in this struggle. That is what the President believes. And, thanks to his efforts we have received valuable assistance from many good friends around the globe, even if we have, at times, been disappointed with the reactions of some."[7]

Those who think McCain will be open to persuasion by reluctant allies on matters as important as whether the U.S. should go to war should look up his record from 2007 ("Our partners must be good allies, too. . . . They must face the threats of our world squarely and not evade their global responsibilities. And they must put an end to the mindless anti-Americanism that today mars international discourse"[8]), 1999 ("I still fear that NATO's political leaders are interfering with General Clark's prosecution of the war"[9]), and basically every time he has supported a military action that Paris has opposed.

3. *He pushed for a new global "League of Democracies," a sort of United Nations without the nasties, where countries with shared values of freedom and democracy could coordinate interventions in places like Darfur and Burma unencumbered by the likes of China and Russia.* An intriguing idea, one that's been rattling around Beltway internationalist circles for more than a decade . . . and totally, utterly, dead on arrival. After eight years of a cranky, go-it-alone White House that won re-election in part by bashing limp-wristed Euro-weenies, the chances of another activist Republican winning enough good faith among grumbly allies to create a brand spanking new America-defined Club of Winners are something approaching zero.

4. *He advocated a "successor to the Kyoto Treaty, a cap-and-trade system that delivers the necessary environmental impact in an economically responsible manner."*[10] Which indeed would be an un-Bush-like way to play nice with the world. If, that is, such a thing would ever pass, let alone produce the intended effects.

Like many or even most of McCain's heart-in-the-right-place reforms, a big new cap-and-trade scheme would combine federal restrictions on private behavior with a regulatory scheme that has dubious prospects at best for success. Existing cap-and-trade markets in Europe, as even Europeans will admit, have not worked at all, partly (in the words of *Reason* magazine science correspondent Ronald Bailey) because "governments have every incentive to cheat" due to the fact that "the process is inherently political."[11] Don't take *Reason's* word for it? How about the tree-huggers at my prior place of work, the editorial board of the *L.A. Times*? Cap-and-trade, the *Times* editorialized in May of 2007, has too many "drawbacks" to be workable, and should be dropped in both California and Washington in favor of a carbon tax.[12]

Yet in a marvelous demonstration of how it's the thought, not the policy, that counts for too many journalists, that same editorial board just nine months later endorsed McCain in the Republican primary, in part because "he supported cap-and-trade systems that could reduce greenhouse gases, and he has stayed that course despite criticism from fellow Republicans."[13] In other words, he supported and defended a policy we know doesn't work, so he's our man!

McCain's newspaper endorsements—he was backed in the primaries by the *New York Times, Washington Post, Chicago Tribune, Boston Globe, Philadelphia Inquirer, Detroit News, Detroit Free Press, St. Louis Post-Dispatch, San Jose Mercury News, Sacramento Bee, Orlando Sentinel, Kansas City Star, Manchester Union Leader,* and *Concord Monitor,* among scores of others—were full of such contradictions. *The State* newspaper of Columbia, South Carolina said that the candidate "would never mislead or dishonor" the country, though McCain himself has serially confessed across multiple platforms that he has "lied" on the campaign trail[14] and occasionally made political decisions "to seek an advantage primarily or solely for myself" instead of the country.[15] Michigan's *Port Huron Times-Herald* uncorked this neat non-sequitur: "For much of his career, McCain has stood by what he believes, no matter how unpopular. He opposed GOP tax cuts in 2001 and 2003."[16] Right, but he also *supported* those same cuts just a few years later, when running for the nomination of a party for whom opposition to tax cuts are not just "unpopular," but a deal-breaker. The *Des Moines Register* praised McCain for "continu[ing] to support comprehensive immigration reform—while watching his poll standings plunge," months after he noisily dropped comprehensive reform because it was making his poll standings plunge.

Nowhere is that journalistic benefit of the doubt more apparent—or more important—than in the assessment of McCain's views on national security. There, in articles filled with evidence to the contrary, the nation's top journalists routinely portray the senator as a grizzled foreign policy eminence straddling the line between neoconservative hawks and the kind of cautious realists who surrounded the first George Bush presidency. In an April 10 piece titled "2 Camps Trying to Influence McCain on Foreign Policy," the *New York Times* gave each side nearly equal weight on a candidate who was not "fully formed," and who has that "reputation for departing from ideological orthodoxy."[17]

In the article itself, the only close McCain advisers quoted—chief speechwriter and confidant (and former aide to neo-conservative hero Jeanne Kirkpatrick) Mark Salter, foundational neo-conservative intellectual Fred Kagan, and McCain's principal foreign policy adviser, Committee for the Liberation of Iraq founder Randy Scheunemann—each said there wasn't really any struggle for McCain's soul, and that his international views were pretty set, thank you very much. The pragmatist/realist contingent amounted to a few people like Henry Kissinger and Brent Scowcroft who the candidate calls now and then. And as Scheunemann told the *New York Sun* in 2006, "I don't think, given where John has been for the last four or five years on the Iraq war and foreign policy issues, anyone would mistake Scowcroft for a close adviser."[18]

Still, the *Times* reporters stared hard enough to see patterns that aren't there. "Before the Iraq war," they wrote, "Mr. McCain generally opposed aggressive assertions of American power abroad."[19] With, of course, those pesky exceptions of Afghanistan, Kosovo, and Panama, not to mention all the countries he named as "rogue states" worth rolling back. To look at McCain's last decade of highly visible foreign policy prescriptions and see a "nuanced" or third way approach between idealists and realists (or "realistic idealists," in McCain's triangulatory phrasing), is an act of ignorance, wishful thinking or both.

You can see the wishful thinking part of the equation on full display in, paradoxically, the best article I have ever read about McCain's foreign policy, by *The New Republic*'s John Judis in October 2006. Moments before Judis laid out in painstaking reportorial detail how and when McCain's views on interventionism changed dramatically from cautious realist to full-throated neo-conservative during the course of the 1990s, he wrote this:

> And therein lies my McCain dilemma—and, perhaps, yours. If, like me, you believe that the war in Iraq has been an unmitigated disaster, then you are likely disturbed by McCain's early and continuing support for it—indeed, he advocates sending *more* troops to that strife-torn land—and by his advocacy of an approach to Iran that could lead to another fruitless war. At the same time, he has shown an admirable willingness to reevaluate his views when events have proved them wrong. The question, then, comes down to this: Is John McCain capable of changing his mind about a subject very close to his heart—again?[20]

Then, after hitting on many of the themes I spell out in further detail in this book—McCain's Vietnam healing at long last, his ensuing embrace of National Greatness Conservatism, his reassertion of the family business of benign imperialism— Judis's fond feelings for the senator still managed to get the best of his judgment:

"Part of McCain's attraction for me and other opponents of the Iraq war is that his hawkishness would give him the credibility to sell a diplomatic alternative to the imbroglio that Bush has created in the Middle East. Indeed, he is probably the best equipped of all the potential presidential candidates to extricate the United States from the ditch into which it has fallen. But doing so would require him to break substantially with his own recent history," he writes in closing. "It's true that little he said to me suggests he will adjust his worldview in the near future, but McCain has surprised his critics before. Perhaps he will do so again."[21]

A thin reed indeed, that "perhaps." And one whose sense of desperate faith absolutely requires considering John McCain to be a sober and searching analyst of the hardest call any president can make: whether or not to send his troops to war. Unfortunately for Judis and the dozens of newspaper editorial boards that endorsed McCain despite loathing the war, the former POW continues to show an almost shocking lack of curiosity about the biggest yeah-or-nays in U.S. history.

In August, McCain and Salter released their fifth book, *Hard Call*, ostensibly to examine and celebrate the most difficult decisions leaders and heroes have to make. Yet despite covering such commanders in chief as Abraham Lincoln, Winston Churchill, Ronald Reagan, and Harry Truman, and writing largely about the making and preparation of war, nowhere in the book is the should-he/shouldn't-he monumentalism of going to war explored. Not even by the 2008 presidential candidate himself, regarding a certain war in Iraq.

"Leave aside the question of whether we would have invaded had we known the true state of [Saddam Hussein's] weapons programs: some have argued we shouldn't have; others, myself included, argued that Saddam still posed a threat that was best to address sooner rather than later."[22] That's it.

McCain watchers have long presumed that the former POW's worldview was forever altered, or at least impacted for decades, by the experience of coming back home from Vietnam and catching up on his reading. A Rosetta stone of sorts for McCain's presumed foreign-policy development was the thesis paper he produced at the National War College in 1974, where he had had "the opportunity to study why and how my country had fought in Vietnam, questions I had become more than a little curious about."[23] As he put it in an introduction to a 2001 version of David Halberstam's Vietnam classic, *The Best and the Brightest*, "There I arranged sort of a private tutorial on the war, choosing all the texts myself, in the hope that I might better understand how we came to be involved in the war and why, after paying such a terrible cost, we lost."[24]

So what was this grand intellectual voyage? Nothing of the kind, it turns out. After the hardcover edition of this book went to press, I obtained a copy of the forty-page report through the Freedom of Information Act, and discovered it had *nothing whatsoever to do with why and how the U.S. fought and lost in Vietnam*. It's about the U.S. military's Code of Conduct governing prisoners of war. For years, McCain has let us believe that his allegedly nuanced foreign policy was nourished by a bracing reality check from 1973 to 1974. Instead, the voluminous printed record continues to show that the candidate doesn't actually care overmuch about whether presidents throughout history should have pulled the trigger on the nation's most controversial wars.

One last thought before I put this edition to bed. During the contested period of the Republican primaries, I would occasionally hear the complaint that I was protesting a bit too much about McCain's supposedly militaristic conception of citizenship, his distrust and occasional hostility toward private behavior and "profit," and his uncomfortably authoritarian tendency to tell Americans (among others) what they "must" do. I must confess that for a few weeks there, as he began sprinkling his speeches with rare-for-McCain testaments to the great things Americans can accomplish when left alone by their government, I almost experienced a little authorial doubt (mixed with patriotic relief!).

But then on April 2, with the nomination well wrapped up and Barack Obama fighting tooth and nail with Hillary Clinton, McCain once again doubled down on the Cause Greater, and re-declared his War on Cynicism:

> But even as we stand today, at the threshold of an age in which the genius of America will, I am confident, again be proven, . . . many Americans are indifferent to or cynical about the virtues that our country claims. In part, it is attributable to the dislocations economic change causes; to the experience of Americans who have, through no fault of their own, been left behind as others profit as they never have before. In part, it is in reaction to government's mistakes and incompetence, and to the selfishness of some public figures who seek to shine the luster of their public reputations at the expense of the public good. But for others, cynicism about our country, government, social and religious institutions seems not a reaction to occasions when they have been let down by these institutions, but because the ease which wealth and opportunity have given their lives led them to the mistaken conclusion that America, and the liberties its system of government is intended to protect, just aren't important to the quality of their lives. . . .
>
> When healthy skepticism sours into corrosive cynicism our expectations of our government become reduced to the delivery of services. And to some people the expectations of liberty are reduced to the right to choose among competing brands of designer coffee. . . .
>
> If you find faults with our country, make it a better one. If you are disappointed with the mistakes of government, join

its ranks and work to correct them. I hope more Americans would consider enlisting in our Armed Forces. I hope more would consider running for public office or working in federal, state and local governments. . . .

The good citizen and wise person pursues happiness that is greater than comfort, more sublime than pleasure. The cynical and indifferent know not what they miss. For their mistake is an impediment not only to our progress as a civilization but to their happiness as individuals.

As blessed as we are, no nation complacent in its greatness can long sustain it. We, too, must prove, as those who came before us proved, that a people free to act in their own interests, will perceive those interests in an enlightened way, will live as one nation, in a kinship of ideals, and make of our power and wealth a civilization for the ages, a civilization in which all people share in the promise and responsibilities of freedom.

Should we claim our rights and leave to others the duty to the ideals that protect them, whatever we gain for ourselves will be of little lasting value. It will build no monuments to virtue, claim no honored place in the memory of posterity, offer no worthy summons to the world. Success, wealth and celebrity gained and kept for private interest is a small thing. It makes us comfortable, eases the material hardships our children will bear, purchases a fleeting regard for our lives, yet not the self-respect that, in the end, matters most. But sacrifice for a cause greater than yourself, and you invest your life with the eminence of that cause, your self-respect assured.

You heard it right: Cynical Americans, according to our potential next president, are "an impediment not only to our progress as a civilization but to their happiness as individuals." Our "greatness" demands an urgent War on Complacency. Private success "is a small thing." And we should somehow all feel guilty and unfulfilled that there are more ways than ever to mix a coffee drink.

Get used to it, America, and don't say I didn't tell you so.

NOTES

PREFACE

1. Richard A. Stratton, a fellow prisoner in Hanoi, told Nicholas Kristof ("POW to Power Broker, a Chapter Most Telling," *New York Times*, Feb. 27, 2000) that McCain was talking about his presidential ambitions as early as the fall of 1970. "He's been thinking of this for a long time," Stratton told Kristof.

2. R. W. Apple, Jr., "McCain, Trying His Best Not to Look Back," *New York Times*, Aug. 31, 2004.

3. David Daley, "McCain is media's main man," *Hartford Courant*, Nov. 21, 1999.

4. On July 29, 1967, in the Gulf of Tonkin, an electrical power surge on the USS *Forrestal* accidentally set off a Zuni rocket, which slammed into the fuel tank of McCain's A-4 Skyhawk, igniting a fire that would kill more than 130 sailors. McCain, who was in the cockpit on impact, ejected, scrambled off the nose, rolled through the flames, and made it to safety.

5. Jon Birger, "McCain's Farm Flip," *Fortune*, Oct. 31, 2006. This article provides a thorough analysis of the issue.

6. The first bit of self-criticism occurs two paragraphs into *Faith of My Fathers: A Family Memoir* (New York: Harper, 1999): "I have spent much of my life choosing my own attitude, often carelessly, often for no better reason than to indulge a conceit." Same with *Worth the Fighting For: The Education of an American Maverick, and the Heroes Who Inspired Him* (New York: Random House, 2002): "Perhaps some of us come to believe that the country cannot part with us." He's more restrained in *Why Courage Matters: The Way to a Braver Life* (New York: Random House, 2004), but then gets right back on the horse in paragraph five of *Character Is Destiny: Inspiring Stories Every Young Person Should Know and Every Adult Should* Remember (New York: Random House, 2005): "Were I to use my own character as an example of how to build yours, I would lack one of the most important qualities of good character—honesty."

7. Peter Canellos, "McCain Makes Use of Mentoring Experience With Dole," *Boston Globe*, June 12, 2007.

8. Teddy Davis, "McCain Woos the Right, Makes Peace With Falwell," ABCnews.com, Mar. 28, 2006.

9. "The Real McCain," April 30, 2006.

10. "The McCain Insurrection," Feb. 19, 2006.

11. Bill Kristol's Feb. 2, 2000, *Washington Post* op-ed ("The New Hampshire Upheaval") is a classic of the genre. "Leaderless, rudderless and issueless, the conservative movement, which accomplished great things over the past quarter-century, is finished," he wrote. "The screams of anguish emanating from K Street and from the Heritage Foundation are evidence that it's a new moment for the Republican Party." Brooks countered in *Newsweek* ("The Battle in the Mosh Pit," Feb. 7, 2000) that the Christian Coalition is "in shambles."

12. Charles P. Pierce, "John McCain Walks on Water," *Esquire*, May 1, 1998.

13. "The Upside of Anger," *Newsweek*, May 23, 2007.

14. David Grann, "The Hero Myth," *The New Republic*, May 24, 1999.

15. Howard Kurtz, "A Running Start? Sen. John McCain, the Media's Man of the Hour," *Washington Post*, June 8, 1998.

16. "Swoon Song," Oct. 18, 1999.

17. *John McCain: An American Odyssey* (New York: Touchstone Books, 1999).

18. While not common knowledge among voters, these matters are commonly acknowledged by the senator himself.

19. Timberg, who tends to give McCain the benefit of the doubt, characterized McCain's role in the carrier shenanigans as "not all that small, and not all that defensible." Oliver North later used McCain's actions as a defense for his behavior in the Iran-Contra scandal.

20. On the comprehensive immigration reform package, McCain insisted that illegal immigrants obtaining a proposed Z-visa would have to pay "back taxes," even though the amendment McCain himself introduced on this issue only required payment of taxes from the date of the visa's issuance, not from the date of illegal entry. On Iraq, McCain has insisted he was never unduly optimistic about U.S. success there, despite a paper trail of statements indicating otherwise.

21. Tucker Carlson, "On the Road," *Weekly Standard*, March 27, 2000.

22. Todd Purdum, "Prisoner of Conscience," *Vanity Fair*, February 2007. A highly recommended profile of McCain.

23. John McCain, at a press conference, Los Angeles, Calif., June 2007.

24. *Man of the People: The Life of John McCain* (San Francisco: John Wiley & Sons, 2002).

25. Author interview with Don Hesselbrock.

26. Macy Hanson, "Straight Talk Is Cheap," *Reason* Online, July 20, 2006.

27. Edward T. Pound, "Straight Talk and Cold Cash," *U.S. News & World Report*, May 20, 2007.

28. The honor code instructs prisoners of war to provide only name, rank and serial number; and engage in active resistance, including attempting escape whenever reasonably possible. It also, however, provides leeway in cases of extreme duress and severe health issues, both of which certainly applied to McCain.

29. McCain and Salter, *Worth the Fighting For*, chapter 1.

30. Cindy McCain, *This Week*, ABC, Oct. 24, 1999.

31. Cindy McCain, appearing on *Dateline NBC*, Oct. 10, 1999.

32. Elizabeth Drew, *Citizen McCain* (New York: Simon & Schuster, 2002), 47.

33. John McCain, at a press conference, Jan. 2000.

34. Matt Welch, "Be Afraid of President McCain," *Reason*, April 2007.

35. See: http://www.clubforgrowth.org/2007/03/arizona_senator_john_mccains_t.php

36. "Confrontation in the Gulf," *New York Times*, Aug. 19, 1990.

37. Adam C. Smith, "Good for McCain that ideas matter," *St. Petersburg Times*, April 8, 2007.

38. His 19-year-old son Jimmy, a Marine, is already there; 21-year-old John S. McCain IV is continuing the family tradition at the Naval Academy.

39. John McCain, "How the POWs Fought Back," *U.S. News & World Report*, May 14, 1973.

40. The most celebrated example was probably David Ifshin, who McCain befriended, forgave and defended against Republican critics in the 1990s.

41. McCain and Salter, *Worth the Fighting For*, xviii.

42. Brian C. Anderson, *South Park Conservatives: The Revolt Against Liberal Media Bias* (Washington, DC: Regnery Publishing, Inc, 2005).

CHAPTER 1

1. From the Larry Mantle collection, *This Is Air Talk*.

2. Review of *For Whom the Bell Tolls*, June 14, 2001.

3. Dan Nowicki, *Arizona Republic*, "McCain Contends With Vocal Critics From Own State, From Own Party," Jan. 21, 2007. According to the article, Hunter received 96 of 458 ballots cast at the Jan. 13 meeting of the Maricopa County GOP, Mitt Romney received 82 votes, Newt Gingrich 53 and McCain 50.

4. Rudolph Giuliani, appearing on *Larry King Live*, Feb. 28, 2000.

5. *Financial Times*, "Lunch With the FT: Tina Brown," July 7, 2007.

6. John McCain, appearing on *The O'Reilly Factor*, May 31, 2007.

7. Aside from those mentioned in the rest of this chapter, a partial list would include: Army Gen. Billy Mitchell; Democratic Arizona Congressman Mo Udall; baseball great Ted Williams; Vietnam hero Sgt. Roy Benavidez; Alabama football coach Bear Bryant; Eleanor Roosevelt; Martin Luther King Jr.; Hungarian Jewish poet-warrior-martyr Hannah Senesh; Auschwitz survivor and psychologist Viktor Frankl; Gandhi; pro-football player and victim of U.S. Army friendly fire Pat Tillman; Winston Churchill; writer Eric Hoffer; Tecumseh; Charles Darwin; dozens of comrades he served with in Vietnam; and many more.

8. John McCain, appearing on Larry Mantle's *Air Talk*, KPCC-FM Los Angeles, Nov. 8, 2002.

9. John McCain, "War Stories: On Memorial Day, Keep in Mind These Books About Soldiers in Battle," *Wall Street Journal*, OpinionJournal. com, May 26, 2007. *For Whom the Bell Tolls* comes in first place, followed by Edward Gibbon's *The History of the Decline and Fall of the Roman Empire*, T.R. Fehrenbach's *This Kind of War*, Bernard B. Fall's *Hell in a Very Small Place*, and Erich Maria Remarque's *All Quiet on the Western Front*.

10. "Inspiration for Life as Public Servant," *Arizona Daily Star*, Oct. 13, 2002.

11. E. B. Potter, *Bull Halsey* (Annapolis, MD: US Naval Institute Press, 2003).

12. John McCain and Mark Salter, *Faith of My Fathers: A Family Memoir* (New York: Harper, 1999), chapter 2.

13. On the USS *Connecticut*, under the command of Rear Adm. Hugo Osterhaus (who, coincidentally, was the author's great-great grandfather).

14. Alton Keith Gilbert, *A Leader Born: The Life of Admiral John Sidney McCain, Pacific Carrier Commander* (Drexel Hill, PA: Casemate, 2006), 2.

15. Ibid., 29–37. In a November 1934 letter to the editor in the *Washington Post*, Slew wrote, "People will gamble. They always have gambled. They always will. They will wager honestly and lawfully in the light of day, or with cheats in dark places." His words are especially ironic given his grandson's efforts to ban gambling on college sports.

16. He rose to rank of Commander in Chief, Pacific Command (CINCPAC), from which he prosecuted the Vietnam War.

17. Karaagac's book-length study (Lanham, MD: Lexington Books, 2000), generates all of one response in a Lexis search and thirteen on Google. Yet it's a valuable companion piece to Robert Timberg's *John*

McCain: An American Odyssey (New York: Touchstone Books, 1999), providing interesting context and analysis of the military traditions and influences on McCain's life.

18. John McCain and Mark Salter, *Worth the Fighting For: A Memoir* (New York: Random House, 2002), xxi–xxvi.

19. George Packer, the *New Yorker*'s influential foreign policy journalist and critic, wrote in the magazine's Oct. 31, 2005 issue ("The Spanish Prisoner: When Hemingway and Dos Passos Went to War") that "because he was better cut out for Spain and politics than either Hemingway or [John] Dos Passos, Orwell kept his bearings, neither turning the war into a stage for his own psychodrama nor wilting under the pressure of ambiguous reality. Almost seventy years after its publication, his 'Homage to Catalonia' holds up against all the recent revelations and controversies about the Spanish Civil War."

20. "Five Best—On Memorial Day, Keep in Mind These Books About Soldiers in Wartime, says Sen. John McCain," May 26, 2007.

21. John McCain, appearing on Dick Gordon's, *The Connection*, WBUR Boston, July 27, 2005.

22. Sept. 28, 2002.

23. "Race Against Himself," March 13, 2000.

24. McCain and Salter, *Faith of My Fathers*, chapter 2.

25. John McCain, appearing on Dick Gordon's, *The Connection*, WBUR Boston, July 27, 2005.

26. September 24, 2002; October 12, 2002; November 3, 2005; and May 24, 2006.

27. The third paragraph in Roosevelt's series marveled, about the Caucasian race thusly: "There have been many other races that at one time or another had their great periods of race expansion—as distinguished from mere conquest—but there has never been another whose expansion has been either so broad or so rapid."

28. He returned from Vietnam a fervent believer in the domino theory, but somewhere along the line changed his mind, without ever (to my knowledge) discussing the implications of discovering that the basis of the U.S. foreign policy he fought for was untrue.

29. John McCain and Mark Salter, *Worth the Fighting For*, chapter 5.5 (it's an interlude between 5 and 6).

CHAPTER 2

1. John McCain and Mark Salter, *Worth the Fighting For: The Education of an American Maverick, and the Heroes Who Inspired Him* (New York, Random House, 2002).

2. Robert Timberg, *John McCain: An American Odyssey* (New York: Touchstone Books, 1999).
3. Kristol repeatedly praised McCain in 1999 for holding principle above politics in the Kosovo affair, then spent the rest of the year talking about how McCain's Kosovo experience demonstrated presidential leadership.
4. "The John Gibson Radio Show," *Fox Radio*, July 10, 2007.
5. Jack once said of Slew, "I knew him as well as anybody in the world, with the possible exception of my mother." John, on the other hand, has said of Jack: "My father could often be a distant, inscrutable patriarch."
6. John McCain and Mark Salter, *Faith of My Fathers: A Family Memoir* (New York: Harper, 1999).
7. Ibid.
8. Paul Alexander, *Man of the People: The Life of John McCain* (Hoboken, NJ: John Wiley, 2002).
9. McCain and Salter, *Faith of My Fathers*.
10. Ibid.
11. Gregory A. Freeman, *Sailors to the End* (New York: William Morrow, 2002).
12. Somewhere during that period, McCain says he attempted suicide. In *Faith of My Fathers*, he said it was just before confessing; to Timberg, he said it came afterward, during the despair. When writing about his experiences in May 1973 for *U.S. News & World Report*, McCain said he was at "the point" of suicide, just before confession.
13. McCain and Salter, *Faith of My Fathers*.
14. *The Nightingale's Song*, chapter 13.
15. *The Nightingale's Song*, chapter 7.

CHAPTER 3

1. San Francisco: John Wiley & Sons, 2002.
2. Author interview with Lyle Tuttle.
3. "Villa Shanel Name Play on Wife's Love of Haute Couture Line," *National Post*, July 2, 2005.
4. David D. Kirkpatrick and Michael Cooper, "By Taking On the Biggest Donors, McCain Is Taking a Big Risk, Too," June 18, 2007.
5. Matt Stearns, "John McCain Is Down, Not Out," McClatchy News Service, July 14, 2007.
6. Liz Sidoti, "Analysis: McCain's Option Is Rebel Roots," the Associated Press, July 11, 2007.
7. David D. Kirkpatrick and Michael Cooper, "McCain Call Raises an Ethics Question," *New York Times*, July 12, 2007.

8. *The Nightingale's Song*, chapter 27.
9. Ibid.
10. "Race to the Finish," *New York Times Magazine*, July 29, 2007.
11. John McCain and Mark Salter, *Worth the Fighting For: The Education of an American Maverick, and the Heroes Who Inspired Him* (New York: Random House, 2002), chapter 3.
12. Bill Muller, "The Life Story of Arizona's Maverick Senator; McCain," *Arizona Republic*, Oct. 3, 1999.
13. McCain and Salter, *Faith of My Fathers*, chapter 6.
14. McCain and Salter, *Worth the Fighting For*, chapter 2.
15. Ibid. chapter 2.
16. Paul Alexander, *Man of the People: The Life of John McCain* (Hoboken, NJ: John Wiley, 2002), chapter 4.
17. Timberg, chapter 11.
18. Alexander, chapter 4.
19. Nicholas Kristof, "P.O.W. to Power Broker, A Chapter Most Telling," *New York Times*, Feb. 27, 2000. This is the best piece of journalism I've seen covering McCain's post-Vietnam, pre-political career period.
20. John Karaagac, *John McCain: An Essay in Military and Political History* (Lanham, MD: Lexington Books, 2000), chapter 7.
21. Alexander, chapter 5.
22. Timberg, chapter 12.
23. Ibid.
24. John Judis, "Neo-McCain: The Making of an Uberhawk," *The New Republic*, Nov. 9, 2006.
25. "McCain Finds It Hard to Mind His Manners," *Arizona Republic*, August 3, 2000.
26. Michael Lewis, *The New Republic*, March 25, 1996.
27. May 25, 1997.
28. Nov. 21, 1999.
29. Amy Silverman, "The Pampered Politician," *Phoenix New Times*, May 15, 1997.
30. *Hartford Courant*, "McCain Is Media's Man Man," Nov. 21, 1999.

CHAPTER 4

1. John McCain and Mark Salter, *Worth the Fighting For: The Education of an American Maverick, and the Heroes Who Inspired Him* (New York: Random House, 2002), chapter 8.
2. "Out of the Fire, Politics Calls; Ex-POW Turns Washington Insider," March 2, 2000. Eisenhower declined to be interviewed, and almost never talks to the press.

3. John McCain, letter to Barry Goldwater, Sept. 8, 1982. Goldwater Archive, Arizona State University.
4. *McCain and Salter*, chapter 1.
5. *U.S. News & World Report*, Dec. 31, 1973.
6. *McCain and Salter*, "A Happier Life in Every Way."
7. "Conservative-Bashed Bush Salutes 'Mr. Conservative,'" United Press International, May 29, 1992.
8. "Barry Goldwater's Left Turn," July 28, 1994.

CHAPTER 5

1. John McCain, appearing on *Good Morning America*, March 24, 2000.
2. "Fox News Sunday."
3. CNN interview, May 12, 2000.
4. "'Recovering' McCain Resumes Crusade; Former Candidate Expanding His Senate Agenda," *Washington Post*, May 28, 2000.
5. "P.O.W. to Power Broker, A Chapter Most Telling," Feb. 27, 2000.
6. John McCain and Mark Salter, *Worth the Fighting For: The Education of an American Maverick, and the Heroes Who Inspired Him* (New York: Random House, 2002), chapter 8.
7. Amy Silverman,' "The Pampered Politician," *Phoenix New Times*, May 14, 1997.
8. Karen Tumulty, "John McCain, Maverick No More," *Time*, July 23, 2007.
9. During my first week of research for this book, a McCain campaign spokesman told me, off the record, that he'd be "crazy" to let me interview the candidate, after the critical things I had written about him in *Reason* magazine.
10. Michael Lewis, "The Subversive," *New York Times Magazine*, May 25, 1997.
11. John McCain and Mark Salter, *Faith of My Fathers: A Family Memoir* (New York: Harper, 1999), chapter 6.
12. John McCain and Mark Salter, *Why Courage Matters: The Way to a Braver Life* (New York: Random House, 2004), 69.
13. Bill Keller, "Who's Sorry Now?" *New York Times*, Dec. 28, 2002.
14. Bill Adair, "The Making of John McCain," *St. Petersburg Times*, Sept. 26, 1999.
15. "Three Generations of McCains in a Single Volume," *The Hill*, Sept. 15, 1999.
16. David Brooks, "One Nation Conservatism," *The Weekly Standard*, Sept. 13, 1999.
17. "A Happier Life in Every Way."
18. McCain and Salter, *Worth the Fighting For*, chapter 12.

CHAPTER 6

1. John McCain, appearing on *This Week With George Stephanopoulos*, ABC-TV, June 10, 2007.
2. John McCain, declaration of candidacy, Sept. 27, 1999.
3. Mitch McConnell, appearing on *The News Hour With Jim Lehrer*, PBS
4. John McCain and Mark Salter, *Worth the Fighting For: The Education of an American Maverick, and the Heroes Who Inspired Him* (New York: Random House, 2002), chapter 6.
5. R. W. Apple, Jr., "National Role Is Seen For Arizona Nominee," *New York Times*, Nov. 2, 1986.
6. Robert Timberg, *John McCain: An American Odyssey* (New York: Touchstone Books, 1999), chapter 16.
7. John Karaagac, *John McCain: An Essay in Military and Political History* (Lanham, MD: Lexington Books, 2000), chapter 9.
8. Susan F. Rasky, "To Senator McCain, the Savings and Loan Affair Is Now a Personal Demon," *New York Times*, Dec. 22, 1989.
9. Paul Alexander, *Man of the People, The Life of John McCain* (Hoboken, NJ: John Wiley, 2002), chapter 6.
10. David Weigel, "More Money, No Problem," *Reason* magazine, May 2007.
11. "Freedom of Speech Now Illegal," *The American Spectator*, February 2004.
12. George F. Will, "Setback for the Censors," *Washington Post*, June 28, 2007.
13. Bradley Smith, "Campaign Finance Reform's War on Political Freedom," *City Journal*, July 2007.
14. "John McCain's War on Political Speech," *Reason* magazine, December 2005.
15. Connie Bruck, "McCain's Party," *New Yorker*, May 30, 2005.
16. John McCain, interview, ESPN.com, Jan. 18, 2005.
17. Michael Lewis, *The New Republic*, Nov. 25, 1996.
18. "McCain Allies Seek Reform And the Money to Get It," *New York Times*, March 8, 2005.
19. Edward T. Pound, "Straight Talk and Cold Cash," *U.S. News & World Report*, May 28, 2007.
20. "Ex-Reformer McCain Depends on Lobbyists," Politico.com, July 11, 2007.
21. "McCain Call Raises an Ethics Question," *New York Times*, July 12, 2007.

CHAPTER 7

1. "Mrs. McCain Is Speaking Up in a Steely Tone," *New York Times*, June 29, 2007.
2. John McCain and Mark Salter, *Faith of My Fathers: A Family Memoir* (New York: Harper, 1999), chapter 9.
3. "Top Aides Leave McCain Camp," *Washington Post*, July 11, 2007; "McCain Campaign Drops Top Aides; New Doubts Rise," *New York Times*, July 11, 2007.
4. "McCain Strategy: Gain Power Early," *Arizona Republic*, May 20, 1999.
5. Amy Silverman, "Don't Cross John McCain," *Playboy*, February 2000.
6. John Dickerson, "The McCain Mutiny," *Slate*, July 10, 2007.
7. "John McCain: In Search of the Old Magic," *The Economist*, May 31, 2007.
8. For example, "McCain's Temper Back on Campaign's Front-Burner," *Los Angeles Times*, May 21, 2007.
9. "Dousing Senator Hothead," *Arizona Republic*, Nov. 7, 1999.
10. "'F*** You': The Inside Story," Powerline.com, May 20, 2007.
11. "McCain Turns Focus to His Fundraising," *Washington Post*, May 23, 2007.
12. "Senator Hothead," *The Washingtonian*, February 1997.
13. "War Profiteering," *U.S. News & World Report*, May 13, 2002.
14. Spartacus, *"Mr. Smith Is Dead."*
15. Howard Kurtz, "McCain, Rising up Against 'Spartacus,'" *Washington Post*, May 13, 2002.
16. "The Politics of Personality Destruction," *New York Magazine*, June 11, 2007.
17. "Senator Hothead," *The Washingtonian*, February 1997.
18. "In This Corner . . . ," *Time*, Nov. 15, 1999.
19. Fred Barnes, "McCain and the Conservatives," *Weekly Standard*, April 9, 2007.
20. "Senator Hothead," *The Washingtonian*, February 1997.
21. "The Life Story of Arizona's Maverick Senator John McCain," *Arizona Republic*, Oct. 3, 1999.
22. Robert Timberg, *John McCain: An American Odyssey* (New York: Touchstone Books, 1999), chapter 16.
23. John McCain and Mark Salter, *Worth the Fighting For: The Education of an American Maverick, and the Heroes Who Inspired Him* (New York: Random House, 2002), chapter 8.
24. "Dousing Senator Hothead," Nov. 7, 1999.

25. Amy Silverman, "Opiate for the Mrs.," *Phoenix New Times*, Sept. 8, 1994.

26. "In Arizona, McCain's Tactics Seen as Power Plays," *Boston Globe*, Dec. 13, 1999.

27. Pat Murphy, "Free Ride," *In These Times*, March 6, 2000.

28. David Gann, "The Hero Myth," *The New Republic*, May 24, 1999.

29. "McCain Minimizes Heated Exchange with Cornyn," *Houston Chronicle*, May 23, 2007.

30. "Despite His Maverick Appeal, McCain's Home Base May Need Bracing," *Los Angeles Times*, Nov. 23, 1999.

31. McCain and Salter, *Worth the Fighting For*, chapter 3.

32. Ibid., chapter 11.

CHAPTER 8

1. John McCain, speech at the annual Alistair Cooke Memorial Lecture, BBC, July 4, 2005.

2. Sydney Schanberg, "The War Secrets John McCain Hides." APBNews.com, April 25, 2000.

3. Robert Timberg, *John McCain: An American Odyssey* (New York: Touchstone Books, 1999), chapter 11.

4. John Karaagac, *John McCain: An Essay in Military and Political History* (Lanham, MD: Lexington Books, 2000).

5. John McCain, interview with Terry Gross, *Fresh Air*, NPR, Sept. 12, 2000.

6. John McCain, interview with Wolf Blitzer, CNN, May 29, 2005.

7. Michael Lewis, "Surrogates," *The New Republic*, May 13, 1996.

8. "Friends, 12-Steppers, Freshman," *Time*, May 13, 1996.

9. "A Strong Bond Through Simple Gestures," *National Journal*, June 6, 1998.

10. John McCain and Mark Salter, *Worth the Fighting For: The Education of an American Maverick, and the Heroes Who Inspired Him* (New York: Random House, 2002), chapter 9.

CHAPTER 9

1. John McCain and Mark Salter, *Worth the Fighting For: The Education of an American Maverick, and the Heroes Who Inspired Him* (New York: Random House, 2002), The "A Happier Life in Every Way" chapter.

2. Jim Powell, *Bully Boy: The Truth About Theodore Roosevelt's Legacy* (New York: Random House, 2006), chapter 1.

3. William Kristol and David Brooks, "What Ails the Right," *Wall Street Journal*, Sept. 15, 1997.
4. Virginia Postrel and James Glassman, "'National Greatness' or Conservative Malaise?" *Wall Street Journal*.
5. Robert Novak, *Meet the Press*, Sept. 28, 1997.
6. Laura Ingraham and Stephen Vaughn, "Is it Time to Redefine Conservatism?" *Washington Times*, Sept. 26, 1997.
7. E.J. Dionne, "Can GOP Govern if it Doesn't Believe in Government?" *Washington Post*, Sept. 18, 1997.
8. Jacob Weisberg, "Con Air," *Slate*, Oct. 26, 1997.
9. Garry Wills, "Get This: A Pro-Government GOP," *The Times Union*, Oct. 16, 1997.
10. Adam Wolfson, "How to Think About Humanitarian War," *Commentary*, July 2000.
11. John Judis, "Neo-McCain," *The New Republic*, Nov. 9, 2006.
12. John Judis, "Great Escape," *The New Republic*, May 28, 2001.
13. John McCain and Mark Salter, *Character Is Destiny: Inspiring Stories Every Young Person Should Know and Every Adult Should Remember* (New York: Random House, 2005), chapter 31.
14. Powell, *Bully Boy*, chapter 2.
15. Theodore R. Roosevelt, *The Winning of the West* (New York: G.P. Putnam's Sons, 4 Vols. 1896), chapter 1.
16. John McCain, "Putting the 'National' in National Service," *Washington Monthly*, October 2001.
17. McCain and Salter, *Faith of My Fathers: A Family Memoir* (New York: Harper, 1999), chapter 8.
18. "The New Hampshire Upheaval," *Washington Post*, Feb. 2, 2000.
19. David Brooks, "Playing It Safe Works for Now," *New York Times*, Feb. 21, 2000.
20. Editorial, *National Review*, March 3, 2000.
21. "TR and his Fan," Feb. 7, 2000.
22. Franklin Foer, "Arguing the GOP," *The New Republic*, March 20, 2000.
23. Franklin Foer, "Great Escape," *The New Republic*, May 28, 2001.
24. Jonah Goldberg, "Grading Greatness," *National Review*, May 21, 2001.

CHAPTER 10

1. "Vietnam War Leaves Legacy of Anguish," *Los Angeles Times*, April 28, 1985.
2. John McCain, appearing on *Meet the Press*, May 13, 2007.
3. John McCain, appearing on *Larry King Live*, May 24, 2006.

4. John McCain, appearing on *This Week With David Brinkley*, June 12, 1994.

5. John McCain and Bob Dole, "Rescue Darfur Now," *Washington Post*, Sept. 10, 2006.

6. "The Unvarnished Man," *Business Week*, June 4, 2007.

7. Ibid.

8. "Shultz: Latin Role Linked to Viet 'Lesson,' U.S. Leadership," *Los Angeles Times*, April 26, 1985.

9. *Arizona Republic*, June 21, 1987.

10. *USA Today*, December 21, 1989.

11. John McCain, appearing on *Larry King Live*, August 27, 1990.

12. "Standoff Looms as Estimate of War Cost Rises," *Boston Globe*, Sept. 23, 1990.

13. "The Man Who Would Be King," *U.S. News & World Report*, Aug. 13, 1990.

14. "Senate Threatens Relations With Nations Not Supporting Mideast Effort," Associated Press, Sept. 10, 2000.

15. John Judis, "Neo-McCain," *The New Republic*, Nov. 9, 2006.

16. John McCain, speech given at Kansas State University, March 15, 1999.

17. John McCain, appearing on *Nightline*, ABC, March 30, 1993.

18. Gregg Easterbrook, "A Conservative with Quirks; Poised for two Ground Campaigns," *Los Angeles Times*, April 11, 1999.

19. Charles Lane, "Swoon Song," *The New Republic*, Oct. 18, 1999.

20. John McCain, speech given at the Center for Strategic and International Studies, April 13, 1999.

21. "The Trillion-Dollar Defense Budget Is Already Here," *The Independent Institute*, March 15, 2007.

22. John McCain, "Putting the 'National' in National Service," *Washington Monthly*, October, 2001.

23. "Do the Nation a Service," *Newsweek*, Sept. 15, 2003.

24. John McCain, *Washington Monthly*.

25. John McCain, speech given at the Concord, NH, Chamber of Commerce, July 13, 2007.

26. *Arizona Daily Star*, Aug. 28, 2005.

27. Howard Fineman, "McCain and the Upside of Anger," May 23, 2007.

CHAPTER 11

1. Tucker Carlson, "On the Road," *Weekly Standard*, March 27, 2000.

2. John McCain, appearing on *Meet the Press*, June 19, 2005.

3. The Associated Press, "McCain Says Resentment Remains Over 2000 Race," Aug. 15, 2006.
4. John McCain, appearing on *Meet the Press*, Nov. 12, 2006.
5. "McCain's Farm Flip," *Fortune*, Oct. 31, 2006.
6. "Prisoner of Conscience," *Vanity Fair*, February 2007.
7. John McCain, appearing on *Hardball*, MSNBC, Oct. 18, 2006.
8. John McCain, appearing on *This Week*, ABC, Nov. 19, 2006.
9. "Weighing a Marriage Amendment," March 28, 2006.
10. "Final McCain Notes: Lightening Round," Politico.com, March 19, 2007.
11. "McCain Stumbles on HIV Prevention," *New York Times*, March 16, 2007.
12. "McCain Gets Boost From Bush's Troubles," *San Francisco Chronicle*, Aug. 20, 1999.
13. Patrick Hynes, "McCain: Pro-life. Period," Dec. 5, 2006.
14. "McCain Faulted on 'Roe' Remarks; Critics See Weakening Of Anti-abortion Stance," *New York Times*, Aug. 24, 1999.
15. John McCain, appearing on *Meet the Press*, Jan. 30, 2000.
16. John McCain, speech given at the Progressive Policy Institute, May 18, 2004.
17. Howard Kurtz, "Journalists and John McCain: Is The Honeymoon Really Over?" *Washington Post*, April 26, 2007.
18. David Broder, "Straight Talking Again," *Washington Post*, April 27, 2007.
19. William Schneider, CNN, July 3, 2007.

EPILOGUE

1. John McCain and Mark Salter, *Hard Call: Great Decisions and the Extraordinary People Who Made Them* (New York: Twelve, 2007), introduction.
2. David Brooks, "The Fatalist," *New York Times*, April 12, 2007.
3. Matt Welch, "Do We Need Another T.R.?" *Los Angeles Times*, Nov. 26, 2006.
4. "B.T.," "Guess John McCain Won't Be Getting That L.A. Times Endorsement," AnkleBitingPundits.com, Nov. 27, 2006.
5. "McCain as TR," Nov. 26, 2006.
6. Tucker Carlson, "On the Road," *Weekly Standard*, March 27, 2000.
7. Matt Welch, "Be Afraid of President McCain," *Reason*, April 2007.
8. "Letters to the Editor," *Reason*, June 2007.
9. "The Life Story of Arizona's Maverick Senator McCain," *Arizona Republic*, Oct. 3, 1999.

10. John McCain and Mark Salter, *Worth the Fighting For: The Education of an American Maverick, and the Heroes Who Inspired Him* (New York: Random House, 2002), chapter 12.

11. May 13, 2007.

12. Paul Alexander, *Man of the People: The life of John McCain* (Hoboken, NJ: John Wiley, 2002), chapter 8.

AFTERWORD

1. "McCain's Manifesto," *Washington Post*, March 30, 2008.

2. David Brooks, "Tested Over Time," *New York Times*, March 28, 2008.

3. Michael D. Shear, "McCain Outlines Foreign Policy: In Speech, He Vows Collaborative Approach," *Washington Post*, March 26, 2008.

4. Ibid.

5. Des Moines Register Editorial Board, "Republican Editorial Endorsement: Why McCain," *Des Moines Register*, Dec. 15, 2007.

6. John McCain, speech given at the Los Angeles World Affairs Council, March 26, 2008.

7. John McCain, speech given at the Republican National Convention, Aug. 30, 2004.

8. John McCain, speech given at the Hoover Institution, May 1, 2007.

9. John McCain, speech given at the U.S. Senate, April 20, 1999.

10. John McCain, speech given at the Los Angeles World Affairs Council, March 26, 2008.

11. Ronald Bailey, "Carbon Taxes Versus Carbon Markets: What's the Best Way to Limit Emissions?" *Reason Online*, May 24, 2007.

12. "Time to Tax Carbon," *Los Angeles Times*, May 28, 2007.

13. "John McCain for GOP Nominee," *Los Angeles Times*, Feb. 3, 2008.

14. "I had not pledged to tell a lie only if it was apparent I really would have preferred not to," he wrote in *Worth the Fighting For*, about his Confederate Flag dodge. "I had promised to tell the truth no matter what. When I broke it, I had not been just dishonest. I had been a coward, and I had served my own interests from my country's. That was what made the lie unforgivable." John McCain and Mark Salter, *Worth the Fighting For: The Education of an American Maverick, and the Heroes Who Inspired Him* (New York: Random House, 2002), p. 386.

15. John McCain and Mark Salter, *Hard Call* (New York: Twelve, 2007) p. 424.

16. "McCain has earned chance to lead nation: Senator outshines rest of GOP field," *Port Huron Times-Herald*, Jan. 13, 2008.

17. Elisabeth Bumiller and Larry Rohter, "2 Camps Trying to Influence McCain on Foreign Policy," *New York Times*, April 10, 2008.

18. Josh Gerstein, "McCain Signals Distance From Bush, Neocons,"
    New York Sun, Aug. 23, 2006.
19. Bumiller and Rohter, "2 Camps Trying to Influence McCain on For-
    eign Policy," *New York Times*, April 10, 2008.
20. John Judis, "Neo-McCain," *The New Republic*, Oct. 9, 2006.
21. Ibid.
22. McCain and Salter, *Hard Call*, p. 6.
23. McCain and Salter, *Worth the Fighting For*, p. 11.
24. David Halberstam, *The Best and Brightest* (New York: Modern Library,
    2001), p. x.

INDEX

60 Minutes, 196
2007–8 Republican presidential primary elections, 205–6, 208, 213, 217

abortion, 181–82
Albright, Madeleine, 163, 166
Alexander, Paul, 26, 39, 198
Alfond, Dolores Apodaca, 132
Apodaca, Victor, 132
Apple, R. W. Jr., xii, 55, 87
Aristide, Jean–Bertrand, 162
Armey, Dick, 69

Bader, William, 120
Barnes, Fred, 113
Beatty, Warren, 185
Biden, Joseph, 109
Bipartisan Campaign Reform Act, xix, 9, 87
Blitzer, Wolf, 126
Broder, David, 186, 208, 210
Brooks, David, xiv, 69, 79, 82, 135–40, 145, 150–52, 189, 209, 222
Bush, George H. W., 66–67, 130, 158, 161
Bush, George W., xii, xiv, xv, xxv, 55, 151–52, 190–91; 2000 primaries and, 44, 71–72; campaign finance reform and, 94; "compassionate conservatism," 82; foreign policy, 149; McCain and, 71, 97–98,
168, 182–83, 186–87; Putin and, 155; Rove and, 18; torture policies, 117; troop surge and, 21–22; Vietnam veterans and, 132–33

campaign finance reform: Keating Five scandal and, 76, 192; McCain and, 54, 67, 85–88, 151; opposition to, 92–95. *See also* McCain–Feingold campaign finance bill
Carlson, Tucker, 139, 174, 190
carpetbagging, McCain accused of, 45, 55, 203
Carter, Jimmy, 43, 52–53, 191
Chait, Jonathan, xiii
Character Is Destiny (McCain): on cheating, 199; on his father, 6–7; on freedom, 81–82; on religion, 183–84, 198; on role models, 3; on Theodore Roosevelt, 141, 142
Cheney, Dick, 149
Christian Right, 68, 179, 202
Christopher, Warren, 161
Clinton, Bill, xiv, xvii, 98, 110, 139; Haiti and, 162; Kosovo and, 22, 166–69; McCain and, 65, 68, 125–27, 160–64; Mogadishu and, 161; opposition to, 80, 91; Vietnam and, 126–28
Clinton, Hillary, 52, 154, 190
Coburn, Tom, 180

Cochran, Thad, 51
Cohen, William, 49, 166
"compassionate conservatism," 82
Cornyn, John, 108–9
Craner, Bob, 35
Cranston, Alan, 88

Daily Show, The, 196
Dalton, John, 113
Darfur, 155
Day, George "Bud," 33, 204
Dayton Peace Accords, 164, 166
Dean, Howard, 72
Dean, James, 26
DeConcini, Dennis, 88, 90
Dionne, E. J., 137
Dittrick, Jack, 29
Dole, Bob, 10, 55, 164

Easterbrook, Gregg, 165
Eisenhower, Dwight, 110
Eisenhower, Judy, 58
Ellsberg, Daniel, 123–24
ethanol, 175–77, 179

Falwell, Jerry, 68, 150, 179, 183
Feingold, Russell, 91, 95
Fineman, Howard, xv, 172
Foer, Franklin, 151–52
Fonda, Jane, 121, 125–26
For Whom the Bell Tolls
   (Hemingway): influence on
   McCain, 3–4, 7–10, 12, 14–17,
   204; Robert Jordan in, 1, 3–4;
   Theodore Roosevelt and, 142

Gibbon, Edward, 204
Gingrich, Newt, 69, 85–86, 91, 136
Giuliani, Rudolph, xxviii–xxix, 2,
   193–94, 205
Glassman, James, 137
Glenn, John, 88, 90
Goldberg, Jonah, 152

Goldwater, Barry: funeral, 77;
   influence on McCain, 7, 14, 51;
   McCain and, 57–70, 77, 82, 95;
   view of government, 79
Good Morning America, 72–73
Gore, Al, 45, 94, 102
Gosinski, Tom, 114
Grann, David, 10
Gross, Terry, 125
Guantanamo Bay prison, 97
Gulf War, 65–66, 129, 133, 159, 167

Haiti, 149, 162, 171
Haldeman, H. R., 123
Halsey, Bull, 4
Hard Call (McCain): on character,
   189, 191, 196–200, 204, 216;
   McCain's role models and, 3
Hart, Gary, 49, 125
Hemingway, Ernest, 3–4, 7–9,
   12–15, *225*
Hensley, Cindy, 43, 49
Hensley, Jim, 43
Heritage Foundation, *222*
Hesselbrock, Don, xix, 42, 53, 57,
   107
Hollywood, 13, 68, 97
homosexuality: gay marriage, 97,
   177–78; military service and, 68,
   161
Huckabee, Mike, 205–6
Hunter, Duncan, 2, *223*
Hynes, Patrick, 181, 189–90

Ifshin, David, 126–27, *223*
immigration reform: 2008
   Republican primaries and, 23;
   effect on McCain's popularity,
   193, 196; failure of, 108–10, 186;
   Gingrich and, 85–86; McCain
   and, 10, 100, 145–46, 174–75,
   203, *223*
Imus in the Morning, 85, 95

Ingraham, Laura, 137
interventionism: Clinton and, 22;
    Darfur and, 155; Dominican
    Republic and, 149; Kosovo
    and, 166–67, 169; McCain and,
    61, 98, 117, 170–71, 177, 203;
    McCain Doctrine and, 167–68;
    Theodore Roosevelt and, 140,
    142, 148–50
Iran, 153–54, 157, 208, 209, 215
Iraq: Baker–Hamilton Iraq Study
    Group, 171; effect on McCain's
    popularity, 186, 196; Gulf
    War and, 159; Iraq Liberation
    Act, 138; McCain and, xviii,
    9, 41, 97, 167–68, 171, 206–8,
    222; McCain on, 153, 214–16;
    Philippines and, 11; troop surge
    and, 21–23, 154, 186; U.S.
    foreign policy and, xxiv–xxv;
    Vietnam War and, xxvii; waning
    popularity of, 172, 174

Jackson, Henry "Scoop," 59
Jeffords, Jim, 151
John McCain: An American Odyssey
    (Timberg), 21, 25
John McCain: An Essay in Military
    and Political History (Karaagac), 7,
    27, 50, 65, 122
Johnson, Lyndon, 62, 121
Judis, John, 54, 138, 159, 160,
    215–16

Karaagac, John: on breaking
    the rules, 27–30; on Keating
    scandal, 88; on McCain's early
    Senate career, 65; on McCain's
    foreign policy, 125; on McCain's
    imprisonment, 32; on McCain's
    influences, 7, 224; on POW–
    MIA movement, 125; on USS
    Midway, 50

Karp, Jonathan, 77
Keating, Charles, 43, 52, 57, 88–90
Keating Five scandal: campaign
    finance reform and, 54, 65, 76,
    101; Hard Call on, 200–201;
    Karaagac on, 88; lessons learned
    from, 192; McCain and, 57–58,
    65, 76, 88, 101; overview, 88–90;
    Paxson Communications and,
    197
Kennard, William, 197
Kennedy, Robert F., 121
Kennedy, Ted, 2, 85, 108
Kerry, John, xxvii, 119, 129–32
King, Martin Luther Jr., 121
Kirkpatrick, Jeanne, 138, 214
Kosovo, 22, 81, 83, 129, 166–67,
    169, 209, 226
Kristof, Nicholas, 49, 74
Kristol, William: Iraq War and,
    22–23; McCain and, xiv, 150–52,
    222, 226; national greatness and,
    82, 209; neoconservatism and,
    150–52; view of government, 69;
    Weekly Standard op–ed, 135–39;
    Wittman and, 150–51
K Street, 222
Kurtz, Howard, 112, 186
Kyl, John, 42, 53, 108–9

Lane, Charles, xvii, 167
Larry King Live, 12, 21–22, 158, 173
Lewis, Michael, xi, 55–56, 75, 99,
    126
Liberty University, 179
Lieberman, Joe, 151
Limbaugh, Rush, 91, 136
Lincoln, Abraham, 135, 149, 196,
    216
Lincoln Savings & Loan, 88–89
line-item veto, 10, 9, 65, 68, 91, 99
Loan, Jack Van, 36

Mahan, Alfred Thayer, xxvi, 11–12, 141

Matheson, Malcolm, 25

Matthews, Chris, xi, 177, 187

McCain, Jack, 6, 11–12, 24–25, 45, 59–61, 141, 149, 168, 199, *226*

McCain, John Sidney "Slew," 4–6, 11, 24–25, 45, 141, 168, *224, 226*

McCain Doctrine, 167–68

McCain–Feingold campaign finance bill, xix; Gingrich on, 85–86; Gore and, 102; political impact of, 93–95, 102; Supreme Court and, 93, 99

McConnell, Mitch, 86, 95

McGovern, George, 125, 174

McGovern, James, 49, 50, 74

McKinley, William, 143

medical marijuana, 68

Meet the Press, 9, 181, 195–96

Mencken, H. L., 148

Military Commissions Act, xix

Milosevic, Slobodan, 163, 166

Mondale, Walter, 126

Monroe Doctrine, 149, 157–58

Montini, E. J., 108, 114

Moran, Terry, 173–75

Murdoch, Rupert, 135

Nader, Ralph, 72, 152

national greatness conservatism, 64, 82, 95–96, 98, 117, 137–38, 140, 145, 151–52, 198, 209, 215

Naval Academy, McCain at, 26–29, 46, 191, 200

Naval War College, 123–25, 191

Nelson, Lord Admiral, 11, 200

Nelson, Terry, 18

neoconservatives, 81–82, 136–38, 152, 166

Nightingale's Song, The (Timberg), xvii

Nightline, 173

Nixon, Richard: foreign policy, 149; Goldwater and, 62; McCain and, 78; Pentagon Papers and, 123–24; Vietnam and, 121–23

Norquist, Grover, xxiv

North, Oliver, *222*

Novak, Robert, 137

O'Connor, Sandra Day, 68

Orrick, Bentley, 26

Overly, Norris, 33

Patients' Bill of Rights, 83, 97, 151

Paul, Ron, 41

Paxson Communications, 197

Peck, Millard, 130

Pelley, Scott, 196

Pentagon Papers, 123–24

Perenchio, Jerrold, 101

Perot, Ross, 72, 122, 152

Peterson, Pete, 138

Podhoretz, Norman, 136

pork-barrel spending, 9, 41, 65, 91, 110–12, 154, 203

Postrel, Virginia, 137

Powell, Colin, 159, 181

Powell, Jim, 135

Powell Doctrine, 203

Project Vote Smart, 180–81

Putin, Vladimir, 155

Rather, Dan, 55

Ravenel, William, 192

Reagan, Nancy, xi, 48

Reagan, Ronald: appointment of Sandra Day O'Connor, 68; conservatism and, 64, 68–69, 82, 150; federal government and, 80, 82; foreign policy, 157–58, 167; influence on McCain, 7, 44, 63–64, 138, 155, 196, 216; loyalty and, 107; POWs and, 48, 122

Reynolds, Michael, 14
Rhodes, John, 42, 52
Riegle, Don, 88
Robertson, Pat, 150, 179, 183
Romney, Mitt, xxviii, 2, 23, 205–6, 223
Roosevelt, Theodore, xvi, xix, xxv, xxvi, 135–52; Hemingway and, 3, 12–13; influence on McCain, 13, 64, 137–48, 150–51; McCain Doctrine and, 167; racism, 144–46, 225; Slew McCain and, 5, 11, 168
Rove, Karl, 18, 151
Russert, Tim, 9, 55, 176, 182, 195

Salter, Lauralie, 199
Salter, Mark, 18, 77, 138, 196, 214, 216
Santorum, Rick, 113
Savings & Loan scandal, 57, 88–89. See also Keating Five scandal
Schanberg, Sydney, 119, 132
Schneider, William, 186
Schwarzenegger, Arnold, xi
Schwarzkopf, Norman, 159
September 11 attacks, 98, 110, 146, 174, 198
Shansby, Gary, 40–41
Shelmerdine, Kirk, 94
Silverman, Amy, 55, 106, 114
skepticism, 14, 22, 64, 79–82, 143, 171
Smith, Bob, 131
Smith, Bradley, 94, 101
Smith, Jay, 52
Stephanopoulos, George, 85, 177, 183, 196
Stewart, Jon, 196
Straight Talk Express, 71, 86, 106, 187, 197; media coverage of, 139, 173–74; questions regarding abortion, 182; questions

regarding contraception, 180–81; South Carolina and, 10, 71
Straight Talk PAC, 99–100
Suellentrop, Chris, 85
Symington, Fife, 53

Tancredo, Tom, 23
taxes: Bush tax cuts, 195–96; estate tax, 152; immigrants and, 222; McCain's flip–flop on, 183; Republican revolution and, 81–82; tobacco tax, 9, 82, 99
Thompson, Fred, xxviii–xxix, 54
Thompson, Hunter S., 174
Thomsen, Dick, 26
Thurmond, Strom, 113
Tillman, Pat, 40, 224
Timberg, Robert, xii, xvii, 222, 224, 226; on McCain and antiwar movement, 125; on McCain and Keating, 90, 113; on McCain as Navy liaison, 49–50, 120; on McCain's education, 25–27; on McCain's first congressional campaign, 42–43; on McCain's imprisonment, 21, 33, 36–37; on McCain's time at Naval Academy, 28
torture: Bush and, 117; McCain and, 35–36, 75, 78, 88, 120, 184, 193
Tower, John, 7, 44, 49, 59
Trilling, Lionel, 136
troop surge, 21, 23, 97, 155–56, 171
Tully, Duke, 43, 52, 59

USS Midway, 50

Vaughn, Stephen, 137
Vietnam, McCain and: courage and, 89; downing of plane, 27, 31, 32; faith in reason for war, 14–15, 217; foreign policy and, 172;

Vietnam, McCain and: *(continued)*
  Gulf War and, 159; healing
  wounds of, 119–34, 138, 215;
  imprisonment and torture,
  32–37, 197; Kosovo and, 167,
  169; political impact of, 61–64,
  156–57; presidential aspirations
  and, 106; recollections of, 75–76,
  175, 183–84; return from, 203;
  temper and, 116, 118
Vietnam memorial, 23
Viva Zapata!, 3, 15, 18

Wallace, Mike, xvi
War on Terror, 155
War Powers Act, 64, 110, 155
Weaver, John, 18, 109, 139, 151,
  177, 180
Webber, George, 40
Wheeler, Winslow, 110–13
Why Courage Matters (McCain), 3,
  76, 198
Will, George, 93, 95
Williams, Ted, 200, *224*

Wills, Gary, 137
Wilson, Edmund, 1, 12
Wilson, Woodrow, 149
Wittman, Marshall, 138–39, 150–51
Wolffe, Richard, 19
Wolfson, Adam, 138
Worth the Fighting For (McCain):
  on 2000 campaign platform,
  198; on campaign mudslinging,
  116–17; on desire to be president,
  76, 81–82; on first election, 44,
  52; *For Whom the Bell Tolls* and,
  4, 8–9, 17; on Goldwater, 60;
  on loyalty to Republican party,
  83; on McCain's imprisonment,
  131; on "national greatness," 98,
  198; on Pentagon Papers, 124;
  on political scandals, 90–91, 92,
  201; on rebels, 21, 37; on role of
  federal government, 68–69; on
  Theodore Roosevelt, 135, 142,
  148; on Vietnam War, 128; *Viva
  Zapata!* and, 15